WILLIAM NOWELL

VALUE MATCH SELLING™

TRAFFORD PUBLISHING™

© Copyright 2006 William Nowell.
All rights reserved. No part of this publication may be reproduced, stored in a retrieval system, or transmitted, in any form or by any means, electronic, mechanical, photocopying, recording, or otherwise, without the written prior permission of the author.

Note for Librarians: A cataloguing record for this book is available from Library and Archives Canada at www.collectionscanada.ca/amicus/index-e.html
ISBN 1-4120-8996-4

Printed in Victoria, BC, Canada. Printed on paper with minimum 30% recycled fibre. Trafford's print shop runs on "green energy" from solar, wind and other environmentally-friendly power sources.

TRAFFORD
PUBLISHING

Offices in Canada, USA, Ireland and UK

Book sales for North America and international:
Trafford Publishing, 6E–2333 Government St.,
Victoria, BC V8T 4P4 CANADA
phone 250 383 6864 (toll-free 1 888 232 4444)
fax 250 383 6804; email to orders@trafford.com

Book sales in Europe:
Trafford Publishing (UK) Limited, 9 Park End Street, 2nd Floor
Oxford, UK OX1 1HH UNITED KINGDOM
phone 44 (0)1865 722 113 (local rate 0845 230 9601)
facsimile 44 (0)1865 722 868; info.uk@trafford.com

Order online at:
trafford.com/06-0752

10 9 8 7 6 5 4 3 2 1

FOREWORD

I learned more during the first 15 minutes I spent with Will Nowell than from any other trainer in my 35 year career as a senior manager. He first encouraged me, and then convinced me, to simply "listen" with my mind wide open. Since that fateful day I have been learning faster, growing as a person and understanding more about business and about people then I ever have before.

Will and his training program are not about the latest "tricks" of the trade or built around some new found buzz word. Rather it is a solid, metrically-based program about developing and then mastering a set of skills - that can be measured. I have been constantly amazed at the quantified success of not only sales teams but entire organizations using his program.

In a business training world filled with half-truths and innuendoes, Will Nowell is a visionary grounded in integrity. He possesses that rare combination of a passion for excellence in all he does, and a commitment to bottom line success. He clearly understands the linkage between an organization's business goals and how his strategic sales system can help to achieve those results.

Will's sales success system can be best illustrated by sharing with you a few of the improved metrics from our organization. During our first year of fully implementing Will's system, we improved our total closing ratio by over

> "In a business training world filled with half-truths, Will Nowell is a visionary grounded in integrity"

200%. Now after four years of continuing compliance with his program, we have improved that closing ratio by another 100%. That translates to an overall sales closing increase of an astounding 308%!

No system, including Will's, can be left to middle management to implement if you want to truly achieve excellence. It takes a total commitment from all levels of management for any program to truly succeed—and it starts at the top. Everyone within the company needs to witness the CEO's personal commitment to implement and then diligently monitor and apply Will's principles. I can attest to the fact that anyone who follows these simple rules will not only have more control over their ability to manage results, but the bottom line will dramatically increase.

Will Nowell is a Master Communicator who combines a brilliant intellect with a gentle humor. That allows him to infuse each learning session with fact-filled, fun-based anecdotes from his vast experience as a leader. His process of immersion learning is one that allows him to open your mind to new ideas ... ideas that are the basis for his wonderful "results-oriented" training system.

Inside this book, you will learn some of the basics of Will's creative and results-driven sales program. However, I suggest that you also make the commitment to visit with Will personally. It is only through personal interaction with Will that you will begin to understand the power of his sales philosophy and VALUE MATCH system.

My first 15 minutes with Will led to successes for my organization beyond my wildest dreams. Now, almost 5 years later, I am still amazed at the insightful lessons learned about the power of listening. I am honored to write this foreword, but even more honored simply to be called Will's friend.

Thomas J. Harrison
President/COO
Aston Care Systems, Inc.

WILL'S PREFACE

Hundreds of books are written each year promising to make you a better person, to improve your financial situation or your personal drive, to give you an advantage over others, both personally and professionally. Hundreds of movies, CDs, tapes, DVDs, etc., are produced each year offering tips and presentations that will make you a millionaire, that will allow you to uncover the secret to a longer life or eternal youth.

Having witnessed the less than stellar performance of these get-rich-quick, fix-it-fast, cure-all-ills guides, it is understandable that many readers would be wary of new promises and more outlandish claims. They ask themselves: Why would I want to buy yet another self-help book when I'm already lining the canary cage with pages from the previous ones? When I'm using the CDs and DVDs as coffee table coasters?

For one thing, this book makes no fanciful promises and over-the-top claims. It offers no "secret" formula or scheme to uncover some mythical pot of gold. For another, this book is not something pulled out of thin air simply to improve my own financial situation (although that would be a nice side effect).

It is rather the result of my own personal journey and the many questions I have asked myself—and am still asking myself—along the way. It is the result of a dialogue, a conversation, an attempt at understanding what it means to communicate with another person on a meaningful level. Most importantly, it is the result of a deep soul-searching on the meaning of being truly human, of being social creatures who need to interact with one another in order to achieve their fullest potential.

"This book ... is the result of my own personal journey ... of deep soul-searching"

The journey starts with a straightforward question: What is it that keeps individuals from reaching their full potential?

When I asked myself that simple question several years ago, I had to honestly and sincerely admit that I did not know. Oh sure, I felt successful in many ways and was thankful for all the bounty given to me. But at the same time, I felt that something was lacking, that despite all that I had achieved I had not truly moved towards fulfilling my full potential.

I knew I had more to offer—to myself and to others. True satisfaction eluded me and I was haunted by the feeling there was more out there to achieve. Or rather, more in me to give. Having asked the question and having looked at myself in the mirror without blinking, I began an ongoing journey that has brought me to this point, an exploration seeking answers on how to get more out of life, how to go beyond the superficial to the rich depths below.

Thus far, it has been an exciting, challenging, helpful and above all fun journey to explore why we, despite our ability to see, visualize and understand where we want to be, often struggle to get there. Why we run into roadblocks that slow us down, that confuse us. Why we are led astray, go off on needless tangents and hit dead ends. Why we <u>allow</u> ourselves to be led astray. Why we can't stay focused on the target, on the very visible target, the bull's-eye of full potential.

The answers to these questions and the path leading back to full potential come in something I am proud to call **VALUE MATCH,** *the subject of this book. I'm not dealing in hyperbole when I say it has changed my life and allowed me to reach heights that I never dreamt were possible. Or that it has opened vistas I didn't even know were there—even though I was staring right at them all the time. This is the unvarnished truth—and I trust you'll permit me to share this journey with you, in the hope that you too might enjoy similar success and achieve similar heights.*

In the chapters to come, we will take the journey together as we investigate the details of this process and as you hopefully discover a new way to tap into the limitless potential inside us all.

It is here that what is essentially a never-ending journey has its true start. I'm positive that you'll enjoy yourselves as much as I did when I first set out. And I'm just as positive that the results will dramatically improve your selling abilities and at the same time make you a better person.

Postscript to Will's Preface:

Some of you folks out there might be wondering about the title of the book and why I've decided to call it "Everybody Lies! Let's Be Honest!" Well, first off, I should tell you that I'm not trying to impugn the noble profession of selling. Far from it. As you will see when reading this book, I hold it in great esteem. Nor am not trying to suggest that everybody "lies" in the sense of being dishonest or underhanded.

Instead, I would suggest that everybody speaks in code. What do I mean by that? Well, most people want to tell the truth. They want to be upfront about things. But out of convenience, fear, not wanting to hurt the feelings of others, or concerns that telling the truth might be misrepresented, they speak in code instead. They use words that, for them, are connected to the truth on some level, usually a factual or literal level.

But, at the same time, these words quite effectively hide the real emotions and values that are behind people's responses, requests, statements and desires. They try to keep them concealed until their fears and concerns are addressed. We're not talking here only about the selling process but with respect to any interaction in any relationship. Now, the reason this happens is obvious but the reason we are not better at decoding those words is not so obvious.

For the most part, we as humans have grown up being taught, both by example and by actions, that asking for clarification when someone says something is not a good thing. As children, we get things such as: "Why so many questions? Are you slow or something?" Or: "How many times do I have to tell you something? Do I have to clean out your ears so you can hear better?" Or: "There's gonna be trouble if I have to repeat myself." The message comes through loud and clear: Don't ask too many questions. Whether you understood or not, pretend you did.

So, we learn to be cautious and wary of telling the truth. We also learn not to be too inquisitive and to avoid intimacy. In most cases, we actually replace our natural curiosity with talking, saying whatever comes to mind. You know the old adage: If you do not have the patience (or the skill) to listen, then talk. It is no wonder that most sales people talk 80% of the time and listen very little (even when they have been trained to do otherwise).

> "We have been taught that asking for clarification when someone says something is not a good thing"

> "This book is all about breaking the code, using the most revolutionary code-busting communication technique"

Thus the stage is set for what we have now. It's an environment where we guess a lot and maybe get it right some of the time but mostly we don't. Or we only get it half-right. It makes for a great deal of inefficiency, low pro-ductivity, wasted time, unmet expectations, and in some cases even heart break. Remember this doesn't only happen in sales or on the job but even in our personal relationships, often doing irreparable damage.

This conundrum, this speaking-the-truth-factually-but-not-actually-telling-the-truth puzzle is responsible for countless hours of running around in circles, missed goals, blown opportunities, and poor results. It is responsible for much of what is wrong with our society today.

This book is all about breaking the code, using the most revolutionary code-busting communication technique to come around in years. As you will see, it is simple, so simple you might be tempted to take no notice of its power to produce beneficial change, to call it too simple to be true and then discard it.

But that would be a regrettable mistake. Many of the most revolutionary ideas to come along have been simple and yet have made a huge impact on the world. For example, our Founding Fathers' idea that government should be built from the people up rather than from the king down created a brand new approach to government and "the pursuit of happiness". Or Newton's idea of gravity conceived from a falling apple. Or Henry Ford's idea of the assembly line and putting a lot of things together one part at a time rather than putting only one thing together completely.

In this book I have attempted to outline and illustrate the principles behind this code breaking technique. I have tried to give you as many real life stories and examples as possible to help you visualize and internalize the information. However, you will not be able to get the full benefit from this book until you commit to learning and mastering these skills and come to grips with what kind of person you are. Your true self, in other words.

If you really read this with a commitment to learn, a desire to improve, and the humility to let your guard down and allow yourself the luxury of failing a few times, then you'll improve your ability to learn the code and how to break it. In so doing, you'll begin a cycle of honesty in your life that will help those around you and improve the quality of your life. That's my guarantee.

So, I hope you enjoy this adventure and I encourage you to make a commitment to be honest from this point forward.

And thank you for allowing me to take it with you.

INTRODUCTION:

THE JOURNEY BEGINS

> *The English language is a form of communication! Conversation isn't just crossfire where you shoot and get shot at! Where you've got to duck for your life and aim to kill! Words aren't only bombs and bullets—no, they're little gifts, containing meanings!*
>
> **—Philip Roth**

What Is VALUE MATCH & Why You Should Care

Values Unlocked In The Introduction

In this section we will learn:

- How to understand the difference between what we call communication and telling the truth
- The importance of developing communication skills both in one's personal and professional life
- An introduction to the VALUE MATCH system and how it can help you achieve your full potential
- How to take advantage of the most important asset we have—the truth as humans
- The VALUE MATCH System versus other sales programs and their promises
- How to communicate with people (be they customers, family or friends) on a truthful level
- The four-fold purpose for writing this book.

Communicating: It's A Skill

As a professional sales trainer and coach, in the last ten years I have helped thousands of salespeople improve their customer service and selling skills. Like a car mechanic breaking down an engine to determine what the problem might be and then fixing it, I have broken down sales techniques and analyzed them to try to understand what was being done right and what wasn't working. And I have worked to fix the problem so that the wrong sales techniques are discarded and effective ones put in their place.

During that time, I have tried to observe and study the "selling engine." What I've noticed bears repeating: Rarely have I found a salesperson with a bad attitude or the wrong motivation. Hardly ever have I found a salesperson without the needed enthusiasm, gung-ho spirit, and go-get-'em attitude that has made American entrepreneurs and businesspeople the envy of the rest of the world. All those I've met and observed want to be successful, all want to earn a good living, and the majority understand the process on how to achieve that success.

So what exactly is wrong with these "selling engines"? The problem arises from their communication skills. Either there is a lack of communication skills per se or a lack of understanding as to which communication skills are needed to make the sale. It's as if the salesperson has the spiel all ready to flow but then suddenly becomes tongue-tied, suddenly trips all over the words. They are ready to roar to full life, anxious and eager to put into practice what they've learned—only to be thwarted at the last moment. And they don't know what the problem might be.

This is not a problem suffered only by professional salespeople, by those who earn their living trying to convince others to buy things. This is a problem each and everyone of us has experienced at some point. The fact is that there is a fundamental challenge we all face: Everybody lies, all the time. Now don't get mad and throw this book away. I don't mean that people intentionally mislead others for their own personal gain. Although there are those few that fall into this category.

> "Rarely have I found a salesperson with a bad attitude or the wrong motivation ... or without the needed enthusiasm, gung-ho spirit and go-get-'em attitude"

I am referring to the rest of the human race. Basically honest people who have learned to speak in code and all the rest of us who have learned to cope with and do our best to interpret the code.

It is also a fact that all humans need to communicate effectively, to get across the deepest meanings for what they are trying to say and to get those across without confusion. This is true whether it's to "sell" themselves, to establish deeper more meaningful relationships with family and friends, or simply to feel more at ease—more "in one's skin"—in social situations. When that doesn't happen, when communication fails or is misunderstood, the consequences can be disastrous—not only for the person attempting the communication but also for those around him.

At one end of the social spectrum, this lack of true communication can lead to a frustrating personal life, wasted friend-ships, and missed business opportunities. It can lead to dysfunctional families and misunderstandings that accrue like barnacles on a ship, slowly eating away at the integrity of the hull, slowly emptying the person out.

At the other, it can result in acrimonious confrontations, both emotional and physical, unpleasant skirmishes and saber-rattling, and even full-scale wars that devastate entire nations and continents. And we've all had first hand experience with enough of those to last us another millennium, thank you very much.

Thus, no one would give me an argument if I were to say that the ability to communicate and break this code is an essential lifetime skill we all must learn as quickly as possible. In fact, it could easily be said that the ability to communicate in an effective manner is what ultimately distinguishes us as human beings, what sets us apart and allows the smooth functioning of the various levels of kinship and society.

> "The ability to communicate is an essential lifetime skill we all must learn as quickly as possible"

It is such an important and integral ability that it can't be left to haphazard trial and error, to blind testing and experimenting. It can't be like someone left alone to work her way through a maze. By the time the person gets it right, it might be too late. The opportunity knocking so nicely might have moved on to another door. Or a person might go through life stifled and frustrated because they never learned the art of communicating effectively and consequently never reached their full potential.

The VALUE MATCH System: An Introduction

VALUE MATCH is a proven system that ensures that everyone who masters it will reach their full potential. VALUE MATCH distills what I have learned about effective communication and breaking the code into a book- a simple, easy-to-understand book that will help readers work towards achieving that elusive potential everyone talks about.

In all humility, I can safely and honestly say that VALUE MATCH is a simple and easy to understand concept unlike anything you've ever heard or read about before. It will show you how to get positive, life-affirming answers to important questions, and how to put those answers to work for you in whatever areas you choose to apply them. Of that, I have no doubt.

The most interesting thing about VALUE MATCH is that it is a skill set that anyone can master. The key that unlocks this skill doesn't lie in being unusually talented or gifted, but in a desire to see others succeed. The only real roadblock to success is your willingness to learn the concepts and principles and commitment to practice the skill. I can say that I have been able to teach VALUE MATCH to young, old, experienced, inexperienced. The only real difference between those who put VALUE MATCH to work for them has been their attitude and commitment to practice the skill.

That's why I have come to call it VALUE MATCH. And whether you're actually selling goods or services to others or simply trying to improve your familial and social skills, the key lies in your ability to match your values with those of others around you. VALUE MATCH can help you do that, by unlocking or making obvious the things that are holding you back from achieving your deepest goals and desires.

Thus, not only is this an entirely different kind of book about sales, salesmanship, and sales management but it is also about your relationships with others—both on the personal and on the professional level. And not only is VALUE MATCH a system whereby you can learn effective and specific selling skills that can be used in a highly competitive environment but it is also a system of values for turning your own life around. A way to dig up and bring to the surface all those hidden treasures and untapped resources you have locked inside you. Call it values. Call it our spiritual core. Call it the accumulated knowledge from millennia of being human. Everyone wants to tap into that well deep inside all of us. Knowing how is a different matter.

After having read this book and after learning how to apply its principles, I know you'll see a dramatic improvement in your business, your personal life, and in the positive, enriching effect you can have on the lives of others. This book is about adding value and empowerment. It's about making you a better person. A person who radiates life-affirming values and richly positive attitudes. A person who isn't afraid to go out and make the most of the opportunities given. A person with an essential core that can withstand any and all assaults from negativity and the fear of failure. My hope is that this book will start you on a continuing journey, a process that will dramatically change your life for the better. No, it's not just a hope. It's a promise. A guarantee.

That's no idle boast. I've helped people make it happen thousands of times already. Or rather: I've helped people help themselves make it happen. A fellow in one of my recent classes asked me to share what my mission was. I said: "To help individuals be more effective in their interpersonal communication skills."

> "My hope is that this book will start you on a continuing journey, a process that will dramatically change your life for the better"

VALUE MATCH and You

I am the head of a company called ServiceTRAC. Among other services, we conduct sales performance research and training, as well as providing state-of-the-art customer service feedback and research to our clients. Through its network of more than 35,000 shoppers, ServiceTRAC provides mystery shopping services. We shop on the phone, in person, via hidden video camera and even on the internet.

Usually, when I tell folks this, they have an urge to throw something at me, especially if they have been on the receiving end of a mystery shop that has not gone very well. I actually see our mystery shopping services as a service to those salespeople. Let's face it. If they were not proud of the results of the shop, isn't it better it was us and not a real customer?

Mystery shops allow businesses to improve their sales and customer relations and reduce dreaded customer turnover. It also allows firms to pass on the knowledge, skills and especially attitudes to their employees in a way that becomes integral to how they treat customers. That, in turn, feeds back to the company and increases the chances of continued success, no matter what the selling trends and fads of the moment might be.

I have had the invaluable opportunity to work intimately with many companies and to measure specific attitudes, skills and knowledge. More generally, I have also enjoyed the privilege of sharing the principles in this book with individuals and organizations from coast to coast. It has been an immense learning experience—both for myself and for the people with whom I have worked.

The results have been amazing. I have seen the VALUE MATCH principles not only lead to increased professional success, but also improve personal lives and help unravel often tangled relationships. Now, I am proud, excited and, to tell the truth, a little nervous about sharing my ideas with a more general audience rather than simply sales professionals and business entre-preneurs.

I know these things don't work well in a vacuum and I look forward with pleasure to your feedback. I also know that this

> "I have seen VALUE MATCH principles not only lead to increased professional success, but also improve personal lives"

is not a static process, not something writ in stone for eternity, and that your thoughts on how the VALUE MATCH principles have helped you will only serve to improve the process. As I stated at the beginning, this is more like a journey than a one-time application, a journey that lasts a lifetime and one during which there is constant learning.

At the same time, I have absolutely no qualms about putting my reputation on the line when it comes to the efficacy and productiveness of the VALUE MATCH system. On an empirical level, I have the accumulated research data to prove every point and to back every statement made in this book. As the saying goes: "The numbers don't lie." And I have the numbers. Lots and lots of numbers acquired through years of providing "hands on" service and testing that service to check on its continued success.

But numbers are only one small part of the equation, only one of the things that goes into successful selling. The human factor is just as important—if not more so. By faithfully applying the VALUE MATCH principles in my own life, I've built a successful, nationally recognized business and have found a satisfying role in society that allows me to contribute to the success of others. Most of all, however, VALUE MATCH has helped my wife and me create a wonderfully happy and rich family life.

Now, I want to share that information with you. I want you to be as happy, satisfied and fulfilled as I have become. It's not an easy task and it requires dedication to the principles and an energetic outlook. But, at the same time, it isn't onerous and the results are more than worthwhile.

> "I have absolutely no qualms about putting my reputation on the line when it comes to the efficacy of the VALUE MATCH system"

Our Most Important Asset? That Would Be You

As human beings, we are blessed with practically unlimited power, enviable ability, deep knowledge, and intense emotional strength, along with plenty of faith, hope, and charity. And, for most of us, the desire to share what we have is just as powerful as the attributes themselves.

So what's the problem? Why is the world wracked with turmoil and dissent? Why are families constantly fighting? Why do friends fall away? Unfortunately, there is something blocking our ability to take full advantage of what we've been given and what we've learned as human beings. That bottleneck is our often limited capacity to communicate effectively with one another. To decipher human coded messages that are sometimes not what they seem on the surface. To give the important stuff a power boost. To unlock the power and spread the faith.

I think of the many wonderful books I have read that share the sales process and communicate strategies for successful relationships, healthier marriages and families, and stronger friendships. I think of the videos and DVDs I have watched and the tapes I have heard, all extolling the virtues of improved relationships and finding one's inner self. Like most, I realize that this information can be valuable and needed, if we're really serious about shaping a better world around us.

So why is it that so much of it goes unused and untapped? Why is it that what should be teaching us to make better use of our resources ends up further frustrating us? I believe it is because we do not have the basic skills and strategies to use the information in a way that makes sense. It is because we can't find a way to make the connection between the process needed and the value we wish to achieve. It is my fervent hope that this book will provide you with these skills and strategies so you can access the value all around you and reach your potential.

And Herein Lies That Difference

Okay, you've probably heard that last statement dozens of times before in other sales skills training programs. Like weight loss pitches all promising to turn you into the next Mr. or Ms. Universe. But the VALUE MATCH system really is different and I have the hard data to back it up. Besides, I make no promises that I can't keep.

Other sales training programs focus almost entirely on the process of selling, specifically of selling something to someone. Most subscribe to the basic needs-satisfaction process. No doubt, you've heard or read about them in one form or another: "Customer Focused," "Customer Centered," "Need Satisfaction," "Need Fulfillment," and so on. This is the sort of thing in which customer relationship marketing strategies specialize. And there are entire on-line web-based learning programs that focus strictly on this archetypal customer whom everyone must learn to serve.

Now, in theory, there is nothing wrong with these sales programs. They subscribe to the idea that you try to learn what the customer wants or needs and then help that customer get it. They encourage salespeople to listen and gather valuable information so they can, at the right time, make a powerful presentation that hopefully fits the customer's needs. There is usually an emphasis on prospecting, especially getting referrals and leads. Particular attention is usually focused on closing and handling objections.

All that is fine and dandy—and one could learn plenty by following such training programs and customer relationship theories. So what's the problem? Why do things sometimes go wrong, both in small ways and catastrophically? Well, the trouble is that, no matter how much one desires to go through the process, no matter how well-armed the salesperson might be,

You can be a wonderful prospector; you can be great at researching your client's desires; you can overcome any possible objection; and you can be a master closer. And still be falling short of your goals. Why? Because, for some reason or other, the customer is afraid and is not volunteering all the facts. Without those facts, without that truth the salesperson struggles through the process and often comes out the other side without having accomplished anything.

This can be just as true, and just as deadly, when dealing with personal relationships. I think all of us can relate to having a close friend or relative who comes to us for help and is then disappointed with the results. They tell us a story, relate some problem or event, and, when we offer a bit of advice based on what they've told us, they respond with: "You don't understand! You just don't get it! Nobody does!" And they're probably right! We don't understand, but not because we have deliberately failed to understand, rather because they have not been completely honest with their situation. The story was incomplete so, of course, we couldn't offer complete and helpful advice.

I'm not being presumptuous or saying this just to be controversial. In my capacity as head of ServiceTRAC, I have listened to literally thousands of "mystery" tape recordings of sales people doing their level best to get through the sales process. They follow the steps; they have the right attitude; they ask for the close; they do everything "according to the book." But they come up empty handed, with nothing to show for their efforts.

Communicating Those Skills

Why? Well, it's not because they've done anything wrong, "according to the book." Rather, it's because they don't have the basic skills and tactics necessary to succeed: the ability to listen to and communicate with customers on a truthful level; the ability to ask what the customer really values rather than what he or she seems to want.

It's not the fault of the salesperson. The truth is our society doesn't teach us how to listen. To really listen so that we're prepared to ask questions. In fact, we're taught just the opposite: to simply <u>pretend</u> to listen, to nod our heads and then to move on to something else. And it doesn't seem to matter whether we've really understood or not. In school, for example, asking too many questions is considered a sign of stupidity. People think you just don't get it. Later, people who ask a lot of questions are thought to be nosy or not minding their own business.

To top it off, no one ever listens to what we say in any case, so we don't get to experience the benefits of true listening. Others know this so they too learn to speak not to be understood but rather to make a point. Or to shout at the top of their lungs, leading to antagonism and hardened positions. In the midst of all this, the thing that suffers the most is the truth, the kernel of values we all carry inside ourselves.

Better and Improved

More specifically and more importantly, the book will change and improve the ways you communicate with your fellow employees and managers, your family, your neighbors, your friends and whoever else might cross your path during your journey through life. It is designed to dig beneath the surface gloss of most communication in order to get to "the important stuff."

By improving your communication skills, you open the doors to a better understanding of your customers, your family, your friends, and yourself. It's automatic. Better understanding allows you to present yourself and your ideas more effectively. Better understanding will cause those who hear you to actually listen to what you're saying. Better understanding will clear away the cobwebs that lack of genuine communication tends to create.

You will make the case for your product, service, organization or promotion or pay raise faster, better, and with more genuine conviction and with ultimately greater success. You'll find yourself in stronger, more meaningful relationships with those around you. You'll feel more confident and able, become more friendly and affable, and come to enjoy more deeply things you've taken for granted. You'll do all that because you know that It's the classic win/win situation.

The Four-Fold Way

I have a four-fold goal and purpose in writing this book. Using the VALUE MATCH system, I want to help you:

1. Change and improve the way you communicate.

2. Improve your relationships with others.

3. Present yourself more effectively.

4. Help others get what they want.

The four goals listed above seem to be modest—and perhaps they are. After all, I didn't list creating a warp drive for interstellar travel, bringing peace to the world, finding a solution for global poverty, or even finding a cure for the common cold. But I believe that, if we can start by changing ourselves for the better, we have gone a tremendous way towards changing our world for the better. And those four, modest proposals, if properly implemented, can be real world changers.

You've no doubt heard the old English proverb: "For want of a nail, the shoe was lost... for want of the shoe the horse was lost ..." The story progresses from horse to soldier to battle to war until finally the entire kingdom is lost. That might be an over-used and sometimes abused truism if I've ever heard one. But that doesn't take away from the essential truth of what it is trying to say—especially in reverse: If we take care of the small details, the nail for example, the bigger things, the kingdom, will inevitably come our way.

England's Westminster Abbey is an amazing place where the church member or tourist faces an overwhelming sense of history, a sense of monumental time and gigantic enterprises that helped tame the world. But not everything at Westminster Abbey has to do with large movements and quests. Some of that history is quite applicable to what we have been discussing above. Take, for example, the poetic and extremely wise words written on the crypt of an Anglican Bishop who lived circa 1100 AD:

When you master the principles of this book, you won't have to worry over all the things that "may have, might have, could have, should have been." You won't have time as you'll be too busy building a happy, healthy and productive life. You'll be too busy solidifying old and creating new relationships. When you learn and practice the VALUE MATCH principles outlined here, the world will turn! And it will turn in your favor. That's a promise.

The Next Step—The First Step

In the next chapter, I will show you what the first step is in learning to live by VALUE MATCH principles. That first step is the acceptance of integrity as the basis for everything we do in life. Integrity, in turn, implies knowing yourself, being in touch with your deepest feelings and emotions. It is only then that you can learn to sell using your heart rather than being a hard-sell salesperson.

VALUE CHECK

- Communication, it's not only important, it's absolutely crucial both personally and professionally
- The VALUE MATCH System: an introduction into how it is going to show you how to reach your full potential
- Taking advantage of our most important asset—the fact we're humans and possess the inherent and latent skills to communicate
- VALUE MATCH System versus previous sales programs
- How to communicate with others on a truthful level with all that false code stripped away
- The four-fold purpose as to why I wrote this book.

> *When we study human language, we are approaching what some might call the 'human essence,' the distinctive qualities of mind that are, so far as we know, unique to man and that are inseparable from any critical phase of human existence, personal or social.*
>
> **—Noam Chomsky**

CHAPTER ONE:

INTEGRITY

> *I am sure that in estimating
> every man's value either in private
> or public life, a pure integrity
> is the quality we take first into calculation, and
> that learning and talents are only the second.*
>
> **—Thomas Jefferson**

Your Values: Do You Know Who You Are?

Values Unlocked In This Chapter

In this chapter, we will discuss and learn about:

- The desire to know exactly what is going on in someone else's mind or heart
- The power of manipulation
- The value of integrity both in personal relationships and in the selling process
- The difference between manipulative selling and the VALUE MATCH process
- The expressing, clarifying and prioritizing of personal values
- How to be a heart-sell versus a hard-sell salesperson.

What's On Your Mind?

Wouldn't it be great to be able to read people's minds? To really know what a person is thinking? To reach in and tune into someone's innermost thought patterns? To leave nothing to chance or misinterpretation? Now, there's a thought!

Seriously, what would it be like if you could read the minds of your customers? Or the mind of your boss? Your spouse? The person next to you on the train? The salesperson making a presentation to Imagine knowing a customer's goals, objections, or reservations before he or she could even say them out loud. Her goals and objections and reservations—and not just what she says they are. Just imagine your negotiating power when you know the true bottom line rather than the amount stated. When you know exactly how far a person is willing to go before they break. You'd be fully aware of your customer's real state of need behind that false "I can take it or leave it" attitude. And they couldn't hide behind half-truths or use words to distract you from goal.

I believe most of us would say: "Yeah! That would be great! In fact, that would be more than great! That would be absolutely fantastic! Where can I sign up for mind-reading lessons? Where can I plug in so I can start probing those minds?"

Here's the problem. Here's the catch.

You think that reading someone else's mind would be great. But how would you feel if other people were able to read mind? Able to uncover innermost secrets? How would you feel about that situation? Ah-ha! That makes a difference, doesn't it? Suddenly, it doesn't seem so appetizing. Suddenly, there's something really sinister and unhealthy about it.

When you turn things around, you realize just how uncomfortable—and I mean truly uncomfortable—you'd be if other people had that ability over you. If other people could probe into deepest thoughts. Viewed from that perspective you can see the real power I'm referring to. It is also why, when you watch those science fiction programs and movies, everyone's afraid of people who can read minds. Everyone wants to rein them in or isolate them.

I can hear some of you protesting: "But I don't want to read the minds of others to manipulate people. Or to take advantage of them. I wouldn't use my power to do that sort of thing. That's unethical. I just want to know if they're telling the truth. Just want to get past the smokescreen that humans like to put in front of themselves when they're doing something."

That's good! And I'm glad you think that way. Real salespeople are always ethical and they never ever attempt to manipulate a customer. Those who do are not true salespeople in my estimation: they're like mind readers who would use their powers to gain mastery over someone else. And that doesn't just apply to salespeople but in all situations and walks of life, be they personal or professional.

Now, That's Manipulation!

Manipulation, defined as the act of influencing others to do what you want them to do in a way that is devious and underhanded, can take many forms. But they all come down to one thing: power over someone else. And there's a reason why the adjective "manipulative" isn't normally used in a complimentary way.

I taught a class recently in which a student shared that she was having a very difficult time asking questions—a key element in helping others get the things they want. And one of the important techniques we teach salespeople. Both curious and puzzled, I probed further to gather more information and to help determine what her problem might be. Her real problem, that is.

It turned out that her husband, a lawyer, always asked her questions to a point where it would really start to bother the woman. It was as if he had her in the courtroom witness box and was conducting a cross-examination. Needless to say, she just didn't like the process and came to identify any form of questioning with her husband's technique.

I was tempted to laugh at first, to file it under an eccentricity or some type of obsessive compulsive behavior. But then she told me that it didn't stop there. He used the information he extracted from her to argue with her, to show her the "error of her ways," and to win most arguments.

In other words, he would use what he got from her as ammunition for his subsequent verbal sparring matches. He used that information to get what he wanted out of a particular situation. In most cases, my student felt that what he wanted was not usually in her best interests. What he wanted often led to frustration on her part and feelings of being psychologically coerced into agreeing with him. That's manipulation!

I sent her home armed with some questioning and listening tools of her own. We taught her the VALUE MATCH principle that enabled her to listen in the face of being asked direct questions. To pay attention to the thoughts behind the questioning and to focus on those feelings and practices as opposed to the actual questions themselves. The true questioning behind the lawyer questions, in other words.

This helped her gain control of that specific conversation—and the Universal Conversation of which that particular dialogue was only a small fragment. She has since been able to feel better about herself, to gain more mastery of her life and to communicate better and more fruitfully, especially with her husband. She has tapped into a vein of confidence and feeling good that ever so much surpasses even a vein of gold or other precious metal.

That's a very good example of improving the quality of someone's life the VALUE MATCH way. She is still interested in what her husband has to say, but she has learned how to better communicate with him. She is no longer manipulated by him and his questions and both are the better for it. In fact, I recently received a letter from this woman that said the process we taught her has helped change her life—and has actually improved her marriage! What a great feeling it was to read those words. It truly was a rewarding experience.

The Integrity Factor

Manipulation has no place in the selling process and should be the furthest thing from the mind of a real salesperson. Being manipulative is equivalent to being underhanded and devious. That is just not acceptable and anyone involved in such practices will eventually come to regret it.

The difference between and comes down to one very important word—integrity. Manipulation and integrity can never occur in the same interaction. When you practice VALUE MATCH principles with integrity and with the intent of having the other person's best interests at heart, it is impossible for you to manipulate that person. When you have the other person's agenda at heart rather than your own, that's integrity.

The goal of the manipulative salesperson is the sale and nothing but. The sale at any cost, including the old joke about selling your soul to the devil to get what you want. That's all wrong. Both personally and professionally. We've all seen and the results of this kind of salesmanship: not very pretty to look at. The trading off of long-term goals for a quick fix benefit is never a pretty sight.

It's not only because it just won't work in most cases (people aren't that easily fooled) but also because it goes against the most important values in our society, the values most of us claim as fundamental. These are the same values that provide the glue that keeps our marriages intact, that allow families to function as healthy units, that make friendships blossom in trust and camaraderie. When one abandons these values just to make a sale, it's like abandoning spouse, family, friends, neighbors. It's like a slap across the face to those who love us and who want us to thrive as human beings.

The VALUE MATCH goal is to build trust with customers, discover the customers' values, and help them get what they want. If you place your focus on these principles and always perform to the highest standards of integrity, the sale will almost always follow. But even if it doesn't, not a problem. It's because it wasn't the right thing in the first place. It wasn't meant to be at that particular moment.

What this means is that you don't have to draw a line between your personal life and your professional life. In our personal lives, most of us naturally think about what those around us want and we want to help them get it: our spouse, our children, our friends. We know this is the right way to do things because it's something that works in a reciprocal way: when we help others get what they want, they help us get what we want.

In other words, in our personal lives, most of us have built-in values. What are these values? How do we recognize them? Values are those ideas, philosophies, morals, ideologies, people

> "The VALUE MATCH goal is to build trust with customers, discover their values, and help them get with they want"

or goals that help us shape who we are or how we spend our time and resources. Values are those things that are the most important to us.

Examples of personal values could be:

- **Personal Health**
- **Family and Friends**
- **Education and Experiences**
- **Focus on Spirituality**
- **Emphasis on Material Wealth**

Some of us think of these values in a conscious manner, read about them, worry about them even discuss them with others. Others simply live by them in a subconscious manner, without even thinking about them. No matter what though, we all have them. In fact, even Machiavelli had them!

I was told the story of a man, now quite old, who was a salesman back during the Great Depression of the 1930s. Those were tough times to be selling things. Few people had any money in those days and fewer still were willing to let go of what little they had. There were plenty of rainy days that needed taking care of before a family could think of new products to buy. While others gave up, this man had a philosophy that kept him going through those lean years.

"If you can't make a sale, make a friend," he'd say.

He always made time to get to know folks even if they couldn't or wouldn't buy his product. He knew that things change, that even Great Depressions will come to an end one day. So he worked on establishing things that don't change: relationships, friendships, bonding, links.

That's why he practiced what I call "heart-sell" instead of hard sell. He always served the best interests of his prospects and customers. Sure enough times got better. Money started circulating again and soon individuals, families and companies could afford to invest some of it.

Guess what happened? Right! When they needed the man's product, they remembered and called up their friend.

"And I had friends all over the country," he said.

He had his priorities straight and practiced integrity. That simple philosophy paid off time and time again for him. He found himself with both friends <u>and</u> sales! Ensuring that you too have your priorities straight and act with integrity is what this book is all about. The rest is guaranteed.

Are You A Heart-Sell Salesperson?	
The Hard-Sell Salesperson Says:	**The Heart-Sell Salesperson Says**
"Let's get you signed up today. No time to waste."	"Let's discuss the next logical step and then go from there."
"We only have one more. Get it while you can."	"Based on what I heard, I think this might be right for you."
"We'll need you to write a check before we can do anything."	"We'll need to secure it for you while we take care of the details."

When you are hard-sell, you sell the facts. When you are heart-sell, you sell with emotions. How do customers buy? They buy with emotions, then justify with facts. It's the same when you are trying to "sell" yourself. How many times have we been told that "love is blind" and that no one knows why two people like each other enough to spend the rest of their lives together?

Sure, we want to know the "facts" about the one we love but our decision is based on emotion. It is based on a reading of the other person, almost as if one could read not the other person's mind but their soul. That's exactly what two people with deep feelings for each other do: they reciprocate a mutual reading of souls, of values. It is thus that a decision is made.

The lawyer-husband of that student of mine we talked about before was a "hard-sell" person. He believed that by manipulating his wife he could get her to do what he wanted—and she'd be happy about it. Of course, that only works for so long. The student learned to read her husband's "heart-sell"—and that made all the difference.

A Defining Moment

Saying one has values is one thing. Knowing how to prioritize and make use of them in one's daily life is another. And it's something much more difficult to do. We all know people—heck, we've probably been there ourselves—who talk a mean value talk. But when it comes to putting those values into practice, suddenly they don't know which foot to put forward first.

When someone can't differentiate between values or can't come up with a way to prioritize them effectively, the values all become equal. They dissipate and lose their defining characteristics. That leads to confusion. It also leads to stasis and the inability to act upon the values that are or should be of most importance, the values that can make a difference in both your personal and professional life.

If you are already leading your life in accordance with the values you've chosen, then congratulations. You're well on your way to taking full advantage of the VALUE MATCH system.

There are some wonderful books on this topic. My favorite is by Steven Covey. Reading this book helped me tremendously in this area. And I highly recommend it to you as a companion to the ideas and principles exposed here.

The Next Step—The Second Step

Congratulations once again. You've taken the first step towards learning to live by VALUE MATCH principles. You've thought about the meaning of values and how values can be an important part of your life. You've discovered that values are something we all hold dear. And you've learned about the importance of aligning your values with the way you conduct your life.

The next step is to take a look at the value of integrity more closely. Specifically, what our integrity alarm means and how you can come to grips with yours.

VALUE CHECK

- The desire to know what goes on in another person's heart and mind: the pros and decided cons of mind reading
- The dangerous power of manipulation and how to get out from under its grip
- The value of integrity in one's life
- The vast difference between manipulative approaches to selling and the VALUE MATCH process
- The examination of personal values—we've all got 'em
- Being a heart-sell versus a hard-sell salesperson.

> *Integrity without knowledge*
> *is weak and useless,*
> *and knowledge without integrity*
> *is dangerous and dreadful.*
>
> **—Samuel Johnson**

CHAPTER TWO:

AN HONORABLE PROFESSION

*A man who is not honest
with himself presents
a hopeless case.*

—William J.H. Boetcker

A Value-Able Lesson About Values

Values Unlocked In This Chapter

In this chapter we will learn:

- How to come to grips with your integrity alarm
- The pride of salesmanship
- There is nothing stereotypical about someone who practices VALUE MATCH principles
- How to come to terms with conflicts that arise when you act contrary to your beliefs simply to advance in your career
- The definition of what a value is and what it does

Your Integrity Alarm

What happens when your actions betray your beliefs? When your mind (boss, sales manager, etc.) says sell the swampland in Florida—and not that good stuff around the Disney compound either—and your heart says: "No way"? That's cognitive dissonance. And that's why you'll botch the sale. Your presentation will be flawed; your timing will be off; your memory will fail to bring up facts and figures; and your heart just won't be in it.

The reason is simple. Your personal integrity will not allow you to manipulate your customer into a bad purchase. That's what sets you apart and that's why you're not a "glad-hander." This is a good thing. It is your integrity alarm screaming for attention, making sure you're listening—at least with your heart.

Your integrity alarm signals when you are about to do something that doesn't jive with your values. We all have one. Only for some, it sounds more loudly than for others. Our integrity alarm helps us make good, ethical decisions. Unfortunately, it can also betray us. In the case of a salesperson who has negative beliefs about the sales profession, those beliefs will set off the alarm. You can go through the motions all day long and still not have any success. Those negative beliefs will always hold you back.

I have a saying: "Dogs, children and customers can smell insincerity a mile way." People can sense when something is amiss. You have to believe in what you do to match values. If you hold negative beliefs about sales, you must change your attitude. I'll go into greater detail on this subject later in the book, but for now I believe we need to focus on getting comfortable with being a salesperson.

Before you can move forward in your career, it is essential that you come to grips with your integrity alarm.

Try the next exercise and see what you think.

A Value-Able Lesson: Part One

Each of us has a unique set of values. We have our own priorities. What are yours? Grab a pen and piece of paper, a pencil and a notepad, or boot up your computer and get into your word processing program and list your top ten values using this definition:

What Is Value?

Our personal values, even when we may use the same words, are unique. We all have unique priorities. Priorities can change instantly. And a value can even be more important than life itself. Here's proof.

Suppose you are on the edge of a long and narrow I-beam suspended ten or twenty stories above the hard, concrete streets. Would you walk across to the other end for a dollar? Of course not. How about five dollars? Ten dollars? Obviously, the answer is a universal: "No way, José."

Now, suppose I up the ante to a thousand, ten thousand, or a hundred thousand dollars—maybe a few of you might actually consider the proposition. And when I get to a million dollars, a few folks will convert their "no way" to a "well, sure." But there are still a lot of holdouts. When I toss in blowing wind and rain those brave "well, sures" would quickly become "you gotta be crazies!"

Now, suppose you're on that same building, ten or twenty stories up, and a baby, a child or a loved one is in danger of falling off the other side. I know that the vast majority of you would risk life and limb to rescue that other person—without a single thought of monetary reward. People who would never consider risking their lives for a million dollars wouldn't hesitate to take the same risk to save someone.

That is what values are all about. And values are what salespeople are all about.

My Values Take Flight

I remember the first time I thought seriously about my values, really thought about them. I was on a long flight, late at night, looking through my day planner. I noticed some pages I had not been aware of before. They were lined pages with the word "Value" at the top and with room to write in up to ten values beneath. I had nothing to do so I proceeded to write down those things that I thought most important, the things I felt were at the heart or should be at the heart of how I spent my time, focused my energy, and prioritized my activities.

Values were on my mind at the time. I had recently completed defining my goals for the next year, the same as I had done for several previous years. On the first sheet I had the routine and familiar goals, including having **X** number of dollars in the bank, achieving **X** number of sales goals, and growing my business to a desired level. But something was missing and I could feel it. I just didn't know what.

As I completed listing my ten values and turned the page to the next section, there were more pages allowing space to write a couple of paragraphs defining and explaining what each value meant to me. I took the time to write my feelings about each value. It was an experience I will never forget. I realized I had not really thought about or articulated values such as family, health, integrity, love of my wife, my spiritual belief in such a way ever before.

I realized that if I just used my goals to guide my activities, I would become a dispirited person. You see, I had just written down that I wanted to be in good health. I wanted to be at a certain weight that allowed me to participate in sports that I enjoyed. I wanted to be healthy as I grew older.

Upon review, I was in anything but good health. I was not losing weight. I was overweight. In fact, here's an example of how poor my health was at that time: I ran a three-mile fun run with my wife in which she had to run backwards in front of me to encourage me to finish — and she was six months pregnant! I was working very hard, spending long hours at my job and traveling way too much. My family life was suffering and my relationship with my children was suffering too. I noticed that wasn't even one of my own top ten values. I was out of alignment.

Steven Covey, author of , wrote about putting first things first by using an example of how to place rocks into a jar. For our purposes, think of those rocks as values. If you started putting the little rocks into the jar first and the medium rocks next, you may not be able to get the big rocks in without breaking the jar.

On the other hand, if you put the big rocks in first, you may or may not be able toget the medium and small rocks in. But if some don't make it, that's okay. <u>They are not as important as the big rocks</u>. So it was with me. I redid my goals. I outlined the different specific tasks and action steps I could do each week and month so that, if I completed them, they would help me accomplish what I really <u>valued</u>. I wrote down goals such as these:

(1) Take my wife Kathy on a date every Friday night.
(2) Bring Kathy flowers once a month.
(3) Volunteer as a coach in at least one team for my children all the time.
(4) Read to one of my children at least once a week.
(5) Spend one-on-one time with a child once a week.
(6) Read a new book once a month.
(7) Spend time each week with my family and my wife on building our spiritual foundation.
(8) Exercise regularly and stay healthy.

As much as it was possible, I made goals specific and achievable. The interesting thing is that finances, the goal that had for so long been my overriding focus, did not even make the list. Not that finances are not important. They are, but they no longer dictate how I live my life. The values I wrote so long ago are special to me. I cherish them and I honor them. I am committed to keeping them in my life.

A Value-Able Lesson — Part Two

List your ten most important personal values.

1._____

2._____

3._____

4._____

5._____

6._____

7._____

8._____

9._____

10._____

Review that list. Make sure you have listed the real top ten. You're not trying to impress anyone. This list is just for you. Remember, there's no right or wrong, so make sure that the answers really reflect your innermost feelings.

Now go over the list and select the three that are most important to you.

#1 Personal Value _____

#2 Personal Value _____

#3 Personal Value _____

Wanted: Value Differentiation

You see, **all values are equal in the absence of a value differentiation**. That means most of us don't think too much about our values or try to prioritize them before we act. We just react to the situation we find ourselves in. We must take the time to think ahead about where we want to be and what is important to us, as I did all those years ago. If I did it, you can do it, too. We are always faced with making choices that are or aren't in line with our values. A value differentiation can be an event or series of events in our lives or careers that sometimes require a quiet moment of reflection and decision on the part of the salesperson.

I challenge you to define your values. What does love of family, spiritual living, honesty, courage, or whatever you've written down really mean to you? Everyone is unique. If we were in one of my classes now we would begin to see two very interesting things:

(1) different people have an entirely different set of values, and
(2) there are significant differences in how different people define those words. A given value, such as spiritual living, can have as many different meanings as there are people in the world.

Let me emphasize this again: One thing I have learned is that when I ask people to do this exercise, I have never had one person come up with exactly the same set of values as someone else. Even in cases where people have the same top three in the same order, those values always have different meanings to the individuals involved.

Each of us has our own, unique way of looking at the world. That's what helps make life interesting. But it also makes life challenging. You have all heard of The Golden Rule. I'm sorry to say that it doesn't apply and that I don't believe in it. Are you shocked? Before you throw away this book and burn my image in effigy, let me share The Platinum Rule:

> "All values are equal in the absence of a value differentiation"

"Do unto others as they would have you do unto them."

This is, I believe, a higher law. It honors each person's uniqueness, their unique manner of looking at the world, their unique needs, and the unique ways they express themselves. To honor this higher law we must change the way we communicate. I'll cover more on this later, but for now just remember this. When a friend, prospect or customer expresses a value such as "I am spiritual" or "I love my family," you should:

- Take time to understand what that value means to that individual
- Find out how they define that value
- Learn why that value is important to them

You'll be surprised at what you learn.

A Value-Able Lesson — Part Three

So, on a personal level, what do your values really mean? Define your values and write them here.

        Value   Definition

#1 Value

_____

_____

#2 Value

_____

_____

#3 Value

_____

_____

    Understanding your own values will help you understand the values and priority of values of your customers. This is key to understanding people and to serving their needs as an effective salesperson.

    Here's the tough part of the exercise, a self-examination.

    How well are you directing your energies, your time, your activities and your life to match those values? Are you living up to your own standards? Values are a 24-hour a day commitment. You can't be honest at home or church, but dishonest at work. You can't value your family, but devote so much time to your career that you forget your kid's birthday. You can't devote hours of visualization techniques toward good health while stopping off for donuts on the way home.

    This is the next to hardest question you'll answer. Be candid and don't hesitate to be brutally honest. (Hey, nobody's looking over your shoulder so you can afford to be a straight shooter.)

- How does your life measure up to your values?
- Are you really living the life you want to live?
- Are you living consistent with your values?
- Do you want to achieve more?
- Do you realize that you really do have the power to live the life you want?
- Are you willing to take action steps to drive those values in your life?
- Where are you failing to meet your standards?
- How can you make your actions match your values?

Your Value-Oriented Goals

I offer another challenge. I would like you to write out nine steps you can take to get you closer to your goals. Make sure that your steps are (1) specific, (2) attainable, and (3) realistic.

1. Value_____

   Value Goal:_____

   Value Goal:_____

   Value Goal:_____

2. Value_____

   Value Goal:_____

   Value Goal:_____

   Value Goal:_____

3. Value_____

   Value Goal:_____

   Value Goal:_____

   Value Goal:_____

4. Value_____

   Value Goal:_____

   Value Goal:_____

   Value Goal:_____

5. Value_____
    Value Goal:_____
    Value Goal:_____
    Value Goal:_____

6. Value_____
    Value Goal:_____
    Value Goal:_____
    Value Goal:_____

7. Value_____
    Value Goal:_____
    Value Goal:_____
    Value Goal:_____

8. Value_____
    Value Goal:_____
    Value Goal:_____
    Value Goal:_____

9. Value_____
    Value Goal:_____
    Value Goal:_____
    Value Goal:_____

Change Starts With You

In his wonderful book, Bill Phillips challenges the reader to change his or her body by making changes in lifestyle and habits. He comments on the fact that the key ingredient to success is to be personally committed to making a change. Once you are committed, you can still cheat, but you are only cheating yourself. He claims that for people to have success, they must be true to themselves. My 12-year-old son Taylor is trying to get into better physical shape. He has committed personally to better eating. For him that means one dessert instead of two or three. Well, at least that's a start. Anyway, Taylor came home from school recently and said he had made a successful decision that day. He was presented with an opportunity to choose a healthy lunch or to go for a delicious, but less healthy alternative. He said: "A thought came to mind. I could cheat and no one would know. But just as quickly I realized I'd only be cheating myself."

When we identify our values, clearly articulate them and set goals and action steps that are in line with our values, but then don't follow through, we are only cheating ourselves. I want to encourage you to take this time to go all the way and take those steps to make positive change in your life as I, and my son, have had the opportunity to do.

> "When we identify our values, clearly articulate them and set goals and action steps ... but then don't follow through, we are only cheating ourselves"

The Lesson Of The Value-Able Lesson

What did we do in that exercise? Where did we go? What did I help you do? Together, we:
1. Identified what is most important to you: identifying your values
2. Clarified and prioritized your most important values
3. Created action steps by asking you to think about how you can align your life with the priority values.

In other words, You haven't been manipulated. You haven't been pressured or forced into a bad decision. You've just been helped on your way to achieving your goals in life by someone who wants to help you get there. That's what we salespeople do!

A Salesperson's Defining Moment

A salesperson is a <u>value differentiator</u>. The precise definition I use is:

Someone who helps someone else identify personal values, clarify those values, prioritize those values, and take action steps that help them realize more values in their life.

A real salesperson helps someone else do what he or she wants to do. And it's all about values.

Are You A Salesperson?

As a salesperson you must know (in your heart and not just in an intellectual way) these essentials:

- **Know yourself and your values**
- **Know why you are here**
- **Know why you are a salesperson**

Without a thorough and deeply-felt understanding of this knowledge, you become a ship without a rudder. You'll just bounce around wherever the storms of life toss you without the faintest hope of ever reaching your goals. Knowing your values provides that rudder. It's key to success in sales.

You Are The Foundation Of Your Own Success

They don't buy from industries, dealer/distributors, outlets or companies. Regardless of the product, the price, the company's reputation, return policies or the reputation of the service department, more than any other factor a sale depends on the trusting relationship between two human beings — a buyer and a seller. That is the ultimate bottom line in sales.

All things being equal (and in the mind of the customer that's the case most of the time), the sale stands or falls on your ability to build a trusting relationship with the prospect. Despite the similarities in product and service, you know that your automobile, house or raw material really is best for your prospect.

But what good is that information if you haven't built enough trust so that the customer can believe your presentation? All the colorful brochures, corporate videos, multi-page web sites, and testimonials in the world are meaningless if you don't build a trusting relationship. You are the only one who can do that. And that's why you are the foundation of your own success. That's good because, again,

A Graphic Tale

ServiceTrac provided one of our clients with dramatic proof of the need for discovering a customer's values. The company—let's call it Printer A—is a great firm, providing printing and related services for business and personal clients. Their nearest competitor is Printer B. Both are national firms.

We were hired by Printer A to conduct an in-depth series of mystery shops and we discovered some startling information. Telephone shoppers calling both Printer A and their nearest competitor selected our client exactly ZERO PERCENT of the time. Prospects who were shopping printing services with in-store visits were only selecting the company 30 percent of the time. Printer A is an excellent firm with state-of-the-art equipment and facilities and an impeccable reputation for quality work.

So what exactly was the problem?

Well, our research discovered that their customers did appreciate the value of the facilities and equipment. But, and it was a mighty big but, they felt the customer service people were stuffy, cold, overly professional and gave off the impression that they just didn't care about the customers. That's what customers felt and, whether those feelings were perceived or real, the problem itself was certainly as real as it could get—loss of sales!

About that time their nearest competitor launched a national advertising campaign. The theme was something along the lines of "Come Home To Printer B." The key word there is "home." Considering the values of the customer base, that was a brilliant strategy. Printer B didn't promote state-of-the-art equipment, modern facilities, computerization, Internet access, or any number of high-tech services.

Yes, they promoted technology, but they also realized that customers wanted more than anything else a feeling of warmth, trust and friendship. They stressed the "warm and fuzzy" feeling customers experience when they visit the stores. It worked and the reason it worked was Printer B's uncovering of customer values and then matching theirs to the clients'.

Sales: You Gotta Love It!

I love to meet people. I really enjoy getting to know others and I mean really getting to know them. I also enjoy helping others solve their challenges and get what they want from life. I sell or buy off my own ideas. Why? Well, I believe in what I am doing. I invest time researching and developing the products I sell. I truly believe they are great. They are the best. I believe that the customers using them—and that includes my training sessions—will improve their lives and businesses. I believe it with all my heart. If I didn't have this passion for what I do, I would not be able to spend my time and energy doing it.

I advise you to be the same way. You need to have a real passion for what you do. Do not continue on your current path if you don't have real passion for it. Get out and do something else where your passion can lead you to real success. Never settle for mediocrity. Since I believe so strongly in my own path, I have a responsibility to sell it to the best of my ability. I have to be good. I have to develop my skills completely. I should be able to help even the most confused, stubborn, or frustrated customer along a decision path to a solution to their needs. If they make a choice and move forward, I want those steps to be with me and my company and product.

More than all that, I have a responsibility to be good at <u>selling</u>. I have to develop the attitude, skills and knowledge to overcome any sales situation and to be successful in the face of any challenge. I take great pride in being a great salesperson. I feel if I am not at my best and a customer does not make a decision to go with me and my company, I have let that customer down. I have also let down my company and myself in the process. That's an every day challenge and I truly love it.

A Holiday Story

Holiday Retirement Corp. is the world's largest developer and manager of retirement apartments. They operate an excellent business and I have been privileged to provide sales training and consulting services for them for many years. I will always remember one of my first projects. As you know, we offer mystery shopping services. We send our representatives posing as customers into an organization to evaluate sales and customer service performance. In Holiday's case we sent shoppers to visit 130 properties and a number of their competitors.

I knew that their staff and management worked well, but I was surprised at how well. You see, we did not tell the shoppers who had hired them or that we had more than 100 shoppers working on the project. In the end, the shoppers picked Holiday properties as the #1 choice, hands down, over the competitors they had visited in the same market.

Intrigued by this result, I decided to do some additional research. I surveyed the shoppers to discover why they made that particular decision. They overwhelmingly said they had found a warm and friendly feeling in the Holiday buildings That feeling was more important than anything else. Feelings were more important than the physical structures, the pricing structure, and the breadth of services—and Holiday offers great value in all of these areas.

I learned that if you, as a salesperson, do not make a positive impression, you are off to a bad start, perhaps one from which you will not recover. This warm and friendly feeling promotes and communicates trust.

Holiday employees learn from Bart Colson, Holiday president, that a warm smile and a listening ear are the most important customer service skills in his company.

Keep it simple, right?

Right!

Customers Don't Care What You Know Until They Know How Much You Care

That phrase is worth repeating until it becomes second nature. Native Americans have a saying that you can't understand another person until you walk a mile in his or her moccasins. A more recent phrase says you have to "get inside their head." The key to selling is to understand your customer's values and matching them with the values of your product or service. Without it you're probably selling something they're not buying.

For example, if you don't know your customer's values, you could easily be promoting your product's price when he or she is really most concerned about delivery, on the job safety or retrofit capabilities. You could be selling from Column A, when they're really interested in the goodies over in Column B.

A real salesperson knows the importance and real value of serving a customer's real needs. That is a genuine service and that's why it's okay to be a salesperson.

In fact, it's not only okay—it's great!

The Next Step

Now that we've learned about integrity, prioritizing values, and the true art of salesmanship, the next step is to come to grips with the "value gap." Specifically, how to lessen that gap between you and the customer, between you and your spouse, between you and your family. Look at the gap like a prism that has been split in two—and that won't reflect light properly until the two pieces are brought back together again.

It's not all that hard—especially if you have that value oriented tutor to guide you. It's a whole lot easier than trying to read someone's mind!

VALUE CHECK

- It's okay to be a salesperson.
- When you practice VALUE MATCH principles, you are not the stereotypical salesperson.
- Before you move forward in your career, you must come to terms with the inevitable conflict that occurs when you act contrary to your beliefs.
- A value is something that drives your decisions, something you use to prioritize your time and resources.
- In the absence of a value differentiator, all values are equal.
- A good salesperson will: identify what is most important, clarify and prioritize the most important values, and create action steps by asking the customer to think about how he can align his life with the priority of values.
- As a salesperson you must know four essentials: (1) yourself (2) your values (3) why you are here (4) why you are a salesperson.
- Cognitive dissonance sets off an "integrity alarm" which is an internal warning device that sounds every time you think you're about to violate your personal value system.
- People buy from other people.
- Customers don't care how much you know until they know how much you care.
- Listen to your integrity alarm. Never do anything that goes against your values.
- Know your values. Identify, clarify, and prioritize them.
- Be a value differentiator.
- You are the foundation of your success.
- Sales is a matter of integrity.

We can change our whole life and the attitude of people around us simply by changing ourselves.

—Rudolf Driekurs

Man's chief purpose… is the creation and preservation of values;
that is what gives meaning to our civilization, and the participation
in this is what gives significance ultimately,
to the individual human life.

—Lewis Mumford

CHAPTER THREE:

FIRST IMPRESSIONS AND VALUE GAPS

> *To be trusted is
> a greater compliment
> than to be loved.*
>
> **—George Macdonald**

> *No virtue is more universally accepted
> as a test of good character
> than trustworthiness.*
>
> **—Harry Emerson Fosdick**

Much More Than A Sale: The Importance of Trust

Values Unlocked In This Chapter

In this chapter, we will thoroughly discuss and learn about five very key and very important elements that help define not just the processing of successful selling but also the essence of developing successful relationships with those around us. Those five elements are:

- The Four Customer (Relationship) Goals.
- The Four Steps Of The VALUE MATCH Process.
- Central Barriers Inhibiting The Process.
- Your Customer (Relationship Development) Is Your Challenge.
- Who Or What Is The Customer's (Relationship's) Worst Enemy?

Sales And Life: A Matter of Relationships

We have just invested some time learning about how true salesmanship works and how, when properly practiced, it is a worthwhile, and if I may say so, a noble profession. It's also a profession that has been part of human interaction since the first days of barter and other forms of trade.

Okay, so maybe saying that we're here to further humanity, promote good will, and spread joy on Earth is a bit of overkill. But we can state without fear of exaggeration that we are certainly doing something in which we believe strongly and about which we feel passionate. And, on occasion, we might even manage to spread some of that elusive joy. Lord knows, we could certainly use some of it!

At the same time, we have also been discussing how the act of selling, be it a product or a service, is so very similar to other experiences we all take part in as human beings. These are experiences that play a large role in shaping us.

We have talked about how the process of selling can be seen as a metaphor for life in general and how successful sales are similar to successful relationships in both our personal and our professional lives. In fact, the art of selling ourselves to others is a key to living a full and fulfilling social life.

That leads us to the 64 million dollar question: If everything is so rosy, why aren't customers flocking to us in droves? Why aren't they coming in to share their problems openly so we can work together to solve those problems and offer solutions? Finally, why aren't most relationships working as well as they should?

> "Why don't you tell a salesperson that your car is on its last legs when you step on to the car lot?"

Well, when it comes to customers, the truth is they still have that old, tired image of the stereotypical "used car salesman" stuck in their minds. They still see us all as Willy Loman clones, willing to do anything, including selling our souls, just to make a sale. They still don't trust us. They keep their guard up, raising the alarm anytime they see a salesperson heading their way.

In fact, you know what? Most of the time, they don't even tell us the truth! That's right. You heard me.

Customers lie all the time.

Or at the very least they prevaricate. They don't tell the whole truth, so help them. They only tell us bits and parts and they make sure to keep the rest under wraps. They make sure the best parts, the most significant parts, are hidden from sight.

Why? You know the answer. Just think about it for a moment. It's a bit like what we talked about earlier when it came to the mind-reading stuff. Why don't you tell a salesperson that your car is on its last legs when you step on to the car lot? When shopping for a new refrigerator, why don't you tell the appliance salesperson that your Christmas bonus was really big this year?

It's simple. You don't trust the sales-person to have your best interests at heart. You're concerned that the person will turn around and use this new information to help manipulate you into an unfavorable "deal." Or get you to buy something you don't want. You're afraid that you'll be taken advantage of by an unscrupulous person who has wangled essential information out of you.

This attitude is basic human nature for most of us. It's part of our built-in survival instincts. Unless we see some advantage to doing otherwise, we keep information close to the vest. We don't share the truth with just anyone—and often not even with our nearest and dearest, let alone with the typical salesperson. It's something we learn from experience, from being burnt by those who think nothing of taking advantage of people at their weakest moments.

This can be deadly to the sales process—whether that involves actual products or attempts to make new friends. As humans in general and salespeople in particular, we must be prepared with the skills to establish a relationship that will foster the **truth**. That will make the truth transparent for all to see. We must be prepared to take that leap of faith and to leave ourselves open to trusting arms: we must be willing to leap, trusting that the safety net is there for us.

This is what is meant by closing the value gap, the difference between what a person says and another hears, the confusion between what a person wants and what the other person thinks he wants. We've all experienced such situations, both in our personal lives and professionally. We thought we meant something and the other person took it completely another way. It's the old joke about a line of people whispering something in one another's ear and how it comes out the other side completely distorted. An old joke but too often also sadly true.

Short of being able to read each others' minds, there is only one way to effectively close that value gap: by building trust, by learning a person's real needs, and by helping people overcome the fears that keep them from committing themselves—whether that means the acquiring of products and services they truly need or the improving of their relationships. We must learn to inspire people to take chances and to put their faith in us.

Now, that's what I call noble—and a far cry from the old used-car salesperson stereotype!

Every Gap Has Two Sides

If you visit the breathtaking chasm that is the Rio Grande Gorge near Taos, New Mexico, you'll notice that this very deep gap in the earth is defined by two very separate rocky cliffs – two distinct sides, in other words, with a large empty space inbetween. That's a pretty fair description of the gap between the salesperson and the typical prospect or customer. Or even between two humans who are having trouble understanding one another.

The bridge that spans the two sides of the Rio Grande Gorge
(Courtesy New Mexico State Highway Commission).

Our job, both as professional salespeople and as human communicators who want to enjoy better relationships, is to do what the engineers in New Mexico did: build a bridge from one side to the other, from ourselves to the customer, from one human being to another. I call the space dividing the customer and the salesperson, one person and another, the Value Gap. The Value Gap is defined by an empty space wherein dwells the lack of truth that keeps the two sides apart.

Of course, the gap between the two sides of the Rio Grande Gorge is a natural phenomenon, something caused by the upheaval of the earth, by wind, and by erosion. The gap between people in their efforts to communicate is definitely not a natural one. It is a sign of frustration and the inability to achieve fulfilling lives. It is a sign that things aren't quite right. Each side thinks they are doing the right thing but for some reason they can't seem to find a way to bridge their differences.

The way to bridge this unnatural divide, this frustrating Value Gap, lies with the VALUE MATCH process. The great thing about VALUE MATCH is that it works both for the customer-salesperson relationship and the personal connections and interactions that all humans face in their efforts to make contact with others. In a sense, it can do double duty.

Let's start with the customer-salesperson relationship. The first thing that needs to be done is to understand what it is exactly that the customer wants and needs.

Below is a graphic representation of the Value Gap in terms of the customer-salesperson relationship and process.

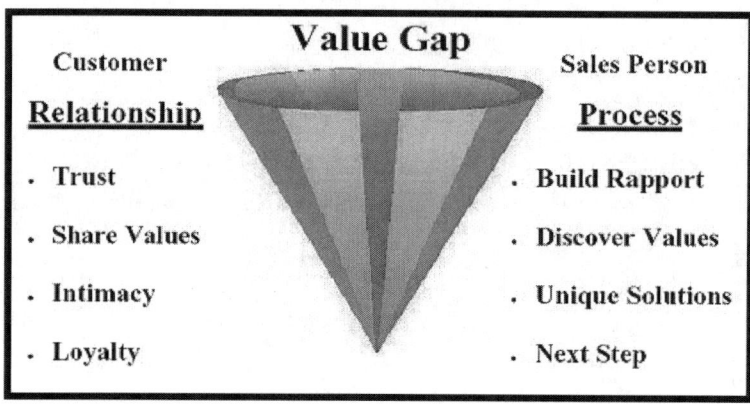

The Value Gap that needs to be bridged between customer and salesperson.

As you can see from the illustration, the customer side of the relationship is defined by a need for:

- **TRUST:** the desire to build a relationship of trust so that he or she can get the advice needed for making an informed purchasing decision.
- **SHARE VALUES:** or, in the absence of that ability, to at least gather information as to the other person's intentions so that one can decide if it is possible to share values eventually.
- **INTIMACY:** to analyze their real needs with someone they trust as a friend, with someone who makes them feel like an individual rather than just another number.
- **LOYALTY:** Once intimate details of the real situation are shared and true needs are discovered, a personal bond is created that is not easily broken, a bond that goes beyond the usual customer-salesperson relationship.

While similar in many ways, on the salesperson's side, the relationship/process is defined by a need to:

- **BUILD RAPPORT:** or, in other words, making a positive first impression, and then building on that to identify common personal values and to develop trust and hopefully friendship.
- **DISCOVER VALUES:** that is, to begin to leverage the initial fragile trust that has been created and to begin to identify and discuss the customer's real needs as opposed to the perceived needs and wants.
- **UNIQUE SOLUTIONS:** Presenting real and understandable solutions that are tailored to the customer's unique situation rather than the usual one-size-fits-all solutions
- **NEXT STEP:** Help the customer take the next step by initiating the decision process and then helping them identify and overcome their fears of moving forward.

Each one of those items represents a step in a process—and it has to be a paired process of the gap is to be bridged. In other words, we have:

- Build Rapport = Trust
- Discover Values = Share Values
- Unique Solutions = Intimacy
- Next Step = Loyalty

What this means is that sales isn't a one-sided presentation with one active and one passive participant.

While the salesperson is going through his or her sales process, the customer is experiencing a very well-defined process of his or her own in order to arrive at a decision as to whether or they want to build a relationship. A good salesperson will know and understand what's happening on both sides of the gap and be prepared to help the customer through the process using the VALUE MATCH skills. This is key to bridging that gap. And always remember that steps cannot be skipped or overlooked. Like in baseball, you may round all the bases but you might still be out.

Your Customer, Your Challenge

One of my favorite sayings from the sales world goes something like this: **"Customers don't care how much you know until they know how much you care."** But getting a customer to believe that you really care for him or her is a lot easier said than done. Especially if that customer has already been "burned" during a sales transaction and is thus understandably wary.

Therefore, it can happen that all too often the very person you want to help the most is the one person who will challenge you the most. All too often your customer enters the sale process like a determined running back dashing for the opponent's end of the football field. He's got his values tucked in like a football and his forearm is thrust out like a battering ram to keep anyone from getting too close.

His goal is to get through the process without letting any salesperson come within arm's length of those precious, closely-held values. He's not going to let any old salesperson take them away from him. And, while he's running that way, head down and forearm out, he's not going to stop to see if the person before him is friend or foe: he's going to assume everyone is the enemy. Anyone in his way is going to get run over.

At the same time, what is this person trying to do? What is he trying to achieve? Most likely, he is trying to solve a problem—

> "Customers don't care how much you know until they know how much you care"

and to make some decisions about whether to purchase a product or service. And the person he's fending off is most often the one most qualified to help him arrive at the right solution, to help him make the right decision. Isn't that ironic?

What exactly is happening here? Well, most often the customer is initially on a search for information that can be taken back and shared with a trusted friend. This can be someone at work, a pal or a spouse who can offer advice on the next step. Isn't that curious? The customer relegates his or her own position to that of information gatherer seeking as many facts and figures as quickly as possible.

Apparently the customer's goal is to get as educated as fast as possible about a particular situation and then leave without making any commitment. He then makes a lateral pass and hands over the buying decision to someone else who may or may not have a clue as to the appropriate next step. But the important thing, the key thing here, is that this "someone else" is a trusted friend, someone who shares the customer's values and is ready to pitch in to make sure the person does the right thing.

It's a major part of your job to become that trusted friend, to start the process whereby you and the customer can achieve value matching and sharing. This is an important step, not only for your own sales success but also for the customer's satisfaction. After all, nobody, certainly nobody in your customer's circle of friends, is likely to know more about your product or service than you. So why should you be left out of that decision-making process? It doesn't make much sense, does it?

Who Is The Customer's Worst Enemy?

Thus, by not having you as a most trusted and best friend, essentially the customer becomes his or her own worst enemy. The customer's unwillingness to trust, share values, and be truthful about the real situation and challenges turns the sales experience into a self-generated less than productive experience. If this situation is left unchecked, it usually means more time is taken up and the results are mediocre and frustrating for everyone involved.

Again, by being overly concerned about keeping things close to his or her vest, the customer actually creates a situation in which it becomes very difficult for him to win. The process takes more time than is really necessary. The customer never gets all the information needed, nor is that information targeted to real needs. He or she doesn't feel that they are getting the whole truth. The customer may actually believe that the salesperson isn't even addressing his or her real needs. The bridge over the gap is never completed. The customer doesn't buy and everybody loses.

Basically, that's the value gap in action. It's the gap between hiding the truth and dealing only on the outside of things or telling the truth and operating to everyone's mutual benefit on the inside.

Remember the "you-just-don't-understand" story? This is the example from everyday life where you and a friend are having a discussion about the friend's personal problem. The friend is relating the issues to you and then you, trying to be helpful, offer some ideas for a solution, based on what your friend has told you. But, instead of being praised for your astuteness and sagacity, you immediately get: "You do not understand!"

The truth of the matter is that the friend is probably right. You do not understand. The thing is that you cannot offer a true solution because the friend either consciously or unconsciously has not shared the true situation and their true feelings about the problem with you. Your friend has kept something back, something essential.

Without that valuable piece of information, your well intentioned and well thought out advice on how to solve the problem is actually off target. You are trying to solve a problem that does not exist and not dealing with the problem that <u>does</u> exist. And all because your friend has not told you the true story or the whole story. All because your friend has decided to keep something back. This is a perfect example of what I mean by value gap.

The Customer's Process: Caution, Proceed With Care

While you, the salesperson, are working your way through the four steps of the VALUE MATCH process, never lose sight of the fact that your customer is going through his or her own process. Both programs are running in tandem and at the same time, and both are tied together. So, it stands to reason that you can only move as fast through your process as the customer can move through his or hers.

As we've already seen, the customer has four steps that he or she normally works through before arriving at any decision—whether that decision involves the purchasing of a product or service or the acquiring of a new friend. It shouldn't come as a big surprise that customers are highly protective of these four special values. As I previously indicated, those four steps are:

The Foundation for Friendship With Your Customer	
The Characteristic Is:	**It's Important Because:**
Trust	It helps to build rapport.
Intimacy	Helps to create unique solutions.
Shared Values	Helps to discover values of the customer
Loyalty	Helps the customer take the next step.

Let's take a closer look at each one of these, starting with a graphic of what the characteristics are and why they're so important in the sales process. Why, in fact, the success of any sale depends on the working through of these four values to create a trusting relationship between the person doing the selling and the person doing the buying—be that real products and services or personal interactions. In essence, who you are becomes more important than what you do when it comes to closing any deal.

What the customer expects out of a sales relationship.

1. Customers want to buy from people they trust.

Let's face it, for the most part, customers just don't trust salespeople. Generally, they don't trust them to do what's best for them, and in particular, they don't trust them to give them the best deal. Sadly and unfortunately, that skepticism is justified in a few rare instances, thanks to the unscrupulousness of a few rotten apples in the sales barrel. Just as there are a few untrustworthy people who masquerade as friends and family members but who only have their own interests at heart.

But clearly these are in the very small minority. Most of us are good, decent folks working hard to provide real service to other decent folks.

Unfortunately, the majority has to pay for the misdeeds of this small minority—because this is what most customers remember. The good experiences tend to be taken for granted; the bad experiences linger on like a bad smell. Right or wrong, that is the situation we face and must overcome. The instant a customer contacts you (even if it's only eye contact), he or she immediately sees you through a filter of skepticism. The customer immediately puts up a guard.

2. Customers want to buy from people who share their values.

It's only natural. Without trust you can never move any further forward with the selling process. You can never get to this second step of sharing values. You can never place your arm around the customer and call him or her friend. This simple observation leads to all sorts of trouble for the poor salesperson.

For example, how can you expect to motivate someone to make a purchase or decision if that person is unwilling to share his or her motivation because they don't trust you? You just can't do it. On the simplest sales level, you could be promoting low price while the buyer is most concerned with safety features or delivery dates. On another level, it all becomes somewhat of a gamble—with the hope that you'll hit what it is that the customer really seeks by simply going through a variety of possibilities.

Again, remember the story of the friend who only pretends to confide in you. I guess if you dispensed enough advice to that person, you could probably hit on a solution that is right for him or her. But who wants to base their friendship on a crapshoot? Who wants to run through a list of potential solutions like some sort of laundry list? We all realize that friendship is more important than that.

3. Customers want intimacy.

The real reasons and motivations why people buy a product or service are often well-kept secrets—either conscious or unconscious. Sometimes the secrets are minor and of little import. Like the reasons why a customer may prefer one brand of laundry soap rather than another.

Other times the secrets are highly volatile and personal. For example, someone looking for an assisted care community for a parent may be holding back on that parent's serious medical history. Someone looking at cars may be embarrassed that certain models are just out of his price range.

A good salesperson creates an atmosphere in which the customer is comfortable in sharing these intimate details. And these details help the salesperson narrow down the potential products and/or services the customer is seeking. Thus, the sharing of these intimate details save valuable time for both of them. It also increases the possibility that the customer will seek out the same salesperson the next time around. This is one case where familiarity definitely does not breed contempt. Rather it breeds closeness and efficiency.

> "A good salesperson creates an atmosphere in which the customer is comfortable sharing these intimate details"

4. Customers want loyalty.

Not only do customers demand to receive loyalty, They want people and organizations to whom they can offer that loyalty without question. Once loyalty is established, the customer is unlikely to share his or her personal information with anyone else, and especially not with your competitor.

Obviously, that's a pretty big hill to climb, and gaining a customer's loyalty is not as simple or easy as it sounds, especially considering a customer's built-in skepticism. For one thing, a salesperson has to overcome the customer's feeling that the salesperson is only trying to gain that loyalty in order to sell the person something.

But the salesperson who earns a customer's loyalty earns a

fierce loyalty. That customer will then be willing to listen to and incorporate your heart-felt recommendations into his or her life. And more importantly even overlook small challenges that commonly occur in the process. In fact, it would then take a mighty big shake-up for a salesperson to consequently lose a customer's loyalty. Just as it takes a mighty big blow to sever a close friendship or break up a loving marriage.

The Salesperson's Task: Closing The Gap

We've just seen how your typical prospect or customer approaches the selling situation—and the various demands such a customer makes before making the decision whether or not to buy. The salesperson, of course, has an entirely different perspective, a different way of looking at what is taking place. But that perspective can't be so far off from what the customer wants that the two processes never actually meet.

For example, your goal can't be that you simply want to separate someone from his or her hard earned money, meet this month's quota, win a free trip, earn a bigger commission, or even close a sale no matter what the consequences. No. You want to help people get the products and services they want and need. That has to be the clear focus for what you do.

Doing that properly means bridging the Value Gap and you do that by mastering the four steps in the sales process. And remember, just as you must move through a sales process during the course of a sale, so must the customer proceed through his or her relationship process. Let's look at these steps one at a time to see how they connect up.

The table below gives a breakdown of the four steps a salesperson needs to take if he or she wants to be successful in the making of a sale. As you can see, there is a sense of direct reciprocity between the person doing the selling and the person who is going to buy the product or service.

Step	Salesperson	Customer	Question	Answers
1	Build rapport with the customer (getting from business to a rapport)	Trust (building a relationship/ making a friend)	Why is it important to build rapport and trust?	People buy from people they trust. People must have trust to share real information. People get advice from friends. People buy on emotion and justify it with facts.
2	Discover the customer's values ("getting inside the circle")	Value Sharing (sharing the truth)	What does it mean to "get inside the circle"?	Discovering the truth. Uncovering a person's true values. By sharing the truth the customer will get a better solution.
3	Present a unique solution to the customer's need (match your unique strengths with the customer's unique values)	Intimacy (sharing secrets)	What kind of solution do you present if you have all the info? What do you need to present the unique solution?	Solutions that benefit the customer, the community and the salesperson. Intimacy and trust. Real needs.
4	Help the customer take the next step (ask a friend to take the next best action step)	Loyalty (working through the challenges)	What is a closing of a deal? How can a lack of intimacy or loyalty affect a close?	The beginning of a relationship. The beginning of solving a problem or problems. Can cause a person to change their mind after a decision has been made (buyer's remorse).

1. Build rapport with the customer.

Make a friend before you try to make a sale. Be there for the other person before offering him or her a product or service—or even friendly advice. Every preceding step builds towards the next one and so on right up to achieving your goal. You want to take these steps one at a time and in the proper order, beginning with building rapport. And you want to make sure that each step has been successfully achieved before moving on to the next.

To skip a step or to get out of order results in nothing more than a waste of time for both you and your customer. Taken out of order, the last step becomes failure. And it is very difficult to try to start all over again because now you've increased the other person's skepticism levels to the point where he or she might no longer be interested in anything you say—even if it could lead to the person getting what he or she really needs.

A handy rule of thumb: If you don't have rapport with your customer, you don't have a foundation upon which to build the rest of your presentation. It becomes a slippery slope and you're the one doing the downward sliding. Without rapport you can't discover, much less meet, the real needs of that customer. Again, wasted time and failure await you at the end of the road.

Rapport allows you to become a trusted friend rather than a mistrusted outsider. People always seek advice from friends, especially on purchases. Doesn't it make sense for you to become one of those friends? After all, of all the friends your customer will ask, who will be better equipped to give the right advice than you? But you can have all the greatest advice in the world and it'll come to naught if you don't build that rapport first.

You will discover a great many other benefits to building rapport. You will make your way through the sales process much faster. There are just fewer roadblocks when a customer has trust. The time you and your customer invest will be much more effective. Let's face it, an awful lot of time is wasted while a customer dawdles or tosses around unimportant objections because he doesn't yet feel a sense of rapport.

> "Rapport allows you to become a trusted friend rather than a mistrusted outsider"

An honest, open, two-way dialog is enhanced by rapport. In fact, it is made possible by a good rapport. You and your customer can get down to the basics without all the unnecessary verbal "tap dancing" that bogs down and often kills the sales process. Lastly, rapport keeps you focused on your customer's real issues so you can find unique solutions to unique problems. You don't waste time with that laundry list.

2. Discover your customer's true values.

You must discover what motivates your customer to buy. This is essential. And you do that by discovering your customer's true values. Earlier I mentioned getting inside. What I mean by that is getting "inside the circle." This is the area where the truth about your customer is most likely to reside.

Some customers will share little or no information. Others will share a lot of information with you. But you'll soon discover that all or most of it will be completely irrelevant to serving that person's real needs. Inexperienced (or sometimes deluded) salespeople often mistake this for legitimate communication. They get caught up in these irrelevancies and details that lead nowhere. They think they are getting to know a customer.

Nothing could be further from the truth because the customer is only sharing what I call that "outside the circle" information. It typically includes such things as name, home address, make and model of car, clothing, education, hobbies and interests and so on. It's also the sort of thing that a good salesperson can retrieve without even having a face-to-face with the other person.

Sure some of that information may be interesting and later on it may even be somewhat helpful in the details of a sale. But it is by definition factual and, as I've already stated, . That is, they buy based on the values associated with the mutually-shared information. They use facts to justify the purchase after the sale.

All the valuable information you really need to serve that customer, to help that person with his problems, is found "inside the circle." Inside is where you'll find such vital information as salary, savings, projected income, debt load, health considerations, bad habits, religion and politics. This is where you'll also find the person's hopes and dreams, vision of life, attitudes and other "fuzzy" stuff that is the true shaper of a human being.

Of course, this is the very information you must have to match your unique solution to the person's unique problem. And your customer will fight like mad to keep you out, to make sure all you get is "outside the circle" material, the stuff they feel is harmless. It sounds crazy, but there you have it: The very information the customer most needs to give you is the very information he resists sharing.

So how does one go about getting this information? How does one break inside the circle? Well, this is where building rapport and trust becomes so important and crucial <u>before</u> you reach the step where you need to get key information. Without rapport the next step becomes a stop. The ladder you were climbing suddenly ran out of rungs and you can't go any further.

It is essential to discover your customer's real values. This is, after all, the core of the VALUE MATCH process, the key to unlocking everything else and having success. How can you match values if you don't know them? Never forget, despite their apparent resistance to trust, customers really want to help you make the sale. Friends really want to tell you their problems and do it truthfully. That's why they're there in the first place. You just need to earn their trust.

> "It is essential to discover your customer's real values. This is the core of the VALUE MATCH process"

3. Present a unique solution to your customer's problems.

Remember we've been saying that every customer has a unique need, a unique reason for wanting a particular product or service. But he or she may not be willing to disclose that reason to just anyone. It is your responsibility to demonstrate how your product or service is the unique solution for that need. But you can't just pick solutions out of a selection of pre-fab explanations and then cross your fingers that one of them might be the right one. The customer will simply leave you standing there.

Again, you have to build on the previous steps to make this step effective. If you haven't discovered your customer's values, you will only present solutions that do not or even cannot benefit the customer. If you haven't gained or earned that person's trust, you will flounder and find yourself lost, thrashing against an invisible barrier that keeps you from achieving your goals.

If you think about it, there are numerous logical reasons why your product is the one best answer to your customer's prayers. As well, there are numerous logical explanations you can give to a person when he or she asks for your advice. When you build intimacy and trust, your customer will provide you with the information necessary to present your unique solution. When you build intimacy and trust, you can tailor your advice to fit precisely and unlock your friend's problem.

4. Make heartfelt recommendation to friend to take the next best action step.

You do that by making a heartfelt recommendation to buy. Regardless of your desire to close, without building rapport, discovering values and presenting your unique solution, you will inevitably set off your customer's integrity alarm. Your motives, as pure as they may be, will be betrayed by your apparent lack of conviction and inadequate presentation. The customer will feel pressured or forced and that gap will just get deeper and wider.

Here's some really good news about this four-step process:

When you complete effectively the first three steps, the last step, closing, becomes surprisingly easy.

Think about that. The one step most salespeople dread becomes the easiest step of all. When you follow the VALUE MATCH process correctly, sometimes closing is almost effortless. It flows naturally from everything else. It's the natural result of the process. It's almost as if you can't lose.

So here's the question: Can you make a **"heartfelt recommendation to a friend to take the next best action step"**? Let's break that sentence down into its component parts and see what happens.

- **Heartfelt:** You have a passion for what you are doing. You believe in your product or service and you feel it is the best available solution on the market. You're not afraid to take a stand and to show others exactly how you feel about it. You make others feel your passion.
- **Recommendation:** You make specific recommendations instead of vague suggestions. You provide a point by point, step by step breakdown rather than some wishy washy proposal.

- **To A Friend:** You have built a friendship, shared values and feel you have the trust of your customer. He is now a friend with all that implies rather than just someone to whom you'll try to sell your products or services.
- **To Take The Next Best Action Step:** This doesn't refer to the next best step for you, but rather the best step to help your customer get the solution to his or her unique need.

When The Sales Process Breaks Down

Of course, not every attempt at selling results in a positive ending. Just like not every effort at helping a friend or family member with a problem ends up being useful. The process can break down completely despite our best efforts. And the reasons for such breakdowns can be as varied as the different types of selling situations.

In my classes and seminars I usually get peppered with questions on this topic. Everyone wants to know why some things just don't work out. Below are some of the most common questions, with my typically brisk and "peppery" answers.

"What keeps customers and salespeople apart, not allowing the sale to go through?"

Usually the gap remains wide due to a lack of time, a lack of trust on the customer's side, a fear of speaking the truth, or a presentation based on a perceived vs. a real need. Any one of these or a combination could be the cause.

"Why do customers sometimes refrain from telling the truth, leading to confusion on the part of the salesperson?"

In a word – risk. The customers' perceived risk in revealing that all-important inside information outweighs their need for the product or service. The VALUE MATCH process is designed to eliminate this fear of taking a risk. Eliminate the fear and you eliminate any reason not to tell the truth.

"What keeps salespeople from getting the truth?"

Generally, the salesperson is lacking in skills and/or knowledge, or has a poor attitude, a lack of focus on the customer's real needs, or an unwillingness to make the effort to get "inside the circle." In other words, they don't want to invest the time and energy needed for the process to work. A similar thing occurs when a friend or family member with a problem comes to someone who isn't equipped to understand what the person is really saying—or doesn't take the time to "listen between the lines."

"Why do salespeople rush the decision process?"

I think the biggest reason is a lack of sincerity and a lack of faith in their sales process. If they knew and practiced the VALUE MATCH process, this insecurity would melt away. Following the process leads to a natural and often easy sale. There's no need to rush because everything happens properly in its own good time. And that's all the time you need. You have to let things play themselves out. Rushing simply breaks the chain.

"What happens when you miss a step in the sales process?"

You stall out and can't move forward. The value gap returns stronger than ever. The key no longer unlocks the values. The process breaks down and you can't complete it no matter how hard you try. Again, take it one step at a time, each step in the proper order. Allow time for the process to work and don't take any short cuts.

The solution to these (and other problems) is simple:
Close The Value Gap

When driving through town and you see a yellow light up ahead, what do you do? Do you follow the law and good common sense, stopping when you judge you can't make it through and going through when there's plenty of time before the light turns red? Or do you step on the gas each time and try to beat the red light, no matter what the situation and conditions?

How you handle yourself in traffic is your own business (and that of the traffic cop and the judge). But how you handle yourself when you see a "yellow light" in sales is my department.

What exactly is a yellow light during a sale? A yellow light is simply a concern or an objection raised by a customer. Unlike traffic yellow lights, this light is unpredictable and can appear at any time. It has only one meaning: It's a clear warning signal to slow down and address the situation, perhaps even a signal to start over.

Unfortunately, many salespeople treat these yellow lights in a similar manner as traffic yellow lights. Instead, of slowing down, they tend to speed up, in the hope that they can get past the customer's objections by simply ignoring them or pretending they don't exist. In the vast majority of cases, the sale falls through when the salesperson tries to ride roughshod over a customer's concerns or objections. I mean, how would you feel if someone ignored your concerns or made light of them?

There are ways to detect yellow lights that flash during the sales process. Some typical yellow lights to watch for include:

Typical Yellow Lights
- **Negative body language**
- **Nervous eye contact**
- **A refusal to look you in the eye**
- **Negative words**
- **Refusal to respond verbally**
- **Any type of negative feedback (looking at a wristwatch, for example, or tapping toes)**
- **Talking faster**
- **Voice tone changes**
- **Unreasonable objections**
- **Unrealistic objectives**

When you encounter these sales pitch road signs, as you inevitably will, the tendency will be to rush ahead and try to "beat" the red light. To push forward with making the sale and striking while the iron's hot, as it were. And that's the worst possible strategy. There may be a traffic cop hiding behind the billboard, ready to stop you in your tracks. Worse there may be a giant semi about to round the corner and crush your presentation, destroying all the good will you've earned to that point and creating a value gap even wider than the Rio Grande Chasm.

> "A yellow light is a clear warning signal to slow down and address the situation"

The professional stops immediately upon encountering a sales yellow light. He or she then backs up and starts over from the point where the warning light appeared. This way you don't have to run a yellow light (or run away from it) because you make it go away. Why struggle with a problem and only make it worse, when you can use the VALUE MATCH process to make it disappear?

Remember that the Value Gap is real. There's no way around it because it is part and parcel of our interactions, of our being human (and our not being able to read minds). The width and depth will vary from customer to customer, from person to person, from situation to situation. But it is a factor you must face and must overcome if you wish to have any success: both as a salesperson and as a human being who wishes to communicate effectively.

It is our responsibility to bridge this gap. The customer just can't do it on his or her own. If they could, they wouldn't have come to you for help. Somehow, we have to change the initial non-trusting relationship into a trusting one. We must become someone with whom our customers can share information just like they would with a trusted friend.

We must help them allow us to help provide unique solutions to unique problems, to build loyalty, and help move them on to the next step.

Just how do we go about doing that?

Let's start with the next chapter where we talk about the **A.S.K.** Principles of Selling.

VALUE CHECK

- Every gap has two sides which requires a bridge for real communication.
- Each of us has a set of personal values which shapes the way we see the world and therefore the way we act and react to the world. Our value filters determine what we need and desire and how we go about acquiring the things we need and desire.
- The customer arrives at a sales presentation with a perspective that includes: (1) trust, (2) shared values, (3) intimacy, and (4) loyalty.
- A value gap occurs because the customer is not secure in his or her belief that the salesperson can be trusted.
- A good salesperson will take four steps to help bridge the value gap: (1) build rapport (2) discover values (3) Present unique solutions and (4) help the customer take the next step.
- The customer is often his own worst enemy and your greatest challenge.
- It is part of every salesperson's job to become a customer's trusted friend so that he or she can bridge the value gap.
- The closing test.
- Watch for yellow lights.

The trust that we put in ourselves makes us feel trust in others.

—François de la Rochefoucauld

CHAPTER FOUR:

A.S.K. PRINCIPLES

> *Nothing can stop the man
> with the right mental attitude
> from achieving his goal;
> nothing on earth can help the man
> with the wrong mental attitude.*
>
> **—W.W. Ziege**

> *A bad attitude is the worst thing
> that can happen to a group of people.
> It's infectious.*
>
> **—Roger Allan Raby**

A.S.K. And Ye Shall Receive

Values Unlocked In This Chapter

In this chapter, we will discuss and learn about the A.S.K. Principles of selling, and the key relationship between making friends and making sales. Among the values to be found in this chapter are:

- **The six aspects of a winning sales presentation.**
- **What motivates the truly successful salesperson.**
- **How a salesperson can become more comfortable helping customers take the next best action.**
- **How to serve your customer through A.S.K.**
- **How to develop your Attitude, Skills, and Knowledge.**
- **The meaning of a can-do attitude.**
- **The six essential sales skills needed to take you inside your customer's circle of trust.**

- **The true meaning of sales knowledge.**
- **The essential knowledge needed for a successful sale: knowledge of a salesperson's own values.**

> "Attitude, Skills, and Knowledge: The three legs of the relationship stool"

The foundation of any successful sales relationship, or any relationship come to think of it, can be seen as a three-legged stool—with <u>A</u>ttitude, <u>S</u>kills, and <u>K</u>nowledge as the three legs. Or A.S.K., for short. Taking the metaphor a little further, these three legs have to be level and evenly balanced for the relationship to remain stable.

For someone to be a balanced, successful salesperson, he or she needs to have a winning sales attitude, master the essential skills and have a firm base of knowledge and information. And it's important to have all three of these in equal abundance. Great attitude without the needed skill and knowledge will only get you so far—and you won't make the sale. Solid theoretical knowledge without the needed skills to put that knowledge into practice might land you a teaching job—but again you won't make the sale. And solid knowledge and good skills without the great attitude will result in an equally "who cares?" reaction on the part of your customer.

Here's another way to look at it: in your personal relations, how would you feel if your partner, a family member or a friend gave you bad advice because they weren't well informed or didn't know to how filter that information so that you can make practical use of it? Not too pleased, I bet.

Worse yet, how would you feel if that same partner, family member or friend displayed a lack of interest and a "who cares?" attitude when you went to them for help or advice? Very disappointed, right? Even if the advice they give turns out to be sound. The attitude put you off and you're no longer interested in listening to what they might have to say.

In the next sections, we'll take a closer look at each of these three legs of the sales relationship stool—and come up with ways to keep each balanced, through the VALUE MATCH selling process.

The "Can Do" Attitude: A Six-Step March

I often begin my day with a "cheer." I think it's not only a healthy but also a fun way to kick-start the morning. It also lets those around know that you're feeling good and raring to go, that you're a cheerleader for life. Thus, as part of the selling exercise, I like to encourage people attending my seminars to come up with their own cheers.

This is how it works: I divide the main group into smaller groups and assign each one to develop a short cheer, which they then have to perform in front of their classmates. Most quickly get into the spirit of things. We rarely encounter really flat and emotionless "cheers," but they do crop up. For example, here's one that no self-respecting cheerleader would ever repeat:

Hey...hey...hey...
Uh...whaddaya say...
We're...er...okay...you know...really, really okay.
Rah...

On the other hand, I recently had the pleasure of watching a team create an upbeat, fast-paced rap song that had two verses and a chorus. Very professional and very enthusiastic. When they finished the entire room burst into laughter and applause. In a sense, the audience had been "sold" on the song.

Aside from being obvious, the difference between the two performances and the two groups was the very subject of the exercise—enthusasm. One group had it; the other didn't. And the difference showed not only in the performance The audience responded emotionally and passionately to the second while scratching their heads at the first, muttering that not much effort had been put into it.

Customers are audiences, too. They need to be entertained and captivated. They need to know you care enough about them to throw everything into your presentation. How they respond is directly proportional to your level of your enthusiasm. If it's not there, chances are excellent the sale won't be there either.

Again, an example from one's personal life might be enlightening. Imagine you're a man courting a woman. You're about to propose to her. But rather than taking her to a fancy restaurant, wining and dining her, and then asking for her hand while passionately telling her how much you love her, you fax over a list of the advantages she'd gain by marrying you.

Correct me if I'm wrong but I think most women would reply with a letter that this point—if not worse! Listing the advantages to be had by marrying someone is a good idea—only not when you're supposed to be showing your heart on your sleeve.

That marriage proposer needs an attitude correction. While some people are naturally enthusiastic, there are ways for everyone to get this "can do" attitude. Listed in the table below are the six key aspects needed for a winning attitude—be it to make a sale or to "sell" someone on marriage.

Having This Attitude:	Helps Successful Salesperson To:
Enthusiasm	Promote customer confidence and trust
Looking for Opportunities	Always have his/her antennae up, meaning he/she is aware of opportunities and recognizes those that others may pass up or ignore
Fail As Fast As You Can	The faster you fail, the faster you learn to succeed. Failure is only failure if you don't learn from it.
Willingness to Learn	Hone or tune our senses to absorb feedback criticism, and information from the environment and the customer
Helping Others Achieve Goals	Help others get what they while achieving personal success
Strive to Improve	Master skills needed for effective sales, especially listening skills to be used both in personal and professional situations

The Six Key Features or Aspects of the Sales "Can Do" Attitude.

Enthusiasm: It's All You Have To Start The Day

Excitement is contagious and spreads like wildfire. Once started, it's also a self-stoking fire. Upbeat, enthusiastic people create positive energy. Which promotes confidence and trust. Which promotes success. Which then promotes more enthusiasm. You only have to look at what takes place when a consistently winning team takes to the football field: the self-confidence of the players; the enthusiasm and spirit of the crowd.

The root of the word can be traced back to the time of the ancient Greeks, those wise, world-shaping people who gave us so many things, including the first democracies and many of the philosophic principles still in place today. The word is traced to the Greek from which breaks down into:

EN ("enabled, inspired, possessed") and THEOS ("gods")

In other words, enthusiasm derives from "enabled, inspired, possessed by the gods." The phrase was originally used in reference to the ancient Olympic Games, featuring male athletes who showed off their imposing bodies and amazing talent and skills for a hugely appreciative audience.

These athletes were said to have enthusiasm. Or, in other words, "they were enabled by the gods" to reach outstanding levels of achievement. As an example, the wrestler Milo of Kroton won in his sport in six Olympics, spanning a period of 24 years. He also liked to show off his strength—in one case by holding a pomegranate in his hand and daring others to remove it, all the while never even bruising the fruit. Now that's enthusiasm!

Today, this expression no longer refers only to those who taste Olympic glory. It can also refer to every other kind of human activity, including the noble profession of sales. You too can proudly display this sign over your door: Your amazing ability can be to serve customers, to share your talents, and to achieve your own personal and professional "Olympian Heights."

Just A.S.K. yourself: "Do I have the Attitude?"

Look for opportunities: Every situation is an opportunity to meet someone new and make a friend

Every salesperson trained in VALUE MATCH principles is always on the lookout for new opportunities. It's a full-time, 24-hour a day, seven days a week preoccupation. After a while, it becomes second nature and instinctual, something you don't even think about consciously any more. You just do it.

The reason is because you never know when a great opportunity will come your way and they are coming your way. It's not only important to be prepared to handle those opportunities. Most people can do that. The real trick is that you have to be prepared to see them when they show up.

Many people will pass up an opportunity, even when it slaps them in the face, because they just aren't looking. You have to be prepared to scoop up the opportunities that others don't recognize. Or that others think aren't worth the bother. It takes a particular mind-set to do that day in and day out. The VALUE MATCH sales process makes that mind-set much easier to develop.

I know people who have made sales in elevators. Instead of staring at the floor indicator, sharp salespeople make friends at every opportunity (there's that word again). Believe me, you can get on the elevator at the lobby and close a sale, find a good prospect, or make a friend by the time the little floor bell goes "ding." In fact, that little "ding" can also be "ringing up" a sale. Okay, maybe you need a few floors to actually pull off a sale but you can definitely get the ball rolling.

It's All Around You

I'll never forget this event. I had just started my company, ServiceTRAC, after quitting my job. It was a great job with all the financial perks and benefits a person could want. You know, health insurance, car, salary and bonus, a nice home, and little travel. The only problem was I realized that I needed a little business to maintain my dream, to achieve my fully potential.

The truth is, however, that after six months of being on my own I hadn't exactly blown the doors off. Or looked like I was going to become the next Donald Trump. Don't get me wrong. My phone was ringing and

I was getting mail. But that was mostly because I was making sales calls like a madman and working from dawn to dusk.

It was in the midst of one of these dawn-to-dusk marathons that I got a call from a large national company informing me that my follow up had worked. They wanted to see me right away to discuss the possibility of working with them. As you can imagine, I was excited for my first real deal. Until, that is, I discovered that this called for a last-minute flight across the country for a two-hour meeting. The cost: $2,000!

Needless to say I bit the bullet and got on the plane. I really had no choice if I wanted to give my business a chance to succeed. While flying I should have been preparing for my meeting, organizing my notes and what I would say, anticipating the kinds of questions that would mostly likely be thrown at me. In other words, doing what the other business folk on the plane were doing.

But as is my habit, I struck up a conversation with the fellow next to me. After all he had on running shoes and I liked to run. We instantly hit it off. We talked about everything. Hawaii, kids, family, football, running, the state of the economy. And, oh yes, jobs.

As it turned out, he was the senior vice president for a large mutual fund company. To make a long story short, he just so happened to be looking for some new ideas on how to spur sales of the products credit unions sold for his company. So after a few letters back and forth following our airplane meeting I signed a long-term agreement with his company to provide our services.

To paraphrase Rosanne Rosannadanna from the old *Laugh In* TV comedy show: "It just goes to show ..." You never know when or where you will find opportunities. And elevators and planes are not the places most people would bother to look.

Fail As Fast As You Can

The desire to succeed is absolutely essential in sales. You have to want it with all your heart and soul. It's one of the things that keeps us going. And you can't be satisfied with yesterday's success. Even when things are going well, they can always go better – and it can always get tough in a hurry.

On the other hand, you have to ask yourself what exactly is meant by "success." And it's not always about material success. The salesperson practicing VALUE MATCH principles is very much like the car company that promised: "We are driven!" For that type of salesperson, earning a commission is very much secondary. It's the drive that counts, the actual making of a sale.

That's why the truly successful salesperson has a unique view of failure. He or she realizes that in a very practical way Failure only exists if we allow it to exist. We can say this with confidence because we prove it day after day. As long as we learn something from the effort, we have succeeded. As long as the desire is there, we have succeeded.

Lest some of you think that this lesson is becoming a little too New Age in its mantra, let's not forget the other side of the equation: we are in the sales game and that's all about numbers. We know that it takes a certain number of calls to get an appointment and a certain number of appointments to get the sale.

And we know a good salesperson makes those calls and appointments. He or she does the leg work, in other words, and doesn't just sit back chanting in the hope a sale will be made. So it stands to reason the faster we get the nays out of the way the faster we get to yes. The faster we get the failed calls and appointments out of the way, the faster we make the sale. And, to boot, we gain knowledge and experience from the process.

A so-called "failure" can actually be the fastest way to success. That's the only way we learn about our mistakes so we can correct them—by actually making them. When you've been rather briskly escorted out of someone's office because you just described the framed picture of his or her son as "the prettiest lil' ol' puppy dog I've ever seen..." well, you've learned something. Even if it's to just be darn sure to ask "who's this?" before offering your assessment of his/her/its appearance.

This brings us to the next item on the list: how to be a good student and an ever more successful salesperson by being willing to learn no matter what the situation or circumstances.

> "It stands to reason the faster we get the nays out of the way the faster we get to yes"

A Willingness To Learn

There's a famous story I've heard tell about an interview with a business tycoon and how he compared himself to President John F. Kennedy in a most interesting way. He focused his comments first by pointing out the similarities between himself and the at-that-time leader of the free world and then a key difference between them.

Just like the president, the man said he had come from a wealthy family. He had connections in all the right places. He had a top quality Ivy League education and a track record of success. Yet, while he was certainly successful, JFK, with a strikingly similar background, had gone on to become arguably the most powerful man in the world.

"What was the difference?" asked the interviewer. The business tycoon's answer was ever so insightful. "When I left college," said the man, "I stopped learning." And then he added: "But JFK never stopped learning."

As salespeople we must be interested in other people, if we're to have any success. We must keep an open and inquiring mind. We must always be alert to the world around us and all its wonders. We must never ignore an idea out of hand without having examined it thoroughly first. Conversely, we mustn't accept an idea simply because someone says it is so.

As with opportunities, you never know where, when or from whom a great idea will emerge. We need to keep learning so we can absorb and understand feedback from our customers, to accept criticism and benefit from it, and to process valuable information as we receive it. It is said that it will not be illiteracy that holds people back in the future. It will be the inability to learn.

As America's great humorist Will Rogers once told us in his incomparable way: "It ain't what you don't know that hurts; it's what you know that ain't so."

A willingness to learn helps us make sure what we know *is* so.

Success Is Derived From Others: You Get What You Want By Helping Others Get What They Want

We mentioned Bill Phillips earlier. Bill has built a great company on his concept of "Body For Life"—and he's deservedly earned millions from it. What has really impressed me, though, is that Bill's success is built solely on the notion that you get what you want by helping others get what they want.

In his case, that's all the things that revolve around helping people look and feel better: through personalized diet, training programs, recipes, eating tips, and workouts. They also hold contests and challenges. In return, he has become one of the most successful diet/exercise program companies in the industry, with more than two million having taken the EAS Body-for-Life Program. That focus has made Bill a multi-millionaire.

Bill Phillips truly understands the term: "No man is an island." What a marvelous way of expressing a fundamental truth! Regardless of whether you are an introvert or an extrovert, we're all in this together and together is the only way we'll ever get anything out of all this.

Bill also understands the psychology of success and failure—and how to get people to focus on the first and banish the latter. On his web site Challenge FAQ, a down-hearted participant asks why they can't seem to complete the Body-for-Life Program: "Why can't I eat right for more than a couple of weeks at a time without blowing it?"

Bill's response in part: "To receive the right answer, you have to ask the right question. If you want empowering answers, ask empowering questions. For example, your question could be transformed to: 'How can I achieve success like so many others have?' When you ask: 'How can I succeed?' your mind is likely to answer: 'Do what they did! Work hard, follow a proven plan, and have faith!' See the difference?"

Now, that's what I can a personalized answer for a customer, one that shows that Bill cares and is interested in giving customers what they want. VALUE MATCH salespeople think the same way. They realize that the best, fastest, most-satisfying

> "Ten percent of the salespeople make 80 percent of all the sales and income"

way to get what we want is to help other people get what they want. That's another fundamental rule.

No matter where you look. No matter what your business. No matter who you study. You will always find that the top sales performers are those people who focus on serving the needs of their customers. To focus on anything else is actually to lose focus when it comes to being a top sales performer.

In a recent survey, salespeople were interviewed and asked what their main motivation was to make a sale. Only ten percent of the salespeople indicated that were motivated by truly helping others. The bulk of the salespeople fall in the middle where their motivation was money.

What may surprise you is that ten percent of the salespeople make 80 percent of all the sales and income. Certainly you will encounter "fast-buck" artists who achieve a certain level of success. And that level can be quite high But the true achievers over the long term are those who serve their clients. They're the ones who come out on top when the sales tree gets shaken out.

On the flip side, money, acquisitions, fear and quotas always serve as the prime motivation for the least successful salespeople. Their focus on these things leads them to forget that the way to success is to look around for opportunities and to look for ways to help others. When you do that, you end up helping yourself. It's a no-brainer slam dunk!

What is your motivation these days?

Sure, you can make this month's quota and some fast bucks by pushing that "lemon" on an unsuspecting customer. But how much repeat business do you think you'll earn in doing so? How many referrals will you get? Do you think he'll recommend you to his brother, cousin or friend down the street? To his contacts at the city's largest corporation?

Think about it. How much business have you just *lost* over your career due to that one "fast buck" sale? I promise you, the amount of business you lose by such tactics over time is staggering. And you'll never even know about it because all those referrals and sales will go to someone else.

Practice: Striving to Improve

Top salespeople never stop improving and the key to continual improvement is practice. Always strive to improve. To become a master salesperson you must master the skills necessary to succeed in sales. And you must continually expand that skill set to include more and more tools. Else, you'll be left behind, working harder and harder for fewer and fewer gains—until the reward no longer seems worth the effort.

This is no different from developing the skills to improve your personal relationships. Through practice, we become better spouses, better friends, better all-around social creatures. Those who remain isolated and never practice their social skills are caught in a vicious circle. Not a pleasant place to be.

One of the most important skills to master is the art of listening. Of course, in sales, prospecting is important. So is building rapport, presenting, closing, and all the other areas from classic sales training programs. But improving your listening skills can enhance every part of the sales process: from building rapport to closing.

I might add from personal experience that improving your listening skills can enhance every aspect of your life, both personal and professional. It can also make the difference between maintaining strong and healthy personal relationships and having those relationships fall apart.

To sum up:

Listening is key to the VALUE MATCH system and there will be much more on this topic in the coming chapters.

What A Difference A Skill Makes

AS**K Yourself: "Do I Have The Six Essential** S**kills?" to your customer.**

Go from his or her words to the definitions of those words and then on to the values associated with them. Listen to somebody's heart and to what makes them tick. These skills allow you to differentiate between conversational chatter and what really is important to someone. You must discover who they really are so that you can present an on-target solution for that unique individual that will make a difference in his or her life.

Successful sales requires six essential skills—of which listening is a key. The table below presents those essential skills.

Having This Skill:	Gives Successful Salesperson:
Relationship-Building	Ability to create and maintain relationships. In sales, you will be building trusting relationships with customers.
Questioning	Ability to discover the customer's unique values. The sales process does not begin until the first question is asked
Listening	Ability to listen carefully and clarify your understanding of the customers' needs. Active listening skills are essential to VALUE MATCH your customers
Presentation	Ability to present solutions and relevant information to your customers
Closing-Overcoming Objections	Ability to encourage the customer to take the next step. Be prepared to help the customer overcome their fears of moving forward
Goal Setting	Ability to set sales goals, describe them clearly, and commit yourself to achieving those goals. Ability to prioritize your customers. You need to make the most of every day

Six Essential Skills for Successful Selling.

The reason so much stress is placed on these skills is so that you don't stop short, you don't waste your efforts outside the circle. Remember that attitude is important but alone it won't get the job done. Learning this skill set may present a challenge, but it is a challenge that will allow you to take the most direct route to sales success.

The Dot Test – A Self Evaluation

Have you got the skills to be a successful salesperson? That's the million-dollar question. Use this simple "Dot Test" to self-assess your sales skills. For each skill, just pencil in a dot in the category—Very Comfortable, Somewhat Comfortable, Uncomfortable—you feel appropriately describes you.

Dot Tests are otherwise known as Likert Scale Tests and have been used to test everything from which store you feel most comfortable as a shopper to police academy entrance psychological tests. Many market researchers prefer them to simply "Yes" or "No" assessments because they can be more subtle and capture nuances better.

Sales Skill	3 Very Comfortable	2 Somewhat Comfortable	1 Not Comfortable
BUILDING RAPPORT			
QUESTIONING			
LISTENING			
IDENTIFYING NEEDS			
PRESENTING			
ASKING FOR THE CLOSE			
OVERCOMING OBJECTIONS			
OVERALL CONFIDENCE IN THE PRODUCT			
OVERALL CONFIDENCE IN SELLING			

The "Dot" or Likert Scale Self-Assessment Test for Sales Skills.

I conduct this test in classes and seminars all the time all over the country. Invariably the participants respond the same way. Most are somewhat comfortable or very comfortable building rapport and identifying needs. They are far less comfortable handling objections and closing. I suspect if we drew a curve of your answers, you'd fit right in with everybody else. Right?

Actually, there's no legitimate reason for all those "not comfortable" dots down there with handling objections and closing. No reason at all. You've heard the expression that if you take care of the little details the big ones will take care of themselves. Sales is a lot like that.

Most of the discomfort comes from not taking care of the details and not taking the steps in their rightful order. Taking the sales process in its natural order is essential because, when you become uncomfortable, you set off your customer's integrity alarm. Your customer's mental "radar" will pick up any lack of confidence in your product or your own selling ability.

At that point, it doesn't matter that you're selling the greatest widget or service in the known universe. Once the customer sees that you doubt your own selling skills and abilities, it's game over. You might as well pack it in and start over with another customer. Or get yourself somewhere to calm down, breathe deeply, and re-build that shattered confidence.

On the other hand, if you handle the early stages of the process correctly, the latter stages, the so-called "big" ones, will fall quite naturally in place. Handling objections and closing will become natural and easy and in many cases they will be virtually effortless. It's like that good old math equation: 2 + 2 always equals 4.

> "Salespeople who are comfortable with the earlier steps are more comfortable asking their customer to take the next best action step"

A.S.K. Yourself: "Do I Have The Knowledge?"

Several key areas of knowledge must be mastered by the salesperson who wants to be successful. I've broken them down into six categories. Five of those—know your products and services, your business, your industry, your competition, and your customers—are basic and standard categories.

The sixth—know your values—lies at the crux of the VALUE MATCH system.

Below is a table outlining the five basic areas in which a salesperson must have crucial knowledge if he or she is to be successful.

Having Knowledge About:	Helps Successful Salesperson To:
Your Products and Services	Present sales points that offer value and solutions to the customer
Your Business	Perform in harmony with the mission of the business Align company's values with those of the customer
The Industry	Keep up to date about the changes taking place so that you can talk knowledgeably about what makes your business unique
Your Competition	Understand what the competition has to offer so that he or she can sell a different and better story
Your Customers	Build friendships based on common values Identify needs unique to customers

The Five Basic Areas in Which A Salesperson Must Have Knowledge For Success.

Let's face it: You can't sell what you don't understand. No one can fake it anymore. There's just too much information out there. Today the consumer can read your brochures, watch your videos, check out your catalogs, research you online and reference your claims with other customers.

The customer has become an educated consumer, someone who can't be fooled very easily. And even if you do manage to fool him or her once, you can rest assured it won't happen a second time—and you've probably lost that person as a customer.

You must know your products and/or the services your company offers. Inside out. You must keep up with the changes in them and related to them. If you're new to the company or the industry, use the same techniques your customers use. Read the brochures and catalogs; view the videos and DVDs; check out your web site for descriptive and technical information; visit with satisfied customers. Finally, dip into the pool of knowledge and ask your more experienced co-workers for inform-ation and tips.

The "good old days" of the salesman all alone except for his golden voice and even more golden handshake are long gone. Not knowing your product or service inside and out, up and down, backwards and forwards, is not only unprofessional, it's unforgivable. And today's customers are quick to pick up on when the salesperson is spreading it thick—and they're unforgiving!

Even more important than knowledge is passion, that deep down understanding and belief that you are representing the best possible option for your target customer. You must have a conviction that your product, service, or company is the best for those people you are serving. You need to be so proud of what you do and how well you do it that it just jumps out of you.

As we've already seen in the attitude section, this quickly becomes contagious. However, although I'm a firm believer that the right attitude and skills are mega-important, you must keep one thing in mind: You can't fake it. You can't simply pretend that the product you're selling is going to do what you say when you know that it doesn't. Or you don't know that it does.

"The 'good old days' of the salesman all alone except for his golden voice and even more golden handshake are long gone"

So how do you do this? The first step is to get a deep and thorough understanding of your product, service and company. It is from this understanding that your conviction must come. You must discover the values of the company and make sure they match yours. Find out who the customers are and learn what makes them tick. When you know these things in your heart, you are then ready to go out and sell.

Yes, I realize this can be hard. You might discover that the product doesn't do what the company says it does. Or that the fine print in the service contract makes the service a lot less attractive than it has been presented. In that case, you have some big decisions to make, including whether you still want to be associated with that particular business. The last thing you want is to be connected with a bad product or service.

Know The Right Questions

As part of your knowledge of the product or service being offered, your customer also expects you to know the right <u>questions</u> *he or she* should be asking. For example, let's say you go to an auto parts store, buy a part, and go home only to discover that it's the wrong part.

Whose fault is that? Ultimately it is the salesperson's fault because he or she should have asked the right questions to determine your real needs. Often customers can only explain a problem on the most basic level. Part of their expectations is that the sales representative knows enough to ask those right questions and provide them with the right solution to their problem.

Know Your Products and Services Questions:

- **What are the five things that impress you the most about your company?**
- **Why do customers buy from your company?**
- **What adjectives would you use to describe your products or services?**
- **What are the most common solutions your customers are seeking?**
- **How do your company's products or services provide those solutions?**

Know Your Company's Vision And Mission

A vision is the long-term goal of the company—be it a one-person operation or a multi-national corporation. It is where the business is going. A mission statement is a brief, written expression of the way we will attain the vision. In other words, it is how it will get to where it is going. Look at the vision as a destination and the mission statement as a map.

Here's an example from one of the more successful hotel organizations in the world, Marriott, and one of 's 100 Best Companies to Work For.

"Vision: We will shape our future as a global organization that grows and prospers by: (1) Being completely focused on satisfying each of our customers, earning their trust and loyalty, and creating long-term relationships with them, (2) always embodying the ideals of the Marriott Philosophy, most importantly the belief that taking care of associates is the key to long-term success.

"Mission: Grow a worldwide lodging business using Total Quality Management (TQM) principles to continuously improve preference and profitability. Our commitment is that every guest leaves satisfied."

It is imperative that you feel comfortable with your company and its product so that your integrity alarm isn't constantly drowning out your sales presentation. As well, this allows you to align your company's values with those of the customer.

Know Your Company's Mission And Vision Questions:

- **What is your company's mission?**
- **What is your company's vision?**
- **What is your role in carrying out the vision?**
- **Are you comfortable in carrying out that vision?**

You Must Know Your Industry

Everything is changing and, in most cases, changing rapidly. For example, a car used to be something used for getting to and from work, grandma's house, the shopping mall, and Yellowstone National Park during summer vacation. Today a car is a computerized, mobile home entertainment center complete with radio, CD player, satellite tracking system, back seat television and DVD, plus access to the Internet.

Whatever your industry may be, change is on the way. Just think about the way the lowly telephone has changed in the last decade alone. If a customer on the showroom floor asks about those changes, you can't just mumble: "I'll…ah…have to get back to you on that, old buddy." And then make a dash for the company's brochure rack. By the time you return your customer is already checking out the models at the next dealership or showroom.

This isn't something that only affects salespeople. Entire industries have been rocked by their failure to understand that, as Bob Dylan sings, The Times They Were A-Changin'. Back during the 1970s American-made automobiles took a beating from foreign competition. The Japanese and German cars were more fuel-efficient, better made and were priced lower than their U.S. counterparts. In a very short time the foreign cars held a substantial portion of domestic auto sales.

Detroit responded and today American-made automobiles are among the best in the world. But the process took a decade or so and it was very painful at times. For example, "motor city" thought it could fight back with a series of X-cars and Y-cars and such-and-such-cars specifically designed to meet the overseas competition. They failed.

Why? An associate consulting with a Nissan (Datsun) dealership at the time asked his dealer about how he would handle Detroit's new competitive models. The dealer said that he wasn't worried because the new cars weren't very competitive at all. He listed reason after reason why the new domestics not only would not, but could not compete with the foreign models: "They just don't have the technology yet to make a competitive car," he said.

He was right and the new U.S. models were, shall we say, less than successful, despite being competitively priced. That dealer's knowledge of his industry allowed him to organize, plan and execute sales strategies designed specifically to point out all the real advantages of his line vs. the so-called "new and unimproved" numbers rolling off the assembly lines up in Michigan. It was only when Detroit acquired and took advantage of the new technologies that American cars once more became truly competitive.

Know Your Industry Questions

- What trade magazines do you read?
- To what trade organizations do you belong?
- In what continuing education do you participate?
- Are you computer literate enough to research your industry over the Internet?

You Must Know Your Competition

Just as your product, your facility and your sales staff are different, so then are those of your competitor. How can you tell a different and better story without knowing how and why? That knowledge lets you point out why yours are differences and how that translates into a better deal for your customer.

Remember, it's not enough that your products or services **are** objectively different and better than those of your competition. You have to let the customers become aware of that fact. You have to be able to present them with the facts about your competitor's products and services and then show them what makes yours more attractive.

We all have stories of inferior or less enduring products outselling better products. Why? Because the customer was made aware of those products and the salespeople did their jobs. It doesn't matter how good your product or service is if you don't get it out there where it can be seen, appraised and sold.

Know Your Competitors' Questions

- In what products does your closest competitor specialize?
- Could you describe and "break down" those products to compare them to yours?
- How does your competition market and advertise their products?

- What market share do your competitors have? Is it growing or shrinking?
- Have you made it a point to get to know the salespeople who work for the competition?

You Must Know Your Customers

Unlike automobiles, customers don't just roll off the assembly line, one model identical to the next. They don't come prefab. Yes, we're all human with common and shared human attributes and, at some level, this is what allows us to be social creatures who get along with others. But, at the same time, each prospect and customer is an individual with unique needs, desires, wants, motivations and values.

It pays to remember that very simple fact. That realization is an important element of a can-do attitude and successful salesmanship. Each person approaches life in his or her own unique way. Everyone is different. These aren't just surface differences either but essential ones. When you discover those essential differences you can show how they match the different and better nature of your own product.

You can then start to build friendships based on this understanding and identify the needs that are unique to a customer.

Know Your Customers' Questions

- How well can you identify your customers' uniqueness and differences?
- Do you know how to match this uniqueness to the products and services you are selling?
- In your personal life, how good are you at reading what your spouse, your friends, your fellow workers really want?
- Do you truly and honestly approach each customer as if that customer is unique?

Know Your Values

While having knowledge of your products and services, your company or business, your industry, your competition, and your customers is essential to successful sales, none of this knowledge will be of much help without one key ingredient: you must know your own values. This is the key to unlocking all the other knowledge and making that knowledge worthwhile and useful.

Sure, there is no doubt that your business, your dealership, your shop, store or department is in many ways different from all the others. And you need to ask yourself: What are those differences and why are they important to providing your customer with the best possible service? You have to know these things so well that they fly off your tongue without thinking about them. You also need to ask: What are your company's values? How do they connect to the greater social values?

These are all important questions. But what it really comes down to is you. Your values. Your role as a team player is essential and, if you can't be an effective part of that team (for whatever reason), then it is in everyone's best interest that you move on. Find another product to sell or another line of work. Too many stay at their jobs for the wrong reasons. Ironically, they're the same wrong reasons as the motivational errors made by many salespeople.

In order to perform in a satisfying and fulfilling way, it's not enough to know products and services, for example, inside out. You must be able to match your values with those of your company so that you can then match them with your customer's values. Naturally, to do this you must know what your company, service or product stands for and how it can match the needs of the customer. But most importantly you must know your own values. Truthfully and honestly.

This is, by far, the greatest knowledge anyone can have. It's the kind of knowledge that isn't learned in books or from watching sales training DVDs. This is the knowledge that is at the core of the VALUE MATCH sales process. It is also the knowledge that is valuable not only when you're trying to sell something but also when you're trying to sell yourself.

So, when you ask yourself: "Do I have the knowledge?" be sure to include knowledge of your own values in the answer. If you truthfully respond that you don't have knowledge of your

> "What it really comes down to is you. Your values. Your role as a team player"

own values, make sure you get it ASAP. A good place to start is to go back to Chapter One of this book.

And, in the next chapter, we'll talk about how you can make your presence felt out there once you've got the basic elements of selling down: **The 30-Second Commercial** or **The Art Of Selling Yourself.**

VALUE CHECK

- The six aspects of a winning sales presentation are enthusiasm, looking for opportunities, a desire for success, a willingness to learn, realizing that success is derived from others, and continuing practice.
- The VALUE MATCH salesperson realizes that there is no such thing as failure.
- The least-successful salespeople are always motivated by money, acquisitions, fear and quotas.
- The most successful salespeople are those motivated by a desire to help others gets what they need or want.
- Salespeople are often uncomfortable helping customers take the next best action because (1) an integrity alarm rings when we are not sure that the solution fits or we haven't built the necessary trust; and (2) we do not build rapport or listen to our customer's real needs and concerns.
- Serving your customer requires that you A.S.K. You must develop your Attitude, Skills, and Knowledge.
- A can-do attitude means you have: a genuine interest in people, persistence, patience, unwavering enthusiasm, initiative, and self-discipline and responsibility.
- Six essential sales skills help take you inside your customer's circle of trust: (1) relationship building, (2) asking questions, (3) listening, (4) presentation, (5) time management and (6) goal setting.
- Knowledge means knowing your product or service; knowing your company; knowing your industry; knowing your competition; and knowing your customers.
- In order for this knowledge to result in a successful sale, the salesperson must possess one other piece of knowledge: knowledge of his or her own values.
- It is then and only then that you can align these values to those of the company and the customers.

*The greatest revolution of our generation
is the discovery that human beings,
by changing the inner attitudes of their minds,
can change the outer aspects of their lives.*

—William James

CHAPTER FIVE:

30 SECONDS OF FAME

> *Doing business without advertising is like winking at a girl in the dark. You know what you are doing, but nobody else does.*
>
> **—Stuart H. Britt**

> *Advertising is the greatest art form of the twentieth century.*
>
> **—Marshall McLuhan**

Love What You Do? Tell The World!

Values Unlocked In This Chapter

In this chapter, we will examine how you can let others know that you love what you do and that what you do best is develop friendships as well as enjoy selling your different and better story so that others can make the best possible decision. We will look at how you can improve your chances for success, take full responsibility for what you do, and share your enthusiasm at the same time. Among the values in this chapter are:

- **The importance of accountability.**
- **Why you should "commercialize" yourself in the era of the sound bite.**
- **How to write your own 30-second commercial.**
- **What makes a good 30-second ad spot.**
- **Making sure the 30-second commercial is yours and yours alone.**

I want to share a very important lesson in my life. Like most true lessons, this one was learned not in the classroom but in the so-called school of hard knocks. I learned this lesson a very long time ago and in a very hard way. When I was a young man and things didn't go my way, I had a tendency to look around me to find out who I felt was responsible. To find someone or something upon whom to lay the blame, in other words. This was a bad habit of mine and one that led to slow progress for me personally and professionally.

Fortunately for me I had an experience early in my professional career that helped me figure out how wrong and unproductive this practice was. I was in my twenties and shared a business with my family. Well, like many people my age, I possessed a lot more enthusiasm than I did either skills or experience. For one reason or another, it turned out things went south quickly in the business.

This left me very bitter and with a chip on my shoulder the size of Texas. This went on for many years because I was convinced the trials I had experienced and the business challenges I had encountered were the outcome of decisions and actions others had made. Oh no, not me, it wasn't my fault. That was my mantra. It was always someone else's fault. Other people caused the problems in the business. They were to blame for these failures. I was certain of that. Unfortunately, those other people also happened to be members of my family so you can imagine the awkwardness of the situation.

This was so wrong! You see, as long as I focused on the others and lay the blame at their feet, I couldn't focus on what was really important: on me and my role, on what I was doing right or wrong, on the responsibility I shared. As long as I believed "they" were in control, I stayed discouraged and depressed. I felt unable to change things.

The explanation is simple. As long as we feel unhappy and put the blame on others for that unhappiness, we have arrived, and can remain stuck indefinitely, in a very bad place. This is a place where we feel useless and lacking in self-esteem. Why? Because we all know that "we can't change others!" No wonder we feel depressed.

> "The secret to happiness is realizing and accepting that you are, as a direct result of your own actions, who you are"

Value Match System

The secret to happiness is realizing and accepting that you are, as a direct result of your own actions, who you are. There is nothing inbetween, no intermediary, no one else to blame or praise. are no one else but . are responsible for what happens around you. are responsible for your success—or failure.

But rather than striking fear in you, this is actually good news and should be taken as a good sign. This means that you have the POWER and you have the ABILITY to change. POWER and ABILITY. Those are strong words, potent words. They indicate strength and self-determination, forcefulness and human capacity. You can change everything you want to change about yourself. You can be whatever you want to be. All you have to do is make the decision to change and then put in motion your plan for improvement. It's as simple as that.

It all comes down to responsibility. Your responsibility! That's the key to happiness. Once you accept that "the buck stops here," you're ready to embark on the great journey towards fulfillment and the achievement of your full potential. All it takes is accepting responsibility for your life.

This is true both in your personal and in your professional life. In your personal life, if you spend your time—no, waste your time—blaming others whenever something doesn't go your way, you'll never get out from under that dark cloud. Unless you take responsibility for your own actions, you'll never learn how to truly love, how to socialize, how to interact with family and friends, how to commit yourself to the relationships you seek and need as a human being.

Similarly, in your professional life, you'll see opportunities slipping away and not know why, not truly know why. Sure, there's always some convenient scapegoat or other. Some blame to lay. But you'll never get to the bottom of the problems until you look in the mirror and recognize who's in control, who needs to take control. It's easy. Selling yourself to others starts with selling yourself to yourself. You are your own most important client.

Being responsible is not simply stating that fact (although that's a good start). Being responsible consists of four separate key areas that you need to examine. The table below presents a break out of these four areas and what you need to do within each one to be a successful salesperson.

Accountability	You always need to measure You can expect what you inspect Establish measurement or performance indicators
Skills Development	Do you practice/monitor/improve? Successful salespeople are constantly learning and practicing skills True mastery comes from constant skill development until the skills are instinctive
Flexibility	There are no perfect solutions Challenges are there to be overcome and to be used to one's advantage
Knowledge	You always stay abreast of what is happening You learn everything possible about the products and services you offer, the industry, the competition, and the customer

The Four Areas of Responsibility and The Forging of Success

It's All About You: The 30-Second Ad

We live in an era in which the "king" of the airwaves isn't a nationally-known "disc jockey," a broadcast or cablecast talk show host or even the anchorperson on your local television station. The real king of media these days is the "sound bite," a short statement that makes a point in a dramatic and memorable way, that gets across its message in one short burst.

The sound bite is an excellent communications tool, especially in this day and age when things seem to have speeded up so much. In a sense, it is the way for us to "taste" an entire message or conversation "meal" through one "bite." Memorable sound bites can become part of a society's historical and cultural underpinning. For example, when Neil Armstrong radioed Earth from the Moon on July 20, 1969, with: "Houston. Tranquility Base here. The Eagle has landed," the message served to crystallize the entire American space program to that point.

As you can see, sound bites can be very effective. So why should we leave the sound bite to the politicians, commentators and editorial writers? The sound bite is there for anyone to create and to use—and that includes you!

As salespeople, we must be prepared to take responsibility for our own actions. We are the only ones with the willingness and the ability to walk our customers all the way through the sales process one step at a time. We are the only ones who can then help them take the next, wisest course of action. It takes a lot of enthusiasm and a "can-do" attitude to perform these tasks in an effective and efficient way—and you have to let your customer get a feel for your enthusiasm if you want to be successful.

> "As salespeople, we must be prepared to take responsibility for our own actions"

How do you go about doing that? Well, one very excellent way to express your enthusiasm for serving the needs of that client is to write, practice and deliver a thirty-second commercial all about... you. That's correct. An ad spot that features you. It's not as outlandish or off the wall as you might first imagine.

Think about all the times you're asked: "What do you do for a living?" And how, unprepared, you fumbled, bumbled or stumbled over the answer. A clear, concise thirty-second "spot," prepared in advance, can have you sounding like the professional you are instead of Porky Pig in a fluster: "I... uh-dib-dib-dib dibby-dib-dib...uh... sell stuff."

That doesn't sound very professional, does it? And you can imagine the impression it makes on a listener. God forbid, he or she happens to be a potential client. But with preparation and a practiced presentation, your own thirty-second commercial can be a spectacular way to open a conversation, to show confidence and to spread the word about your product or service.

When someone asks me what I do, here's how I answer the question:

Hi, my name is Will Nowell and I'm really glad to get to know you. I'm an inspirational and motivational speaker based in Scottsdale, Arizona. I've been doing this for years because I love it. I really do. I get to help sales people, sales teams, managers, individuals, groups and families bring out the best in themselves. One of the best things about this work is making a real difference in peoples' lives. I'm looking forward to the opportunity of helping you and your team too.

If you want to devise your own, here are some key elements I try to include and the reasons why.

Name	Introduction
What You Do	Explanation
How Long You've Been At It	Credibility
Why You Like It	From The Heart
Invitation To Do Business	Why Not?

Some Elements for a 30-Second Commercial

In my seminars and classes, and even in my own office, I will unexpectedly select someone and offer a $5 reward if he or she can come up with an effective 30-second commercial on the spot. Ad lib an ad, in other words. The first time I do it, they're usually flustered, and some even sound like good old Porky. But in no time at all they'll be seeking me out in the hallways: "Hey, Will, get your five bucks ready!"

Dave's Dilemma, Dave's Delight

In a seminar some time ago, I called on a really nice, but totally unprepared, fellow named Dave. I asked him for his thirty-second commercial and he blew it. I mean, he really blew it. The poor man just stood frozen in front of the seminar audience and couldn't even manage a decent mumble. He just couldn't do it.

I was really embarrassed for his embarrassment. I gave him some words of encouragement and told him to keep at it, that he would eventually get the hang of it. But, for months, I felt horrible about the incident and sincerely felt that Dave just wasn't cut out for sales. He was just too shy and self-conscious when it came to speaking in front of others.

Later, I was called upon to give a major national seminar for the company he worked for. The stage towered above the large audience. Huge screens backed me for presenting state-of-the-art images. Speakers boomed my message throughout the large auditorium and spotlights focused all eyes to the stage. It was, to say the least, an extremely intimidating setting—even for someone with my experience.

At the end of my presentation, as is my wont, I asked for volunteers to come up and recite a 30-second commercial. Guess who jumped up and rushed to the stage? Literally ran and leaped onto the stage? You guessed it. It was Dave! The very Dave whose embarrassment I shared when he tanked his 30-second commercial so many months earlier!

He then took the microphone and, in the middle of that intimidating environment, gave one of the best 30-second commercials I've ever heard. Enthusiastic, richly-worded, inspirational. He got a tremendous applause as he walked off the stage. Suddenly, Dave stopped, walked back, took my microphone and said: "I want my five bucks!" The crowd went wild.

Writing Your Own 30-Second Commercial

Few types of presentations are as powerful as a salesperson who can recite a great 30-second commercial, especially when performing his or her spot "on the spot." In an ad lib fashion, as it were. But, despite the spur-of-the-moment feel to these ads, there are four elements that all such presentations must have in common if they are to be as effective as possible. These elements are:

- **ENTHUSIASM:** Speak with a smile on your face and a bounce in your voice. You can often "hear" the smile in the voice of a good, professional announcer. You've experienced the same thing on the telephone. You can just tell when the party on the other end of the line is genuinely happy or faking the presentation. The enthusiastic person makes you believe, makes it enjoyable to listen—be it a presentation or just a salutation. You're excited about yourself, aren't you? Of course, you are. You're excited about your job, right? You're excited about your product or service? Then show it! That's how you get others to share your enthusiasm.

- **CONFIDENCE:** Your customer or potential client won't believe your "spot" if you don't believe in yourself, if you don't believe in what you're pitching. There's that integrity alarm again. Work out any doubts in advance. Practice your performance again and again until you can give it convincingly even with just a moment's notice.

- **EFFORT:** You have to make every effort possible at all times to make yourself available to prospects and customers. You have to put in the time and the work needed. You have to metaphorically learn to put your foot in the door and be prepared for when opportunity comes knocking—be it in an elevator or an airplane. Otherwise, how can you possibly be in a position to deliver your commercial?

- **PRACTICE:** Whoever said that practice makes perfect was absolutely right. In every human endeavor, from sports to spelunking, the more you practice, the better you get. And the more it becomes second nature to do things right. Even if you never actually deliver a perfect pitch, you'll certainly do a more professional job than if you don't practice. Practice builds your confidence, allows you to sound as professional as you really are, and helps keep that integrity alarm from going off.

The advertising man is a liaison between the products of business and the mind of the nation. He must know both before he can serve either.

—Glenn Frank

As a salesperson, you bridge the gap between your product or service and the mind of your customer, the mind of the nation. No one else can perform this essential service the way you can. No one else is an a position to bridge the two so effectively. So it's very important to let everybody know about it, to clue them in on what you do. Leaving it up to mind reading is not the way to success!

How you tell your story is your business. How you create your personal ad spot is up to you. You can make your commercial hard-hitting or soft around the edges. Direct or indirect. Cute or deadly serious. Whatever works for you and your situation. Whatever fits your particular personality. The important thing is that it must be commercial. It should apply to you and to no one else. With some tweaking, you can also tailor your commercial to different situations.

For example, the information I teach applies to the timid, first-time sales person just getting her feet wet as well as the experienced sales champion with hundreds of sales under his belt. But I vary my approach to those different groups to match their current level of skills, knowledge and confidence.

Don't get me wrong. I would never talk down to any audience. That's an absolute no-no and a surefire way to lose sales. But I will not address a seminar of Fortune 500 CEOs in the same manner I would a group of graduating seniors from Smallville High School. I'd use the same commercial, but with a slightly different approach to better reach the very different audiences.

Go ahead. Write out your commercial. Time it so that it is short and effective. Hone the words till you get them exactly right. Until they are . Put it aside for a while and then go back to it.

Then, once you feel you've got it just right, practice out loud. Stand there and let it blast until you can deliver it like the top announcer at one of those 50,000 watt, clear-channel powerhouse radio stations. Be sure to include the "why I really love my job" step. That immediately connects you to your customer on that all-important emotional level. It will help get you "inside the bubble."

> "As a salesperson, you bridge the gap between your product or service and the mind of your customer, the mind of the nation"

Before you try it out in the real world, run it by a few friends or co-workers to get their input, criticism, and suggestions. Make sure your enthusiasm shows through and try to make that enthusiasm infectious. Challenge friends and co-workers to write their own 30-second spots. Go back and present your revised commercial, taking in any suggestions you feel are worthwhile.

Then, as they say in the world of audio/video production: "Three... two... one... action!" You're ready to make your "sound bite" do its bit for your increased success both as a salesperson and as someone who simply wants to communicate better.

In the next chapter, we will look at the first steps—basic but extremely important—to be taken when building rapport and trust between yourself and your customer: the creation of the circle of trust and the first journey inside that magical value bubble where the truth lies. These are valuable lessons that should be used for the building of any lasting relationship, be it professional or personal.

VALUE CHECK

- We live in an era of the communication "sound bite," a short statement that makes a point in a dramatic and memorable way.
- An excellent tool for expressing your enthusiasm is a self-written thirty-second commercial about you, your job and your capabilities.
- To present an effective personal 30-second commercial you must have enthusiasm and confidence, you must make the effort, and you must practice your performance.
- Your commercial must be *your* commercial and yours alone.

When someone stops advertising, someone stops buying.
When someone stops buying, someone stops selling.
When someone stops selling, someone stops making.
When someone stops making, someone stops earning.
When someone stops earning, someone stops buying.
(Think it over.)

—Edwin H. Stuart

CHAPTER SIX:

THE CIRCLE OF TRUST

> *Trust thyself: every heart vibrates to that iron string. Trust men, and they will be true to you; treat them greatly, and they will show themselves great.*
>
> **—Ralph Waldo Emerson**

> *Without friendship and the openness and trust that go with it, skills are barren and knowledge may become an unguided missile.*
>
> **—Frank H.T. Rhodes**

Trust And Truth: Hand In Hand

Values Unlocked In This Chapter

In this chapter, we will take a first good look at the concepts of rapport, trust and the truth. Whether making a sale or establishing a relationship, gaining trust is a key step. In this chapter, we will show how to build the foundations of that trust and how that can then help you take the relationship to the next level.

Among the values unlocked in this chapter are:
- **Building rapport**
- **Initiating and maintaining trust**
- **Being able to work with the truth**
- **Turning stranger into friend**
- **The Personal Value Circling of wagons**
- **Getting into the circle**
- **Staying within the circle.**

At The Core, There's Rapport

There are plenty of definitions of "rapport": "a relation of mutual understanding or trust and agreement between people" is one; "a feeling of sympathetic under-standing" is another. But personally I like "intense harmonious accord." This leaves no room for doubt as to the nature of the connection. Some compare it to the relationship between a therapist and her client; others to what a successful married couple or two very close friends might experience.

But what exactly lies at the base of this connection between two people? In the sales experience, rapport is built upon the idea that you and the customer share values, personal and fundamental values that the two of you have in common. Once values are shared on a personal level, the customer begins to feel he or she can trust you, can place their trust in you and in your judgement.

And guess what happens then? That's right. They begin to confide in you. They begin to tell you what's really on their minds, what they really want. In short, they begin to tell you the truth. In fact, I'll let you in on a little secret: If you handle the situation correctly and honestly, you might actually hear what I call the magic phrase:

"To tell you the truth..."

> "If there is no trust, no way to know truly that you can rely on someone, people would not be able to connect in any way other than the most superficial"

There you have it. Five simple but extremely important words. Five words that serve as the code to unlock the VALUE MATCH sales process. Once you hear, "To tell you the truth," you are ready to ask important questions that will help you and the customer take the next step and reach the next level. It's a thrilling situation to be in, like the famous "Eureka!" or "I found it!" of Archimedes, more than 2000 years ago. Once you hear, "To tell you the truth," you have been admitted entry into the person's Personal and Needs Value Inner Circles.

There is nothing more valuable than being privy to the other person's beliefs, thoughts and feelings in the selling process.

Come to think of it, there is nothing more valuable than that in any type of relationship. In fact, without it, no true relationship would be possible, which may explain the number of marriage breakups we witness these days, the lack of connection between and among people who aren't willing to put in the work to gain each other's trust.

If there was no trust, no way to know truly that you can rely on someone, people would not be able to connect in any way other than the most superficial. Nothing true or sincere could get done. We'd all be walking around with fake smiles pasted on our faces, acting like automatons—just like the folks in that movie, , who live in a black-and-white 1950s sitcom and are deathly afraid of change.

The truth is, if you're afraid of change, of moving forward, then you'll never get things done. You'll never accomplish anything important. You'll never know the truth because everyone will protect his or her personal value bubble and not allow anyone else inside. I mean, ask yourself this simple question: If you're not willing to open up and make yourself vulnerable, why should anyone else? If you're not willing to take chances… ? I think you get the point.

And what could really prove disastrous, you'll never develop a true relationship with a customer. No matter how many widgets you sell him. You'll remain on the outside looking in. You'll never be able to shout "Eureka!" Widgets come and go; relationships can last a lifetime—and beyond. Which would you prefer to sell?

Of course, it can't stop there. Simply having the customer admit to truth-telling gets you in. Opens the outer doors as it were and creates a viable relationship. You now need to advance to the second level. It is then up to you to continue the process so that you can get into the inner sanctuary. It's up to you to make certain that you remain within the truth-telling circle and help discover the customer's true needs. The last thing you want is to have your bubble burst just when you're making headway.

After you've helped pinpoint the real needs of the customer rather than what they might have told you at the start of the dialogue, don't be surprised if the customer expresses a pleasant

> "Widgets come and go; relationships can last a lifetime—and beyond"

shock—and surprise at your ability to practically read his mind! One of the joys of true salesmanship is the ability to give the customer exactly what he or she wants—even before they ask for it.

But remember. While this is exciting, you are nowhere close to being done. The race has a long way to go and there are many steps that need to be taken. For example, once you've made your first successful foray into the customer's inner circle to uncover those needs, you'll most likely need to go in again—to discover what is really holding the customer back from making the decision to buy.

Relationship   **Needs**   **Fears**

(To Tell The Truth)   (That's Amazing)   (That Is A Great Idea)

As the graphic above illustrates, the matching of values takes place at three levels: From true relationship to true needs to true fears. It is your job as a salesperson to help customers articulate these in a way that moves the process forward. The ultimate result is the discovery of solutions. In the following chapters, you'll learn a lot more about specific tools that can be used, including the VALUE MATCH Question and Answer Module, to advance the process.

You know when you're on the inside of each of these circles. We have already discussed the first clue. Once you have successfully penetrated the Relationship/Trust circle, you will hear the words: "**Well, to tell you the truth**." Later, when you have successfully uncovered the real needs of the customer and effectively presented a solution that matches those needs, you will have them say: "**That's amazing**!" And lastly, when you working with the customer to help them overcome their fears to move forward, you will be able to say: "**That's a great idea!**"

For now, it is important to know that each successful entry into the customer's Personal, Needs and Fears Value Circles builds on the previous effort. Whether it's to further establish a relationship, uncover the customer's needs, or work through the fears holding the customer back, each entry into the inner circle of trust brings you closer and closer to that state of "Eureka!" that all salespeople long to achieve.

Facing The Facts

As a salesperson, what do you offer your customer?

I'm not referring to your stocks and bonds, the four-on-the-floor monster car, the aircraft carrier, or the model plane featured in your company brochures. I mean what do you really offer to all those customers out there? What is your bottom line sales presentation? What do you offer when everything else is stripped away?

If you're like most salespeople, you have only one thing to offer regardless of the nature of your product or service. You offer:

VALUE: How the product or service will uniquely meet their individual needs

It is the opposite of That's fine. Facts and factual material, fact sheets and colorful brochures are important in any sale. Part of any full and effective presentation. Every customer has a need for facts, features, benefits and proof. In fact, every customer demands such information. It's part of the trust circle and no sales will make it out of the gate if the salesperson provides false, inaccurate or only partial information about a product or service.

But the truth is that making a sale is a little more complicated than simply presenting the full spectrum of facts, features, benefits and proof. The truth is that:! To be blunt about it, when you sell with just the facts you're not selling the customer what he or she really wants: "Value". And you're barely skimming the surface of the true sales process.

Does the customer in the be-medalled uniform want an aircraft carrier? Yes… and no. That customer wants to buy an aircraft carrier, no doubt. But what he really wants is to defend the lives of the nation's people, to help make the nation safer. What he really wants is to provide the security so that moms and pops can go about raising their children without fear of attack from those who seek to destroy a way of life and the freedom that goes with it.

Does the woman across the desk want stocks and bonds? Again, perhaps on the surface she does, but I don't think that's her ultimate goal. I think what she really wants is a safe and sound future, a worry-free retirement and security for her children and grandkids. I think what she really wants is someone to tell her the best way to go about doing that, right?

Does the guy with the bad toupee and the calfskin driving gloves really want a monster car with 500 horses under the hood and a hemi? Surely he does—and surely he doesn't. What he really wants is to pretend he's 18 years old again, primping in the rear view mirror before picking up his "chick".

Does the bright-eyed and eager child want a model airplane? Of course—and of course not! That child really wants to go "zoom" in the back yard and imagine he or she is breaking the sound barrier alongside Chuck Yeager. That child wants to let the imagination run wild, wants to soar up among the clouds. His model plane is simply the jumping off point.

Don't get me wrong and make no mistake about it. A VALUE MATCH salesperson always provides honest facts and figures, always tells the truth about the products and services being offered. But a VALUE MATCH salesperson also takes the extra step to address the more important emotional needs of the customer, to find out what a customer wants and the emotions that lie behind his or her needs and desires.

Stay In Step

When an army, a marching band or a group of young scouts wants to get from one place to the other in the most efficient manner possible, they march in step. That's the best way for a troop or group to get from here to there without tripping over each other. Otherwise, one will bang into the other and everyone will come tumbling down in a heap. And we all know how difficult it is to get going again after that!

For a sale to be made as efficiently as possible, a salesperson must try to do the same thing. He or she must try to always stay in step with the customer. Never falling too far behind or getting too far ahead. Most often that means becoming the parade director or drum major.

Staying in step means knowing at exactly what point the sales process stands at any particular time and taking the appropriate measures to keep it flowing smoothly along. It also means recognizing the difference between facts and emotions as they apply to the current sales presentation. To do this you need to connect with your customer in three key value areas:

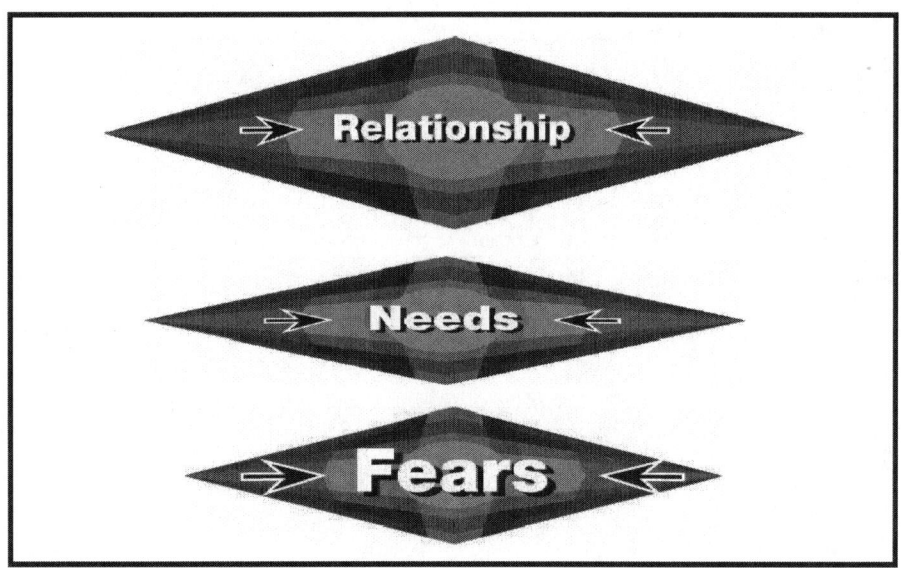

Matching values at these three levels between you and the customer is the solid rock upon which the sales process is built. In truth, matching values at these levels is the impermeable rock upon which all relationships are built.

This is a lot easier said than done, a lot more work than first imagined. I think we all know that. Facts are simple to lay out once you get them. Numbers, statistics, percentages—they're all clear cut. But, when it comes to matters of the emotions, talk may be easy but actually getting things done requires a lot of legwork. Walking the walk, as the saying goes.

Oh sure, things are fine if you've already established a friendship. Unfortunately, one of the problems is that a customer is essentially and by definition a stranger. He or she is most likely someone you've never seen before. A cold call, in the sales vernacular. Two strangers who start off with little in common, other than the fact few people actually trust a salesperson, setting you up with a couple of strikes against you before you even start. And it becomes your job to get one stranger to reveal and discuss vital, personal issues with another stranger.

How do you do that? By entering the stranger's circle of trust and turning that stranger into a friend. And how do you do that? By staying in step with your customer, and by guiding your customer along the way.

Circle The Wagons

A standard scene in the old classic "horse operas" about the wild, wild west was the Indian attack on the wagon train making its way through hostile territory. Upon seeing the tops of feathers over the hillside and hearing the sound of drums in the distance, the wagon master would shout: "Circle the wagons!" The would-be settlers would then form a defensive circle while Jack Palance or Iron Eyes Cody led his horsemen around and around and around, hoping for a breakthrough, for a crack in the barrier.

Every customer who was, is, or will be does exactly the same thing. They circle the wagons the moment they sense problems. Those "wagons" form a Personal Value Circle with a warning for strangers to keep out. These "wagons" create a barrier that prevents the invasion of the space within.

What does a Personal Value Circle look like? Visualize a large motion picture screen—one of those wide, white, blank screens—right before your eyes. Now, mentally draw a large circle right in the middle of the screen. Be sure to leave lots of room and white space around the edges. This is your standard Value Circle.

Now imagine a series of words forming on the outside of that circle:

Outside The Circle Words
- **Hobbies**
- **Home town**
- **Favorite baseball team**
- **Interests**
- **Job title**
- **Favorite car**
- **Recipe for chili**

You could go on and on adding similar information. But I think you're beginning to get the point. Irrelevant or at least not very important information is located outside the circle. This is information a customer doesn't mind sharing and there's no real risk in letting it go. In other words, it's information you really can't use. In fact, it's the kind of information that you could probably pick up anywhere.

What does it mean? It represents a type of trivial pursuit that will have us chasing around and around without any positive results and without the gaining of any real knowledge about the person standing before us.

On the other hand, if you were friends with someone, what sort of information would you be willing to share? And expect to be shared with you? I suggest it might include some or all of the following (depending, of course, on the nature of one's friendship and the degree of trust that has been established):

Inside The Circle Words
- **Income**
- **Health challenges**
- **Projected career path**
- **True desires**
- **Plans for the future**
- **Hopes**
- **Fears**
- **Real needs and wants**

What does this indicate? What does it tell you? It tells you that you have to get inside that circle. That it is absolutely imperative for the sales process for you to do so. What do the words and information above indicate? That here is where the truth emerges. That this is where a person's soul, if you wish, expresses itself. What type of sharing is this?

This is true sharing: This is information we do not share with strangers—unlike the score of the previous night's baseball game. And, as was noted above, as a salesperson, you are a stranger to start with. But hopefully not for very long—if you play your cards right and follow the VALUE MATCH steps. The graphic below illustrates the difference between outside and inside the circle responses.

To better demonstrate this, I recently asked a group of successful salespeople to share what they thought were the types of values customers looked for when it came to sales success. Their initial response was quality of the product or service, speed of delivery, accuracy of information, state of the art of product, customer service, etc.

Then I asked the same people what <u>they</u> looked for in a relationship with other companies in order for them to continue doing business with those firms. Those responses were quite different. They included things like trust, honesty, integrity, low stress, ease of communication, and so on.

I'm sure you've noticed that the two lists are not at all the same—and how different they really are. The first list is full of concrete facts, full of particulars with references to a product or service. The second list is full of emotions, sentiments, words that go well beyond any particular product or service and that could be used for any relationship, personal or professional.

It's emotions that allow us to develop relationships that last during difficult times, that are rock solid at their base with the possibility of building ever new structures. The first list everyone can claim as their own, standard sales territory, in other words; the second list only a privileged and select few are allowed to share. The second list is made up of what some people call the "heart-to-heart," a dialogue between very close friends.

The salesperson who can engage in a "heart-to-heart" with a customer is most definitely on the inside of the inner circle of that customer—and can call himself or herself a friend. That, in turn, paves the way so that they can also present themselves in a different and better light. The salesperson is now ready to introduce a truly unique and valuable solution that meets the customer's deepest needs.

In The Circle Or Out The Door?

Do you want to be inside the customer's inner circle of shared values or trapped on the outside looking in? If you leave that important decision to your customer, you will always be out there in the cold, standing on the doorstep or looking in helplessly through the barred window of opportunity. You won't be in a position to help anyone – not your customer, not your company and not yourself. It's a feeling of helplessness you definitely don't want to experience.

Let's face it. Customers love to talk about facts and figures. They'll rattle on and on about the color, the make or model, the mileage, the CD stereo sound system, the latest gadget add-ons, comparative prices, needed accessories, or whatever. And who can blame them really? After all, there's no personal risk in those topics, no danger of exposing oneself and one's innermost feelings to a stranger.

Unfortunately, there's no forward motion either. It's like being in a sales quagmire where the fruits of one's labor are so, oh so, temptingly close but excruciatingly beyond reach. It's like being the salesperson equivalent of that poor unfortunate in Greek mythology by the name of Tantalus. Remember how he was banished to Hades and punished by never being able to quench his thirst or sate his hunger, despite the abundance of water and luscious fruit all around him. That's where the word comes from! Oh so close yet oh so far.

What's to be done? How do you turn the merely tantalizing into reality? By following the VALUE MATCH process. A VALUE MATCH salesperson takes the responsibility to politely push things along, to develop the attitude, skills and knowledge to get and stay inside the circle. He or she realizes that everything happens inside the circle where those personal values hide behind the "circled wagons." And the only way to get inside is to take the time to befriend the customer.

Inside the circle is where you learn about:
- **Your customer's ability to pay**
- **The need for reliable transportation to get the kids to school**
- **His or her fear of traffic accidents**
- **The time he lost an important job because the car broke down**
- **Mom's health problems and the need for dependable transportation to the ER**

Those and others like them are the real reasons customers make purchases. They're the emotional responses that go beyond any facts and figures. They're at the heart of the matter and the place where sales are made.

A Brief Q&A Session

Below you'll find a few questions that should help illustrate my point—and also drive that point home a little harder. Before looking at the answers, take a minute to provide your own.

Questions:
1. When you visit with a new customer, what do you talk about?
2. Why do salespeople spend most of our time outside the circle?
3. As a salesperson working with a customer, should you invest your time inside or outside the circle? And why?
4. Why is it so difficult to spend time on the inside of the circle?

Answers:
1. We usually spend most of our time talking about things that appear on the outside of the circle. Too many of us spend all of our time there. A VALUE MATCH salesperson invests his or her time working with the customer inside the circle because that is the only place to truly serve the unique needs of that customer.
2. A lack of trust. Building trust is essential. Without it, the customer will never open up, let you inside the circle, and reveal the personal values you must have to serve his or her true needs.
3. Obviously, after all we've said, you want to be inside the circle with the truth—and to spend as much time as possible there. As long as you remain on the outside, you will be working with facts alone and facts just aren't enough to do the job. Of course, you need to work on the outside for openers. No one will let you in just like that and so it's important to indulge in "small talk." But then you need to get inside.
4. Each customer will have a different reason or a set of reasons for wanting to get back outside the circle. These could include a lack of trust, running out of time, a different or hidden agenda, fear, and so on. Every time a customer tries to leave the circle, it's your job to see that you both remain inside.

Once you get inside the circle, you have to stay there. Unfortunately, your customer will often have just the opposite desire, will often try to push you out again. Two key skills are important to staying inside and maintaining the needed intimacy. These are your abilities to <u>ask questions and to listen</u>.

This bears repeating: the ability to ask the right questions gets you inside the circle; the ability to listen keeps you inside. To sum up:

- **We all spend too much time on the outside**
- **Customers ask questions about the outside but *desire what is* on the inside.**
- **You have to get to the inside of the TRUST circle before you can get to the inside of the NEEDS circle.**

Aside from taking these up in detail in the next chapter, we will also look at the heart of the VALUE MATCH Model, reveal how matching values between you and your customer is the secret to successful sales, and underline the importance of words, in particular the keeping of your word.

VALUE CHECK

- A customer has two options in a given sales situation: (1) hold back or (2) move forward.
- A VALUE MATCH salesperson keeps things moving forward at all times by applying knowledge of what is holding the customer back.
- Most sales presentations are limited to features, benefits and proof.
- Successful sales presentations focus on the emotional issues behind a customer's needs and wants.
- Connect with your customer in three key areas or on three levels: (1) Personal, (2) Needs and (3) Fears.
- Values outside the circle are information people are willing to share with people they do not know: pleasantries on the weather and the latest baseball scores, for example.
- If you're working on the outside, regardless of how well you think you are doing, you're in trouble. You're Tantalus and the fruits of your labor will always escape you.
- Values inside the circle are the things people are only willing to share with selected and trusted friends.
- Customers are often their own worst enemies because they focus on discussing topics outside the circle.
- You, as a salesperson, have to learn the art of nudging them along until they're willing to divulge what's inside the circle.

Friendship is never established
as an understood relation ...
It is a miracle which requires constant proofs.
It is an exercise of the purest imagination
and the rarest faith... True Friendship
can afford true knowledge.
It does not depend on darkness and ignorance.

—Henry David Thoreau

CHAPTER SEVEN:

THE VALUE MATCH MODEL

> *Words are the voice of the heart.*
>
> **—Confucius (K'ung-fu-tzu)**
>
> *Words differently arranged have a different meaning, and meanings differently arranged have different effects.*
>
> **—Blaise Pascal**
>
> *The words of truth are simple.*
>
> **—Aeschylus**

Keeping Your Word? A Valuable Asset

Values Unlocked: Words Are The Secret

In this chapter, we will look at the meaning of words and how to align those key meanings with values in order to get "inside the value bubble" whether it's your potential customer, a family member or close friend. We will also look at the ways to break down the gap between customer and salesperson when it comes to the use of words and their meanings. Among the values unlocked in this chapter are:

- How words mean things
- The iceberg of words
- The diamond of meaning
- Effective questioning
- How to really listen

Words Mean Things

We have already discussed the importance of getting inside your customer's personal "value bubble" or personal "circle of values." But how exactly do you know if and when you are inside that value bubble? You know you're inside when you have successfully identified the customer's personal values, his or her needs, and the fears that might be holding the customer back from taking the next key step in the sales process.

Breaking down each one of these, we get:
- **Personal**: **You know you are inside when the customer says: "To tell you the truth" and you have identified the personal values of the customer. This helps to identify where you and the customer have values in common and is the basis for true rapport. This allows the salesperson to then ask more personal questions related to the customer's needs.**
- **Needs**: **You know you are inside when the customer trusts you enough to say: "Isn't that amazing?! You have exactly what I need. What are the odds of that?"**
- **Fears**: **You know you are inside when you are able to say to the customer: "That's a great idea." If you can do that, then you will have little problem moving forward.**

Once inside your customer's personal circle of values, that's not the end of it. It's not like a permanent pass. You have to be able to hold onto that position, all the while as the customer keeps a close eye on you. There are two major keys to maintaining that position:
- **Your ability to ask intelligent and appropriate questions**
- **Your ability to listen to your customer.**

Just like any other form of human communication, the basic tools of the trade in sales are words, yours and those of your customer. Use them well and they will serve you well. Abuse them or misuse them and you're in trouble, possibly serious trouble. It's as simple as that. Ask yourself: can I ever hope to gain the trust and confidence of my spouse or my friend if my communication with them is twisted by slippery words and undefined meanings? Of course not. The same thing is true for the salesperson.

Too often we're sloppy with our choice and use of words, forgetting that words really do mean things, that they have a significance. To make matters worse, words can hold a variety of meanings for different people, which can undermine your efforts at clear communication. When we proceed with conversation using different word definitions than those we've agreed to, we create miscommunication and that can only mean mistakes and missed opportunities.

This is also the meaning of propaganda, the use of words to confuse others and to convince them to do something they wouldn't otherwise do if they had been told the truth. This is not what a salesperson aims for. Not only is it against our core values but it leads to mistrust on the part of the customer once they discover the lie. And they will discover the lie. Mark my words. Once a customer mistrusts your words, good luck trying to get back into his or her inner circle.

Always remember:

When you are listening, you are selling.
When you are talking, you are buying.

Words can have no single fixed meaning.
Like wayward electrons, they can spin away
from their initial orbit
and enter a wider magnetic field.
No one owns them or has a proprietary right
to dictate how they will be used.

—David Lehman

> "Because words mean things, it is imperative that the salesperson discover those meanings as they apply to the individual customer"

Where I live in Arizona, I've experienced summer days that have reached temperatures of a blistering 122 degrees. Of course, that means our winters are, to say the least, mild. Naturally we in Scottsdale and the Valley of the Sun get a lot of "winter visitors," temporary guests escaping the cold, snow and ice of Minnesota, the Dakotas, the Midwest, and even Canada.

In the winter, these folks are used to temperatures that dip well below zero and stay there for months at a time. The different reactions between "Zonies" and "Snow-birds" to the word "cold" perfectly illustrate why word meanings can be so fraught with danger for the salesperson—and why context is so important.

One evening I saw two couples heading out to their favorite restaurant for a quiet evening meal. The temperature was in the upper fifties. The locals were dressed in long pants and sweaters. One even wore a woolen cap. They were bundled up. The winter guests wore sandals, shorts and polo-style, short-sleeved shirts. Both parties were completely comfortable and, clearly, both had entirely different concepts of cold.

If you were selling one of those couples an air conditioner, a fur coat, or just glass of lemonade, the way you used the word "cold" in your product demonstration could have a dramatic impact on your success. In particular, if your meaning of "cold" was not aligned to that particular couple's meaning of the word, then you might find yourself out in the cold when it came to making a sale!

In a class of ten to twenty people, I can get ten to twenty different definitions of the word "cold," or any other word for that matter. That's simply because we are all individuals with particular tastes, needs and experiences—and particular histories. The salesperson needs to discover the context in which the customer uses the word.

Put another way, it is important to understand the differences in the way different people use words. An astute salesperson asks himself or herself:

- **What are some of the common words that come up in my interactions with customers?**

- What are some of the different meanings and definitions for those words?
- What are some of the values associated with each word and/or meaning?

The illustration below indicates how a typical conversation works: words emerge from both ends, each with its own meaning. The object is to ensure that those meanings are understood and that the shared values grasped.

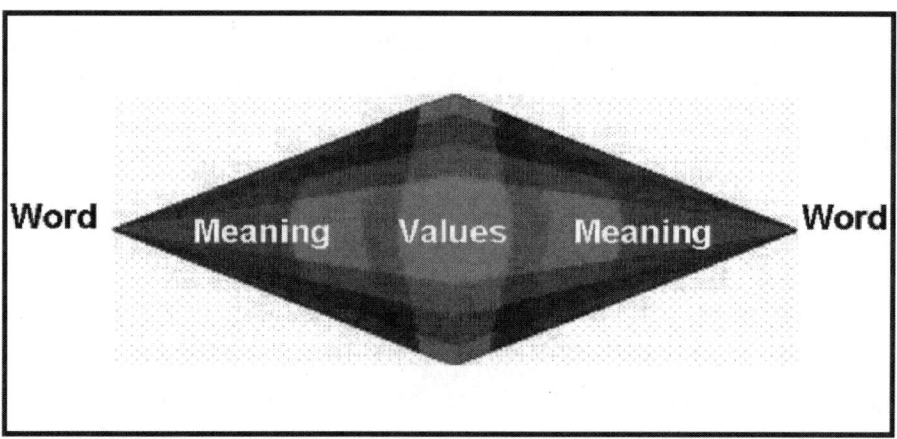

Understanding the Differences Between What Is Being Said and What Is Being Meant.

In most cases, this isn't that difficult or arduous a task. And you don't need to be a linguist to decipher the various meanings. The meanings of words aren't infinite. They lie within a particular spectrum or range. Not even the word "cold" or "comfortable" for example can ever be interpreted as meaning "rabbit." It is up to the salesperson to be aware of this range of possible meanings. That awareness comes from knowing the customer.

Just A Tip: The Iceberg Of Words (listening is not a thinking man's sport)

We can compare an individual's use and meaning of a word to the tip of a very large iceberg. For each individual user of the word, that tip, the particular meaning, is very small. It's just a point and it is very specific. But as the word is used by others, the size of that iceberg grows. The meanings "below the surface" accumulate and accrete. At the same time, it is important to remember that the three levels of the "iceberg" are all connected: from individual use of a word to collective meaning to the value beneath it all.

This is only natural. Within a certain range, every person has his or her own meaning or interpretation until the size of that one little word grows enormously. You and your customer could be using the exact same word or key phrase, but could be miles apart on its actual meaning. And this doesn't only happen in a selling situation. How many times has it happened to you that you and your spouse are "not on the same wavelength" although you're using the same words to explain yourselves?

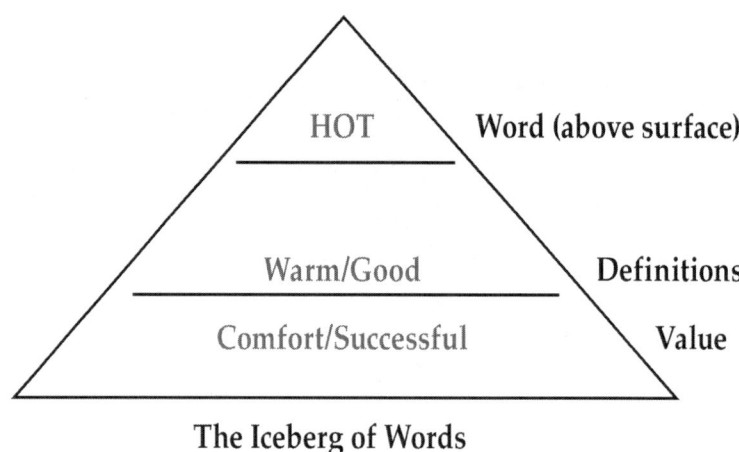

The Iceberg of Words

As you can see, when it comes to understanding and making yourself understood, every word you use is important. The Zonie couple looking at air conditioners may need an industrial-strength unit that can maintain a "comfortable" 63 degrees month after month throughout a brutal four-month summer. The snowbirds might just want something to keep the breeze blowing at a "comfortable" 73 degrees through their short and sweet few weeks of summer. So we have what would be cold for one group as comfortable for the other; and what would be too warm for one group as comfortable for the other.

In fact, when it comes to comfort, the words "cold" and "hot" might not even be all that pertinent. For example, people with allergies might be motivated more by the unit's ability to filter pollen, mold and mildew than by it's ability to cool. This is certainly true here in the desert where Spring and Fall temperatures are pleasant, but allergies tend to run rampant.

Thus, people use words that might seem to mean one thing on the surface but something else when it comes to the value they want to get across. Coded words, in other words, for their true intentions, facts and features to cover their emotional "values". We need to be skilled at helping them and us uncover the values that are connected to their words or that may be hidden by their words. The skill that's needed is listening. I like to say: "Listening is not a thinking man's sport."

The Diamond Of Meaning

What happens when you put two icebergs together end-to-end? You create a diamond. It may be at first a diamond in the rough, but a diamond nonetheless and one that can be polished. Here's another question: What gives a diamond its value? The answer is *clarity.* **That's what gives value to communication, too. Only when the communication is clear can you understand each other and continue the process of providing goods and services. Only then do you create the** *diamond of meaning.*

VALUE MATCH Model Of Communication

The VALUE MATCH model is the way we should communicate with our customers throughout the sales process. Understand that during a sale, the conversation must always revolve around the customer's agenda, not the agenda of the salesperson. Too many inexperienced salespeople rush in with an armload of features, benefits and proof—their own agenda—without ever discovering the needs—the real agenda—of their customer. This can be a fatal error.

Listening the VALUE MATCH way is the critical skill needed to use the VALUE MATCH process.

As indicated by the illustration below, the VALUE MATCH model consists of four steps:

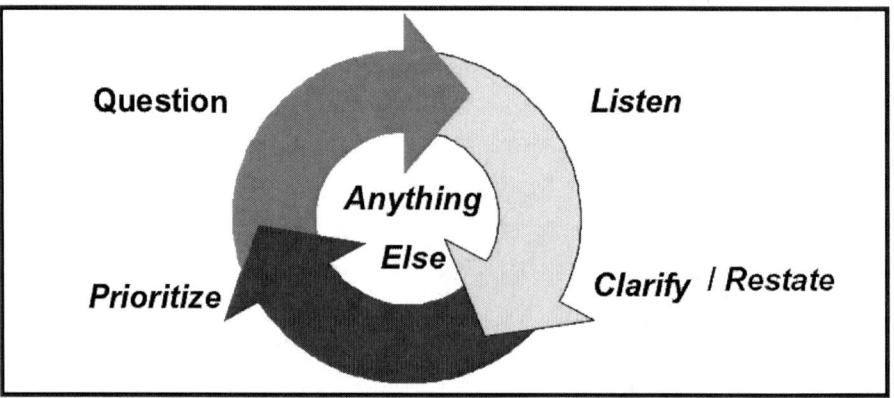

The VALUE MATCH Communications Model is the way we should always communicate with our customers.

- Question
- Listen
- Clarify/Restate
- Prioritize

Notice that the model is cyclical and recursive. Just as in life, what goes down comes 'round. And what goes 'round comes down. Reversing that order can lead to less than satisfactory results. Let's examine those steps one at a time.

- **QUESTION:** This is the step where you gather information about your customer's needs, desires and values. Your questions must be focused on the customer's agenda, not what you want to do, say or hear. Asking intelligent and appropriate questions creates an environment in which your customer feels safe and secure in expressing his or her true needs. Questioning also keeps you in control of the situation.
- **LISTEN:** You have to make an active attempt to hear and understand the meanings of your customer's words and key phrases, to understand the customer's world. It's not a passive activity. You have to get in there and mix it up. This is a pivotal point in the sales process. You have much to gain and much to

lose here. The direction of the process, to hold back or to move forward, will depend considerably on how well you listen. It's absolutely necessary to take notes during listening. The activity shows that: (1) you are paying attention to what is being said; (2) you care about what the customer is saying; and (3) you pay attention to detail.

- **CLARIFY/RESTATE:** Here, you confirm your perception of what the customer has told you about his/her needs, desires and values. This step can only take place effectively once you are clear about the meanings of your customer's words and key phrases. Notice I'm not using the word "paraphrase" and that's important. Paraphrasing is by definition an inaccurate process. When you change your customer's words you also change meanings and that can only lead you into dangerous territory. When you restate, restate precisely what your customer has said to ensure you understand exactly what the customer has said. Use the same words if need be. Here's why:
  - Restating helps the customer know that the salesperson, that stranger he or she needs to trust, is really listening.
  - Restating determines if the salesperson has understood precisely what the customer means by what he or she has said.
  - Restating prioritizes the most important customer needs and values when multiple answers are given.
  - Restating and therefore dramatically increases the value of the conversation.
- **PRIORITIZE:** In this step you confirm your perception of the order and importance of what the customer has said about his or her needs, desires and values. Often, the customer will attempt to talk about the less important of his or her priorities. Or might simply get confused about those priorities. Again, this is understandable. The real needs and values are very personal and it is sometimes difficult for a customer to open up and talk about them. It's the salesperson's responsibility to keep the customer focused on the most important topics inside that circle of trust.

Most salespeople get into trouble when they do not follow the VALUE MATCH Communication Model. There is a great temptation to start "selling" right away, to push the product or service. But in reality, when you don't follow the model you aren't selling. You can't even begin to start selling until you have truly asked, listened, restated and prioritized.

It's very important to remember: He or she has a list of questions, wants to listen to your answers, restate them and get them prioritized. The real key here is to be sure that you ask the questions first. That gets the process rolling in the right direction. That ensures you're in control and providing the proper guidance.

Always stay focused on your customer's agenda and respect their feelings and thoughts. If you are doing things right, you will be discussing personal and private values. Recognize that these are the most important topics and give them the proper respect. Remember that, while the customer is in charge of the "what" of the conversation, the salesperson is in charge of the "when" and the "how." That's why you have the ability, the power and the responsibility to keep the process on track.

The salesperson determines the direction of the initial conversation and the questions that guide the process. It is key that you learn how the customer defines the situation and what values are most important to that individual.

The illustration below now shows the entire VALUE MATCH Model process—from both the customer's and the salesperson's point of view. As you can see, the process brings together the customer's Needs and Wants together with the salesperson's Services and Solutions through the Communications Model to arrive at the VALUE MATCH Solutions at the center of the diamond.

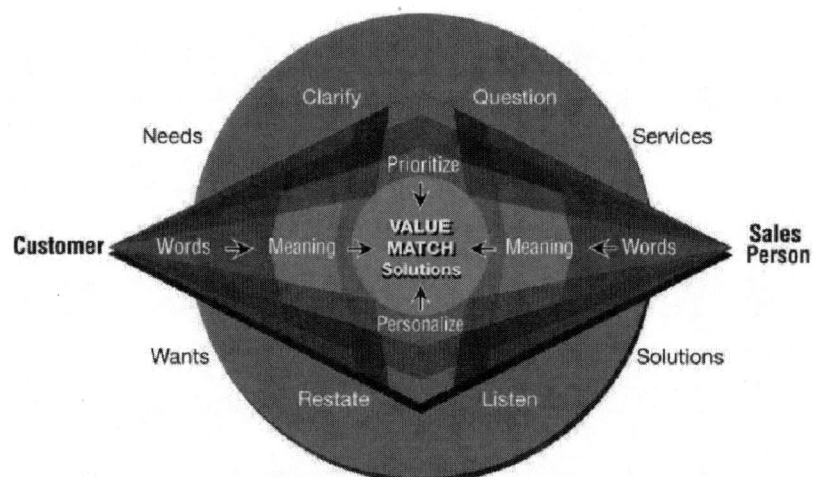

The VALUE MATCH Model as Viewed from both the Customer and the Salesperson with VALUE MATCH Solutions in the Middle of the Diamond.

Question Everything!

As a salesperson, you need to learn to use questioning or probing as a way to gather information about your customer's needs, wants and values. You have to keep those questions flowing. But, at the same time, your questions have to be intelligent, specific, and appropriate. You don't want to waste time with meaningless conversation.

You want to ask highly-targeted and incisive questions so that you can listen to the true meaning of the answers. At the same time, you don't want to come across as if you're conducting a police interrogation of the customer. Your probing and questioning has to come across as a genuine conversation with the customer, something that you might have with a new acquaintance.

After the initial process has started, the secret to effective questioning and listening is to ask questions about what the customer has said and nothing else. Really. By staying focused on what the customer says, you can always stay in control and never be seen as pushy or nosy.

Now, to effectively obtain information while using the VALUE MATCH model, I would like to share with you some time-tested and proven rules I have discovered. They will take some discipline to use effectively but "hey" when you let 'em work, they work like magic.

Rule #1: Use The Three Effective Questioning Techniques

A VALUE MATCH salesperson makes good use of the three basic types of questions:
- **Open-ended questions**
- **Clarifying/Restating questions**
- **Value-added questions.**

Let's look briefly at the attributes of all three types of questions and the reasons for their effectiveness.

Open-ended questions are questions of a general nature designed to encourage the customer to provide more or additional information. They are most useful during the first stage of the sales process. They are also a rather effective technique when you want to change the subject or gather information in a different direction. Open-ended questions can't be answered with a simple "yes" or "no". Or with a conversation-stalling one-word answer.

"Mrs. Smith! What brings you in today?"

The customer just can't give a one-word answer to a question like that, so she to provide additional information.

Use open-ended questions for the majority of your presentation because they encourage your customer to be more involved in the process. These types of questions do not allow him or her to become a passive participant. The customers need to respond and to provide information as they do so. They also keep you, the salesperson, from unconsciously dominating the process, from talking too much at the wrong times, in other words.

One of the first things journalism students learn in Reporting 101 is the "Five Ws and the H" rule. It states that, when covering a story, they need to get the:

- **W**ho
- **W**hat
- **W**here
- **W**hen
- **W**hy
- And **H**ow.

"Who is this purchase for?"
"What is your definition of 'modest'?"
"Where do you see yourself in ten years?"
"When is that delivery deadline?"
"Why are you in our little store this morning?"
"How would you describe the perfect solution to your problem?"

"If you can't ask a question with 'what,' then don't ask it"

The simple rule I follow is: "If I can't ask the question with 'what,' I don't ask it." Again, these kinds of questions are an assured way to keep your customer talking and therefore providing more and more information. The table below describes how a salesperson can best go about using open-ended questions with a customer.

Suggestion	Description and Example
Be short and to the point	Indicate a general area you would like to know about:
Get the customer talking	Shift the responsibility for talking to the customer. This frees you to listen and take notes:
Generate needed information	Prompt the customer to provide information needed to: • Qualify the customer • Build rapport • Develop a relationship • Relate with empathy • Formulate additional questions
Restate with short statements	Short re-statements indicate you not only heard with a customer said but also understood: Short statements may help you target another area that needs discussion:

How to Use Open-Ended Questions in the VALUE MATCH Process.

Clarifying/Restating questions encourage the customer to expand on his or her answers, or to further define a key word or phrase that's come up during the conversation. Clarifying questions are specific and to the point. They are designed to encourage additional responses.

"You say you like to read mysteries and fiction. Which one do you like better?"

"You say you are short on time. What do you mean 'short on time'?"

"When you say an engine with 'pep,' Mrs. Smith, what do you mean?"

Before asking this type of question, it is important to ask a clarifying questions to make sure you and your customer are "on the same page" and that you have heard the customer correctly. The way to clarify is to restate what has already been said, as in the above example. Note again that we never paraphrase because that just gets us further and further into imprecise and potentially dangerous verbal territory. This is extremely important. A customer may agree with your restating question, but then again, he or she may change the key word in the phrase in question.

"Oh, no, Mr. Salesman. I *don't* want an engine with poop. I want a reliable car, one with pep."

Once you reach agreement on the word or phrase, then you can ask for a more complete definition, which helps move the process along. Clarifying/restating questions may try your patience. The process can go through several cycles before it is complete and you may need to use all your skills and abilities to manage the situation. That's okay. You do what you have to do because only after you have a clear understanding of exactly what your customer is saying can you move to the next step. The table below shows how to use clarifying questions.

Use It To:	Description and Example
Elicit additional information	Once a customer has answered your clarifying question, you should have a clear idea about what he or she really thinks and be in a position to move the conversation to the value side of the circle. You: (Clarifying question)
Restate and verify information	Restating what you heard in <u>their words</u> will verify and confirm your understanding and keep the conversation moving in <u>their direction</u>. You: (Clarifying question) Customer: "Yes, you're right." (Verify information) You: (Open-ended question)

How to Use Clarifying Questions in VALUE MATCH Process.

Value-added questions are used to help your customer more clearly focus his or her feelings or emotions associated with a particular topic or area of concern.

"I understand you want a reliable, and especially a roadside assistance plan. Why is that important to you?"

More generally, value-added questions help the customer to explore and share their feelings about a topic. They also guide a customer towards being truthful with themselves and with you about the situation. The table below shows how a salesperson can effectively use value-added questions in the sales process.

Use It To:	Description and Example
Help the customer see the value of a particular product or service when compared to others	Value-added questions reveal the customer's needs and help you move forward in the qualifying process. You: Customer: "I love an Olympic size pool because it allows me to stay fit and that's important to me."
Help the customer search for feelings about the issues at hand	Value-added questions encourage the customer to talk about issues resulting from the current situation. You: Customer: "Well, my son and his family will be close and I can spend more time with them."

Using Value-Added Questions in VALUE MATCH Process.

Proper use of the three types of questioning techniques will turn a scattershot approach to gathering information into a precise, well-targeted and productive process.

Basically, you always:
- **Question – Listen – Repeat and Prioritize while focusing your questions and listening to the words the customer uses.**
- **At the same time, you "peel the onion" so to speak by first asking general questions, then clarifying questions.**
- **Then you ask value-added questions to get to the heart of the situation or the customer's motivation.**

Rule #2: Avoid "No-No" Words And Questions

No-no words are any words that require or encourage a single-word answer such as or some similar one-word answer. These types of questions and the answers they elicit can create roadblocks to your presentation. They break up the two-way flow of real information because it is difficult to formulate effective follow up questions. It's as if you've created a bridge for the value gap and then proceed to dismantle part of it. Or put up barriers so that it becomes more difficult to get to the other side.

Sometimes the problem with one "no-no" word or question is that the first response to such a question sets off an avalanche of such answers. This is the reverse of the old closing technique of getting the customer to say "yes" several times in a row. It leads to negativity and frustration on the part of both you and the customer.

But the real issue with no/no questions is that they are all about the questioner's agenda. You can't be on someone else's agenda and ask these types of questions. The only questions you can ask and be on their agenda is about something they said. Period. The test: If you ask a question and I ask why you asked it, and the answer is: **"Because I want to know,"** that by definition is your agenda. Try it sometimes. You can't ask a question about my agenda using a no-no word to start the question.

Certainly, there is a time and a place for no-no words, but that time and place must be of your choosing. And you should choose Could, would, should, can, do, are, is, does, and will are among the no-no words.

YOU: Could I interest you in a new SUV?

SHE: No.

So where does a salesperson go after that? You try some damage control.

YOU: Would you be interested perhaps in a family van, then?

SHE: No.

Do you see how you can easily paint yourself into a corner with little way out? You're trapped and there is little you can do now to make it right. Odds are you've lost a potential customer. Further probing is most likely useless.

YOU: Should I leave you alone now?

SHE: Yes.

> "The real issue with no/no questions is that they are all about the questioner's agenda ... the only questions you can ask and be on their agenda is about something they said"

Other no-no words to avoid include:
No-No Examples

- **"Do"** you like my suit? "No"
- **"Did"** I tell you I'm Irish? "Who cares?"
- **"Shall"** I leave you alone? "Yes"
- **"Are"** you really tired of me? "Yes"
- **"Is"** this the worst sales presentation you have ever had? "Yes"
- **"Might"** I get someone else for you to work with? "Yes"
- **"May"** I call you to follow up? "No"
- **"Can"** I ever fix this? "No"
- **"Have"** you any heart? "No"

Any question you ask beginning with these words can be answered with a single word. This will hinder your future ability to ask good questions of your customer and most likely lead you away from discovering the customer's agenda, needs, wants and desires. This is the end of the line as far as that customer is concerned.

Using a no-no word during a presentation is the sales equivalent of climbing a mountain, but then cutting your rope halfway to the top. It can be a long, bumpy, unpleasant tumble and it really hurts when you hit bottom. And you won't find the customer there waiting to commiserate with you on your misfortune.

Never ask no-no questions, which always involve a no-no word someplace. Here are five types of "no-no" questions, followed by an example of each type. The experienced salesperson should make it second nature never to use this type of questioning, especially when you are just starting the conversation with the customer.

- **TWO PART QUESTION:** *"How long have you lived in that apartment and do you plan on renting much longer?"*

The problem here is that our salesperson has asked two questions in one. This always confuses a customer. Worse, the no-no words encourage a yes/no response to the second part of the question and will likely cause an abrupt answer to the first part as well. This is not a very good way to get information effectively.

- **TOO LONG QUESTION:** *"What did you think about that new movie where the guy gets stranded on a desert island and has to live off the land until he finally builds a raft and sails away to safety only to find out everything back in his old life had changed or how about the one about that gladiator in Rome who fights with the emperor and wins, but dies anyway?"*

A question that is that long and drawn out can't really be answered well because nobody could possibly keep up with all the information within it. If you want real information from the answers, keep your questions short and sweet and to the point.

- **YES/NO QUESTION:** *"Can you make this purchase today?"*

Such a question can only be answered with a yes or a no. This leaves the salesperson with no "wiggle room" to get out of the verbal mess he or she has created. would be a much better, open-ended question.

- **DIRECT QUESTION:** *"How much do you make a year?"*

Direct questions definitely have their place, and they will need to be asked at some point because it is the type of information that is important to any sales process. But you must prepare that place well in advance of the delivery. Otherwise, you are likely to (1) not get the information you want, and (2) antagonize your customer. Direct questions are also known as "none of your business" questions, the type of questions best left for when the customer is filling out an information sheet that is marked "Private and Confidential".

- **LEADING QUESTION:** *"So, when will you be ready to leave that deposit?"*

When a salesperson asks such an obviously leading question, he or she telegraphs a serious interest in the answer. The danger is to appear more interested in making the sale than in serving the customer. Another danger arises from the fact the customer senses this weakness and will try to go for a bigger bargain, one which he or she will then take to another salesperson.

The most important reason not to use these NO NO questions is because they keep you on your agenda and off the other person's agenda.

Rule #3: When Clarifying/Restating, Ask A Question About The Answer And Ask A Question About The Question.

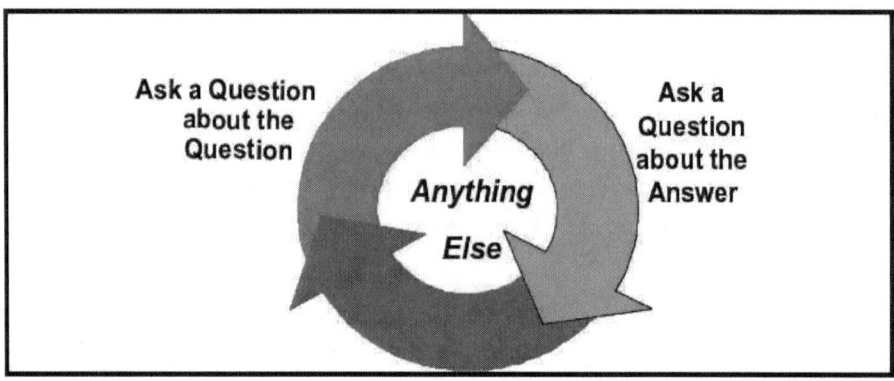

No, that's not the title of a bad country-western song. Or a Chinese riddle. It is, however, an excellent rule of questioning and for soliciting further information from your customer. It also helps to clarify and confirm and lets the customer know that you've been listening. As I noted earlier, the trick is to question everything. Here's an example of asking a question about the answer:

YOU: What is the situation?

HER: Well, we were thinking of buying a car because our car is getting too small.

YOU: So, what I hear you saying is that your car is getting too small, is that right? (Correct follow-up question: "When you say 'too small,' what do you mean by that?" Incorrect follow up question: "So where else have you looked for a car?")

When you restate something, the trick is to ask a question about the question. Here's another example:

YOU: What is the situation?

HER: Do you have some sedans that we can look at?

YOU: So you are asking if we have some sedans that you can look at, is that right?

HER: Yes, that is correct.

YOU: When you ask if we have some sedans, what do you mean?

HER: Well, we are expecting and we will need a little more room and my drive to work is going to be a little longer so gas mileage will be important to me.

YOU: So what I hear you saying is that you are looking for a sedan but also for something with a little more room and that will get some good gas mileage, is that right. It sounds like you are in the right place, I can think of a couple of options for you to look at.

Our salesperson, you, might be selling any number of products or services: play stations, nannies, baby-sitting services, community youth programs, or encyclopedias. That's not the point. The point is that you asked appropriate questions, listened, clarified, restated

You can never ask too many of the right kind of questions. Customers are much more willing to confide in you and allow you into the inner value circle if you show that you are genuinely interested in what they are saying and what their feelings are. That's only human nature. It's the sort of thing we accomplish every day with our spouses, our children, our friends, and our neighbors.

Putting It All Together

Let's put all this to the test. Let's see how these steps could work in a real-world situation. In this case, that situation is the selection of an assisted living facility for a family member, the kind of decision that can be both emotional and stressful. We'll pick up the dialog well into the conversation.

Restate What You Actually Heard

MRS. JOHNSON:... and that's why we're here? Do you think you can help us with mom?

SALESPERSON: Mrs. Johnson, based on everything you have told me, it sounds as though there are three key issues: addressing your mother's medical needs, finding an environment where she is safe and secure, and finding an environment where you can feel good about the quality of her life and care. Is that right?

MRS. JOHNSON: Yes. Absolutely.

At this point, Mrs. Johnson might just as easily offer a "yes-but," as in or some other concern. In fact, she could absolutely agree with everything you've said and still have major concerns that have not yet been addressed.

Ask The Customer: "Is That Correct?"

SALESPERSON: So, you're saying that being close to the other family members is important for you and your mother. Is that correct?

MRS. JOHNSON: Yes. We're a very close family.

SALESPERSON: I see. Is there anything else you should tell me?

Always keep searching for that one more piece of information that might be important to your customer. It's usually there, somewhere, if you just keep looking. When you ask, "is that correct?" he or she may or may not say something significant. If he or she does, determine if the new information is a key issue. If you are in doubt...just ask another question.

Prioritize The Key Issue

Customers often give multiple—and even contradictory or not quite matching—responses to a question. Sometimes they do this because they're not secure in their own minds as to their real needs; sometimes as a stalling tactic; and sometimes just to explore options.

Your task, should you choose to accept this far from impossible sales mission, is to identify the key issue the customer places before you. Remember, choose only the top one. If the customer provides more, cull out the rest. Don't forget about them but keep them on the sidelines for the time being. Then you need to take the key issue and use that in your process.

In this case:

SALESPERSON: Out of the three things you mentioned, which one is of most importance?

MRS. JOHNSON: Well, the most important issue by far is the quality of care.

Your customer is going to be hit with a lot of information. Ideally, he or she will absorb all or most of it. You don't want to overload a customer with the least important information before getting to the most important.

By the time you reach that point, it just might be too late.

Go straight to the important information that addresses what you've discerned as the customer's most important issue. Remember, however, that what you've picked out as your customer's key issue might not be what he or she may have stated as his or her key issue—at least not in the very first statement of those issues.

You need to keep asking questions and be astute enough to listen for the words that will help you dig out a customer's true wants, needs, desires and values. Only then can you be certain that you are addressing his or her top priority. For example, the first time you ask a customer what his or her main concern with respect to a product or service, the customer might answer that price or cost is at the top of the list. But, later, after further probing, other concerns might take over: quality of care, for example, in an assisted living facility; amenities; distance from the family home, etc.

It's up to you to keep probing and asking questions. You can't just say, when a customer goes elsewhere with his or her business, perhaps to a more expensive facility: "But you didn't tell me that these other concerns were more important than the cost. If you would have told me, I would have explained and prioritized those concerns." Might as well not bother closing the barn door at that point.

The Heart Of The Matter

Confucius said that words are the voice of the heart. Words really do mean things and they are the tools of our trade. Like weapons, they can be used to hurt or harm, defend the realm, or bring home the bacon. How your words are used and for what purpose really depends upon where your heart is. Using your words to "heart-sell," to become a trusted friend and advisor to your customer, means that you are a VALUE MATCH salesperson and your word truly is your bond.

In the next chapter, we will look at the inevitable result of the right kind of probing and questioning, the building of trust and rapport between you and the customer—and how that is the true foundation for any successful sale. Or any successful relationship, for that matter. We will look at the actual VALUE MATCH process for achieving that trust, along with a demonstration of the steps you need to go about doing it. We will also look at two invaluable VALUE MATCH tools that will make the process easier and simpler.

VALUE CHECK

- All words have meanings and these meanings can differ among individuals, often making communication difficult
- It is important that the person speaking and the person listening are on the same wavelength when it comes to what a key word means
- When two people come to an agreement as to the meaning of a word, they achieve "the diamond of meaning," the first step in the VALUE MATCH process
- The next step comes in the use of effective probing or questioning techniques by the salesperson to uncover a customer's true needs, wants, desires, and values.
- Just as important as questioning is the skill to really listen to what the other person is saying—and not just saying but actually trying to tell you (often beneath the surface of the words).
- The next step is to take your customer's stated and unstated issues and concerns and to prioritize them in order of importance—and to immediately address the first three.
- It is from this that the VALUE MATCH Solutions are achieved, with the salesperson allowed within the customer's personal and needs value circle.
- Congratulations! From this you can move on to build a solid foundation for that successful sale.

The power of words is immense.
A well-chosen word has often sufficed
to stop a flying army,
to change defeat into victory,
and to save an empire.

—Emile De Giradin

CHAPTER EIGHT:

TRUST AND TRUTH

> *We never stop investigating.
> We are never satisfied
> that we know enough to get by.
> Every question we answer
> leads on to another question.
> This has become
> the greatest survival trick
> of our species.*
>
> **—Desmond Morris**

Building Trust: Foundation of A Successful Sale

Values Unlocked In This Chapter

In this chapter, we will look at the first contact between you and your potential customer. Without success in this initial contact, the rest of the sales process is not going to happen. Thus, your ability to build rapport and handle the initial contact effectively is critical to the entire sales process. One of the key purposes of this chapter is to show you how you can achieve greater rapport with the potential customer—or how to re-establish rapport with an existing customer—through the use of a key tool: the VALUE MATCH Balanced Scorecard.

Among the values unlocked in this chapter are:
- **Six keys to making positive first impressions**
- **Controlling the process of building rapport**
- **The VALUE MATCH Balanced Scorecard, Forms One & Two: To Build Rapport and Establishing Credibility**

I couldn't think of a better bridge between a chapter on questioning in general and a chapter on the specifics of building rapport than the insightful quote above from writer and naturalist Desmond Morris, that acute observer of human nature.

Building rapport, which leads to trust, is an essential component of the initial stages of the sales process. If you fail to build a strong foundation, the steps that follow will be at best a stumbling, faltering effort leading to an inevitable fall; at worst, it may lead to a fall from which you may not recover with the result of losing your customer to someone else.

This chapter begins a different aspect of this book. Rather than simply talking in general terms, we are now going to the VALUE MATCH principles to the sales process. We're going to break down these principles step by step and show you how to go about using them during an actual sale.

Building Trust Builds Sales

In a previous chapter you read all about the importance of building rapport, specifically about the need to have customers feel confident enough to let you in and to tell you the truth. Building rapport is a critical skill. It is also a skill that can be learned. Not everyone is born a super salesperson. Besides, building rapport is something we all need to do—even if our career choice has absolutely nothing to do with traditional sales.

Building rapport is all about building a relationship with a perfect stranger. It's about establishing compatibility so that you and your customer feel as though you can relate to each other. It's about a customer moving from a place where he or she is cold and defensive and feels all alone to where he or she is willing to share with you their personal values. That's right. Until they're willing, even anxious, to share all the important stuff on the inside of their circle. But that's quite a shift and they need help getting to that point. Chances are they're not willing to do it on their own. They're looking for an ally who can help carry the burden of responsibility.

Building rapport is all about creating an environment and setting the stage so your customer can relax. So that you're no longer that complete stranger. It's about controlling the agenda so he or she has the opportunity to share values. It means paying attention to the conversation. It means both talking and listening attentively. It means getting down and personal. This is how you recognize those opportunities to show interest in the things that are important to your customer.

In this chapter you will learn specific strategies, tools and tactics that you can use to build rapport effectively. Remember when trying to build rapport:

- **People want to be noticed.**
- **People crave to be appreciated.**
- **People want to deal with those they can trust.**
- **People judge based on first impressions.**

Setting The Stage

The first step in building rapport is making a positive first impression. I call it "setting the stage." As we all know, the stage must first be set up and properly positioned before anything else can happen. Then and only then can a play or other performance follow. The same thing takes place in the sales process.

Although it only takes a few seconds to make a first impression, those impressions have a long lasting effect—and can easily determine your success or failure in the process that follows. In fact, a bad first impression might very well mean that no process will follow, that the customer will be "turned off" and you're done like toast. Might as well move on at that point.

It all comes down to what I call the "baby duck" effect. Those cute little baby ducks instantly bond to the first thing they see. With ducks it's called bonding, with humans it's called imprinting. But remember that the very reverse can also happen: that first imprint can leave a sour taste and any bonding will be of the negative variety. And you'll end up one ugly duckling without the possibility of turning into a swan!

In fact, the initial impression is so strong that, if we start off on the wrong foot with a potential customer, the negative feelings could stay with that person for some time, perhaps forever. You could be the most intelligent, coolest and nicest person around, but if you make a bad first impression, your customer will ignore all of the smart, cool and nice things you do, say, or, more importantly, know. He or she will search out to reinforce the initial bad impression.

> "You could be the most intelligent, coolest and nicest person around, but if you make a bad first impression, your customer will ignore all of the smart, cool and nice things you do, say, or know"

Suddenly, that single hair out of place, that tiny scuff mark on your shined shoes, those almost imperceptible frayed threads on your jacket will all be noticed and filed away as proof that you are not really what you say you are. That negative first impression in your customer's mind just won't allow you to be intelligent, cool or nice. And you may never get a chance to correct that first impression.

That's just the way it works, isn't it? Think about it. Isn't that the way you were when you met your daughter or son's last flame for the first time? And isn't it the way you were when you went out on your first date? In fact, it could be argued that making a good first impression before a customer is even more imperative than in a personal relationship. Often, we are more forgiving in social situations—and have plenty of time to correct a bad first impression. Not so with a business relationship between a salesperson and a customer. Few such luxuries exist.

So, it stands to reason that we should do all we can to make sure our first impression is positive. Only then can we set the stage for building trust and begin the sales process.

Build On The Basics

First impressions aren't a matter of accidents or come what may—and they can definitely be controlled. The basics for making a positive first impression are:

- **It's all in the name**
- **The importance of touch**
- **Perfecting the process**
- **Your environment**
- **Hygiene and dress**
- **Etiquette for over the phone contacts**
- **Most importantly: Listen**

It's all in the name

Using your customer's name frequently serves two purposes. One, it flatters this stranger who has just shown up on your showroom floor and begins breaking the ice so you can move toward building a relationship. Nothing sounds sweeter to a customer's ear than the sound of his or her own name. It's an essential part of the rapport-building process and it helps to establish a sense of familiarity, giving the customer a sense of belonging.

Two, and just as importantly, it helps you remember the name. Some people can hear a fact, such as a name or a number, and remember it forever. Most of us aren't wired that way. So, repeating your customer's name throughout the presentation is the best way to imprint it on your brain. The key to learning, after all, is repetition.

Here are a few tips to remember about remembering:
- **Be prepared** to hear the name and listen for it. Don't let it slip by as so many salespeople do. There is nothing more embarrassing and potentially deal-breaking than not remembering a customer's name.
- **Say** the name to yourself three times the moment you hear it.
- **Write** it down immediately. Your prospect won't mind and will even be impressed by your professionalism and concern for getting things right. Make sure you get the correct spelling. If you're uncertain, ask: "Is that 'Mr. Gray' with an 'a' or 'Mr. Grey' with an 'e'?"
- **Repeat** the name out loud. "Pleased to meet you, Mr. Grey."
- **Use** some type of word association. Associate the prospect with another Mr. Grey you know or know about. Or associate it with an object such as something found on the "grey market"; or, if you're an avid reader of Western novels, with author Zane Grey, or with Earl Grey tea. Of course, use some discretion with this technique so you don't pop off with: "Glad to meet you, Mrs. Earl ... ah, Zane ... T ... er ... oh, heck!" Use whatever memory trigger works for you in that situation with that client.
- **Use** the name throughout your presentation.
- **Use** the name when saying goodbye.

Importance of Touch

Touch is a significant and important component of human communication, especially when it comes to emotions.. But it is a rather ... well ... a "touchy" subject. Too little and you appear cold and aloof. Too much and you appear to be one of those insincere "gladdaseeya" types or perceived to be invading the other person's private space.

Worse, even with the best of intentions, you could receive a punch in the gut, a slap in the face, or a lawsuit for harassment. A strong and brief handshake that doesn't crush your customer's hand or linger until the sunset is a good beginning. Everything from that moment on should be appropriate to the sales situation.

To what extent can touch influence an outcome? There was a study done in Michigan where the researchers left a quarter in the return box of phone booth. Then later when someone was inside, they went back and asked for the quarter, saying they'd accidentally left it behind. Initially only 25% of the respondents gave the quarter back or admitted they had even seen it. But when the researcher put a hand on the person's forearm while asking, 80% gave the quarter back. That is the power of touch.

Perfecting The Process

The state of your sales process tells your customers how you really feel about serving their needs. Do they have to wait around before a salesperson approaches or does someone walk right up and offer an introduction? Are they passed around from person to person or treated like royalty? Does your organization leave them on their own for long periods or do they always feel they're in capable and caring hands?

I know someone who had just purchased a new car and had to bring it in for an under-warranty repair. His salesperson had agreed to provide a loaner car for the day, but when the customer arrived neither the salesperson nor the loaner was there. Several people made half-hearted apologies, but no one took the trouble to help a customer in trouble. The process broke down and that customer bought his next car from another dealer. Worse, he told everyone he knew to do the same.

When was the last time you looked at your customer and asked for his or her point of view? Perfecting your sales process has to be an ongoing work in progress.

Your Selling Environment

Your selling environment is critical to the process. A technique I recommend for salespeople is to enter your store, organization or facility as if you were a "walk-in." As if you were just touring the mall and decided to drop by for a look-see. Forget everything you know about the product, your company and the people who work there. Look at the situation with the eyes of someone who has just shown up for the first time. What do you see?

Like it or not, the environment is considered a reflection of the product, the company and the service provided. As a "walk-in," what greets you? What stands out? What doesn't? And, more importantly, how do you feel? Your product could be the finest in the world; your company renowned for its integrity; your service second to none. But if your environment doesn't say those things right off the bat, chances are that's one customer you're going to lose.

Our company, ServiceTrac, mystery shopped a location a few years ago. The shopper gave a scathing report and could not find anything positive to say. The shopper made particular mention of the fact that the environment was dirty. Additionally, the salesperson had a run in her stocking and her dress was cut in one little spot. Those are small things, but they speak volumes (negative volumes) to an observant customer. There was just no way to say anything good about the shopping experience, especially the salesperson.

As you can imagine, I did not enjoy sharing the report with the salesperson. But I did it and she was understandably embarrassed. She admitted that the report was correct. She even said she knew about the imperfections, but thought no one else would notice. Boy, was she wrong!

The story has a happy ending. Following the negative report, the salesperson made a 180-degree improvement in her attire and her environment. Not only did her subsequent mystery shop improve, but so did her sales. Funny how that works, eh?

In many situations, especially for those sales folks out on the road, *you* are the selling environment. You create your own environment and are totally responsible for it. That provides a nice segue into the next first impression category!

Hygiene and Dress

Your hygiene and manner of dressing make a strong statement about your quality as a professional salesperson. By extension dress and hygiene make additional statements about your product, your company and the quality of your service. It's hard to imagine being something, no matter how good it is reputed to be, from someone who is sloppy in his or her attire and does not maintain impeccable personal hygiene.

The rule of thumb: Dress as a professional. But what does it mean to dress as a professional? Clearly, that definition varies by product and by customer. A three-piece suit that is totally appropriate for a presentation to the board of directors in a Manhattan skyscraper will be out of place and appear down right foolish under a tin roof building on the chicken farm.

The key is to always dress appropriately for the situation – farm and field or front office. Use good judgment when it comes to this area. My motto: Just a little better: My policy is to always be a little better, faster, nicer or whatever than the customer. I want to set an example of enthusiasm and professionalism. I want to be dressed just a little better. I want to speak just a little faster. I want to be just a little happier.

Why? Because I want to lift others up and help them feel better, get more excited, be happier. When others are engaged and excited, you have created the right environment for selling. Emotion sells and we want our customer to be on the emotional side. That puts them in the mood to confide in you—and eventually to buy.

I think of it like an electrical circuit. People contact you or you contact them when they have a need. They want a solution. They need to solve a problem. They are excited and anxious to learn about what you can do to help. There is electricity. Sparks fly. They reach out tingling all over.

Then they come into contact with you and your company. You have every opportunity to keep them turned on. However, what happens the first time they feel neglected or sense that things are not going well? They lose the electricity, the spark fizzles, and they become keenly aware of the fact that they are buying something. They begin to look at things factually and the electricity gives way to hard cold facts. When you lose emotion, you lose your selling edge and the customer begins to look at things that are simple and generic. Your competitive edge has suddenly vanished and you become just another salesperson selling a product.

I think about the scene in the movie "Somewhere In Time" where Christopher Reeve is happy as can be living in the past with his sweetheart. Then, out of the blue, he sees a modern coin and, in an instant, he is transferred back to reality (unhappily). He is staring cold hard facts in the face and the dream is gone. As a salesperson, you can't allow your customers to lose their electricity. In fact, you need to up the voltage!

Mind Your Phone Manners

Phone etiquette is more important now than ever. These days it's natural for a potential customer to pick up a phone, shop, compare, research and buy over the wires or airwaves. When you take that call you're on the front lines. You make a first impression. That impression can be a golden opportunity to build rapport or a surefire way to lose a sale. How many thousands of sales have been lost because a potential customer hears "Hold, please," followed by the dreaded hum of the telephone line? Or the even more dreaded sound of Muzak? You can hear the phone slamming down clear across the state line.

Here are a few good tips to help improve your telephone courtesy:
- Always answer within three rings
- Identify yourself and your location
- Listen for non-verbal responses and clues such as excitement in the voice, a long sigh, clicking of the tongue, which could indicate impatience.
- Be careful about your own non-verbal signals. Are you clicking your tongue? The telephone works in two directions, you know, and the customer is always listening.
- Get the caller's name right away. You'd be amazed at the number of times this basic slips by. And be sure to get the correct spelling. Is it Mr. S-M-I-T-H or S-M-Y-T-H-E?
- Take notes of your conversation.
- Get the caller's phone number, address, mailing address and e-mail address.

When making outbound calls, it is important to be cheerful, upbeat and positive. You can even use a little humor from time to time. Here are a few that I've used:

WILL: Hi, this is Will Nowell. Is Mrs. Anderson in?

SECRETARY: I'm sorry, Mrs. Anderson is on the phone.

WILL: Wow! How does she do that! Is she sanding on one foot? How the heck does she maintain her balance?

Even if the secretary or receptionist is a critic and doesn't break into uncontrolled laughter, you will probably achieve your goal. That goal is to build rapport with a contact. Here's another one:

WILL: Hi, this is Will Nowell. Is Mr. Jenkins available?

SECRETARY: I'm sorry, he is tied up right now.

WILL: Wow! Where do you have him? Is he comfortable? Was he out of control or are you guys just playing a joke on him?

Or:

WILL: Hi, this is Will Nowell. Is Ms Tangleweed available?

SECRETARY: I'm sorry, she's out to lunch.

WILL: Does she know you talk about her this way?

All kidding aside, doing all you can to set the stage for success is a smart thing to do. Agreed?

You see—setting the proper environment can give you the solid foundation you need to begin a strong sales process and to ensure your success. At the very least, you get a chance to practice some one-liners!

The real secret... LISTEN. That is right, Listen. The most powerful way you can make a first Impression positive and lasting is to simply be interested and caring and listen to the prospect or customer. People go through their days battling their way through countless situations and conversations trying to break through the haze and confusion and get someone who will actually listen to them. It does not happen very often.

When is the last time you feel you were listened to? I bet if you think about it you may come to realize that it does not happen very often. You have to repeat things two or three times, you have to give instructions more than once, you practically never really share something important because it is rare to find someone who cares. I realize that this sounds cynical but it is true.

We live in a society of speed and haste where most people are just caught up in their own worries and objectives and so we have gotten used to this reality. You want to make a real positive first impression? I will give you a sure fire way to knock someone off of their feet. Just Listen to them, let them down load, be interested in what they have to say. It may only take a few minutes but it will be the best investment of time you will ever make. It is not always easy. In fact, some customers make it down right hard to do. But I will give you some ideas about how to overcome that obstacle. For now it is enough for you to simply set a goal. In every interaction make a conscious effort to give your prospects your undivided attention for the first few minutes of every conversation You will put a smile on their face and make a difference in their lives and most importantly make a killer first impression.

Who's In Charge Here?

If you're practicing VALUE MATCH principles, then you are definitely in control. That's important because the salesperson has the responsibility to move the sales process along and to ensure it doesn't get sidetracked or stalled. When a customer is in charge of the process, you run the risk of having the sales process get off track. Remember, customers are often their own worst enemy. As well, some customers refuse to cooperate with the salesperson. Sometimes they are not even sure about what they want.

As we learned in an earlier chapter, the salesperson always listens to the customer. Always. But, at the same time, the salesperson attains and maintains control of the agenda from inception to completion. I say:

> **You are in control of the <u>WHEN</u> and the <u>HOW</u> and the customer is in control of the <u>WHAT</u>.**

This little saying is very important and is one I hope you remember. As a salesperson you want to keep the process moving forward. But, at the same time, you want to be very careful not to miss or skip any critical steps. And the customer's agenda always comes first.

One of the best ways to maintain control is to have an effective strategy, to use the proper and well-maintained tools, and to apply tactics appropriate to the specific sales situation. A good salesperson can't afford to use off-the-shelf solutions.

Strategy: What Do Customers Want?

This is a tricky question, one that does not have any straightforward or easy answer. And salespersons have been scratching their heads over it probably ever since that first salesman tried to convince a reluctant customer to trade in his worn-out wheel for a newer model. In fact, most often, it can only be addressed as follows: *Most of the time customers are not really sure of what they want. They haven't worked out a very clear picture in their minds and things are somewhat fuzzy around the edges.*

They know however that they do NOT want to be sold. They do not want to experience what they believe is a high pressure sales pitch. They do not want to share personal or private information. They fear being manipulated by a tricky salesperson with the gift of gab who will force them to buy something they feel they neither want nor need.

Customers, like all human beings, want to be in control. Or at least they want to feel as if they are in control. They want to ask questions. They want to gather information. They want to be in charge. The challenge is as we talked about previously. Unless the customer builds trust, they will not, cannot, share what's really on their minds and in their hearts. They will refuse to share what they value, their perception of the problem, their view of the solution, and, especially, what they really want or need.

Bottom line: *In the face of dealing with a customer who may be his or her own worst enemy, your strategy and your task is to help the customer through the process.* To begin the process:

YOU have to help the customer move comfortably from business to personal matters—and then back to business again.

What do we mean by that? Basically, a customer comes into the situation with a series of questions he or she has prepared and most likely rehearsed over and over. These are questions that are focused on the basic business issues pertaining to the potential purchase and are designed to keep the salesperson outside the circle. They are also fact-finding questions, fairly sterile in nature, and barely skimming the surface of the sales process. Questions such as:

- "How much is it?"
- "What's included in the price?"
- "How soon can you do it?"
- "Can you do X, Y and Z?"
- "Is there an extra cost for that?"
- "Tell me about the cost."

The list could go on forever with every question remaining strictly on the surface, and not getting to the heart of the matter. Such questions put everyone on the same level. It makes it easy for the customer to compare options. The problem is, this is all generic information. It's not personal. It doesn't get you or the customer inside.

The strategy of this step in the sales process is to move the customer from outside to inside the circle. This is difficult for most salespeople who believe the challenge to be just the opposite. But if you look at a typical sales interaction you will see that people want answers to their questions and concerns—often unasked questions and unspoken concerns. From our research we have seen that most salespeople spend very little time building rapport because of the pressure put on them by the customer to get to the facts.

Let me give you a few examples:

> SALESPERSON: Hi, Joe's Carpet Barn. How may I help you?
>
> CUSTOMER: Well, I want some carpet in my house. I've seen your ad and I have a few questions.
>
> SALESPERSON: Sure. I'm glad you called and I am happy to help you.
>
> CUSTOMER: How much is your plush carpet? How soon can you deliver a 12-by-12 section? Do you install it yourself?
>
> And so on and so forth with one fact-demanding question following another ...

Or:

> SALESPERSON: Hi, Bill's Copy Shop And More. How may I help you?
>
> CUSTOMER: I want 100 50-page booklets bound with spiral binding and I need them today. Can you do it? How much do you charge?

As you might recognize, what is happening in these typical scenarios is that the customer is in control. There is no rapport and the information requested is very generic. If the salesperson responds to the questions as directed by the customer, the salesperson will do all the talking and the customer will have all the information. The customer is just shopping. He or she will get the information, say "thanks," hang up and call the next store in search of the "best deal." The problem is that the customer doesn't realize that price or speed of delivery or whatever isn't the most important issue.

If you think about it, there are a lot of issues more important than price. For instance, our carpet shopper may not realize that the cheapest plush carpet isn't stain resistant or that the installation isn't guaranteed or that the warehouse is six-weeks backlogged with orders. The copy customer may ask about quality not realizing that there are significant differences or ask about alternative methods of delivery not realizing that there are more efficient methods of delivery. If any of these things are important to the customer and the salesperson fails to get that information, both parties lose.

Let me give you an example:

Opening Up The Garage Door Salesperson

A clever customer can acquire enough information from a salesperson to essentially negate the sale. I know. Here is a personal example of a customer controlling the sales situation. My garage door was not working so I called one of the dealers in my area to get some information. I was certain that I'd have to go to the expense of installing a new door opener.

The service person who answered the call was friendly, courteous, and informative. Of course, the first question I asked was: "How much do you charge to install a new garage door opener?" He replied: "$500." So then I asked: "What would it cost to have someone just look at the door?" He replied: "$70 for the first 15 minutes."

I was aghast so I asked why so much for just looking. He said that he could fix most problems very quickly and I was paying for the experience. Made sense but I wasn't ready to fork out that kind of money for a look-see. So I decided it was time to learn a little more about garage doors.

"So what can cause these doors to go bad?" I asked.

"Oh, any number of things," he replied.

"Like what, for instance?"

"Oh, a lot of times folks just have a circuit breaker out."

"Oh, really."

Since I was on a cordless phone, I walked to the garage where the circuit breaker box was located. Controlling the conversation, I kept the salesman answering a bunch of outside-the-circle questions the whole time while I checked the circuit breakers. The circuit breakers were all okay.

"What else could cause a door to jam up like this?" I asked.

"Sometimes the door will just bend a little. Being even slightly out of shape can affect how the mechanism works."

"Oh, really!" I said.

Since I was in the garage, I continued peppering the man with questions while I examined the edges of the door. No problems there.

"What are some of the other causes of this kind of problem?"

"Well, you know those little sensors on each side of the door?"

"Where would those be?" I asked.

"Down there about six inches off the floor," he said.

"And what could possibly be the problem there?"

"Well it's easy for a wire to get crimped or to be pulled out of a connection."

Aha!

Bending over to examine the sensors, I asked: "So, if a little wire was pulled out and you plugged it back in, chances are the door would work again, right?"

"Oh, sure, " he said.

As I plugged in the loose wire, walked across the garage to flick the "up" button, and watch my formerly-stalled door begin to work perfectly, the salesman asked: "And what size door are you looking for?"

"Oh, I'm not really ready to commit to a new door, just yet. But thanks for your time. And, for being so friendly, courteous and informative."

V.I.R. (Very Important Rule): *Control the sales process or you will be controlled by someone else's agenda.*

To sum up: Customers literally do not know what they want and, if we let them lead the sales process, more than likely each of us will lose. Neither customer nor salesperson will come out a winner. We need to be skilled at helping the customer make a transition from business to personal issues and we need to start that in the initial sales conversation, during our first contact.

Now, let's demonstrate the way the garage door salesperson could have handled the call.

ME: Hi, I'd like to get my garage door fixed. How much would it cost?

HIM: I understand that you would like to get your garage door fixed and you want to know what it costs. Is that right?

ME: Yes.

HIM: I would be happy to help you with that. Can I ask you a question?

ME: Sure.

HIM: What is your situation?

ME: Well, I have had the door for two years and it is a little noisy but today it just stopped working.

HIM: Well, how do you feel about this?

ME: Well, I want the door to last me and I am concerned about the noise but right now I just want it to work.

HIM: Well, I can fix the door very quickly, but while I am there, I can perform a 12-point check up to have your door running quietly and ensure its long life. How does that sound?

ME: Great. How much will it be?

HIM: Just $70 for the visit.

ME: Let's get it scheduled.

In this last example, the salesperson took control, helped me focus on the key issues and value which far outstripped my fear of the cost. You too can handle each sales situation this smoothly and with this type of outcome if you learn how to apply the VALUE MATCH MODEL.

Now, let's talk about several practical tactics and tools a salesperson can use to further improve his or her chances of a successful sales process: the VALUE MATCH Balanced Scorecard approach ("The Greeting: To Build Rapport").

VALUE MATCH Balanced Scorecard: To Build Rapport

We can talk until we're blue in the face about first impressions and the importance of trust and rapport in the sales process. But we also need to show how it's done in specific and practical terms. We need to give step-by-step examples. That's what the VALUE MATCH Balanced Scorecard (BSC), the first tool in the salesperson's indispensable toolkit, is all about. Basically, if it is not on the form, don't say it, and it if is there, don't leave it out.

From experience, I have discovered that this tool is one of the most effective in learning the VALUE MATCH sales system. It is intended to be used in conjunction with the VALUE MATCH Inquiry worksheet **which is a note taking form that helps you stay on track in the heat of the battle. The BSC and inquiry form we are demonstrating here is generic and can easily be customized for your situation**. Through the use of these two tools, you will be able to quickly obtain and store valuable information for quick reference and use whenever you need it at any point in the sales process.

The BSC is intended to move the conversation from one logical step to another as quickly as possible without "pushing and shoving" your customer. The VALUE MATCH Inquiry form is divided into three main sections with space provided to take notes at each stage of the process as it moves forward. But because these sheets are limited in space, it's a good idea to focus on <u>key words</u> and phrases and write those in the appropriate boxes. That way you can remember the conversation. Some other things to be aware of:

- Always ask permission to ask questions. This makes the customer more comfortable and there isn't the feeling that you're conducting an interrogation or trying to drag information out by force.

- Always work within any time constraints that the customer might mention. Work with the customer to reassure him or her that you can accomplish their goals and answer their questions in the time available and then move on with the process.

Balanced Scorecard VALUE MATCH Process— To Build Rapport and Credibility

Because the topic of rapport-building is so important in the VALUE MATCH sales process, I have developed the BSC tool to help teach this process which clearly outlines how to build strong rapport. The first form below, known as the **Balanced Scorecard VALUE MATCH Process: "The Greeting"**, is the first of five forms in the process and should be used in conjunction with the VALUE MATCH Note Taking Form included in the Appendix. The second form below is the **Balanced Scorecard VALUE MATCH Process: The Company Story** and is there to achieve the goal of establishing and building credibility. Please Note: The BSC can be modified to fit both in person and phone sales. I have included phone BSC's in the Appendix as well. The Forms may need to be customized for different sales situations.

The third, fourth and fifth forms are used with the VALUE MATCH Needs Inquiry Form discussed in the next chapter. The sixth form—Getting Into A "Closing" Posture—is valuable when you're ready for your presentation, discussed in Chapters 11 and 12.

These forms offer you the opportunity to keep score as a way to determine how well you are doing in the creation of rapport with your customer and establishing rapport and credibility. Successfully completing these important skills and tactics with a customer can lead to building <u>stronger rapport</u> and <u>building credibility</u> during the VALUE MATCH Process. Circle the score for each task if accomplished, and total the score at the bottom.

Remember:
- **First impressions help build a foundation of trust**
- **The best way to build first impressions is to listen**
- **Focus on actually listening to the words and repeating each word back to the customer**
- **Always remember to take notes, concentrating on key words and phrases as memory aids**
- **Be ready for Zingers.**

Balanced ScoreCard™: Building Rapport

	Be ready to take notes. Have both VALUE MATCH Note Taking Form and Balanced Scorecard Greeting form.
	Meet customer at the door so that he or she isn't made to wait. Shake hands firmly and briskly.
	Make introductions. Be positive, upbeat and smiling. Carry a clipboard on which to make notes.
	Question: What brought you here? What attracted you to our firm (facility, business)?
	Question: What would you like to accomplish today?
	Response Skill: "So, <Repeat what customer said>. I would be happy to help you with that. Do you mind if I ask a question or two first?"
	Option 1: Question: What is the situation? **(Listen)**
	Response Skill: "So, <Repeat what customer said>. How do you feel about the situation?
	Listen to the answer and empathize.
	Option 2: Question: Are you familiar with our business? *At this point, you can proceed to the second Balanced Scorecard Form: Building Credibility*
	Overcoming Zingers
	Identify and repeat the zinger.
	Ask what is meant by the zinger.
	Why do you ask about <here mention the particular zinger>?
	Answer the zinger, remembering that the answer must lead back to the process.
	Total

Remember:
- **Listen to the "what" and the "why"**
- **Take the opportunity to tell your story in a way that matches what is important to the customer**
- **Be prepared for Zingers**

Balanced ScoreCard™: Building Credibility
	Be ready to take notes. Have both the VALUE MATCH Note Taking Form and Balanced Scorecard Company Story form
	Make sure that both you and the customer are comfortable.
	Question: "What will be important to you about the firm (facility, business) you choose to work with? What do you know about our company?"
	Response Skill: "So, what I hear you saying is <Repeat what customer said>. What do you mean by that (use key words or phrases). Repeat answer.
	Question: Why is that important to you? **(Listen)**
	Response Skill: "VALUE MATCH". Relate what the customer has just shared to one or more points of your story.
	Option 1: Question: What is the situation? **(Listen)**
	Feature #1
	Feature #2
	Feature #3
	Feature #4
	Overcoming Zingers
	Identify and repeat the zinger.
	Ask what is meant by the zinger.
	Why do you ask about <here mention the particular zinger>?
	Answer the zinger, remembering that the answer must lead back to the process.
	Tie Down.
	Total

A word about Overcoming Zingers

Zingers are those out-of-the-blue questions, remarks, and/or statements brought up at any time by the customer. If not answered properly, these can throw off the sales pitch or cause you to lose control of the process. The technique I teach to overcome zingers is simple—and we'll look at it more closely in Chapter 12—but here I would like to use my son Bret as a way to illustrate the principle.

The Bret Close

This is important. When we meet a customer for the first time, there may be questions, issues, or pressures that are present that, left unaddressed, will hinder your ability to communicate. Sometimes these interfering issues are there as a convenience to the customer. Basically, the distraction helps the customer maintain a safe distance from the salesperson as in the example above: the mention of their time being limited or the mention of limited finances.

A wise salesperson does not bring these issues up on his or her own. These types of issues are facts and are usually not relevant to the real issues. Examples of such issues include time constraints, specific questions **about the product or service**. If these issues come up initially then the salesperson needs to address them and the manner in which they're addressed can really make a difference.

> **Let me illustrate this with a story about my 15-year-old son Bret. Thus, the "Bret Close". I employ my son Bret to clean the pool. And he does a pretty good job. Bret also loves skateboards and has a habit of breaking his skateboards quite often. Usually his pay for cleaning the pool is money to replace skateboards. I'm sure you see the situation: Bret quite often needs to be paid his pool income immediately.**
>
> **When this happens, I arrive home and before I can clear the entry Bret asks me for some money. Typically I want to ask him some questions and go on but Bret continues to bring up the issue and is very reluctant to talk and is persistent about his money until I use <u>The Bret Close</u>.**

ME: Bret, I understand you want an advance on your pool pay, is that right?

BRET: Yes.

ME: When you say you want your pay what does that mean?

BRET: I need to go out with my friends to a movie.

ME: So, if I can get the money for you before you need to go to the movie will that work?

BRET: Yes

ME: Bret, I promise I will pay you tonight before you need to leave for the movie. Is that OK?

BRET: Sure.

Guess what? I never hear the question again and I can then ask Bret how his day was and get a real answer.

If a customer has issues, make sure you hear them out and reassure the customer that you will address or respect that issue. This will put the customer at ease and allow you to regain control.

You don't have time to do it wrong. Now you might be saying to yourself: This could take too long. I don't have that kind of time. Well, guess what? You don't have time to do it wrong and, in fact, the stronger the rapport, the easier and more productive the rest of the time you spend will be. Actually, in most cases, this step can take place in minutes if handled properly. And most successful salespeople do this seamlessly.

Let me give you some examples ...

Phone: Ring Ring

SALESPERSON: This is KB equipment. How may I help you?

CUSTOMER: I'm interested in learning what it costs for an Air Handler?

SALESPERSON: I will be happy to get you some prices. Can I ask you a couple of questions?

CUSTOMER: Sure.

SALESPERSON: What is the situation?

CUSTOMER: Well, I manage 30 buildings and we need to replace all of the air handlers next year.

SALESPERSON: That sounds like a big job. (Note: I don't suggest you ask for more details now. Save that for later when you have more information). How do you feel about that?

CUSTOMER: Well, I'm frustrated. Everyone I talk to just gives me prices and what I really need is a little help with the budget and planning.

SALESPERSON: I can certainly understand how you feel. I've been there. (Relate personally).So, if I can help you with your budget and planning that is what would be helpful? You have come to the right place.

SALESPERSON: What kind of support do you have?

CUSTOMER: Not much. It's just me and my boss.

SALESPERSON: What kind of support do you have from your boss?

CUSTOMER: I need to do all the ground work and make a recommendation. He will go with the recommendation.

SALESPERSON: How do you feel about this arrangement?

CUSTOMER: I like it. I'm autonomous and have the responsibility. But I also have to take blame if it doesn't work out so I have to be sure to make the right decision.

SALESPERSON: I appreciate that. I've been in similar situations. (Relate). What other responsibilities do you have?

CUSTOMER: I'm in charge of personnel and finances as well.

SALESPERSON: What is your favorite part of the job?

CUSTOMER: Finances. I like to know where we are. I like to be in control. It spills over to my hobbies as well. I'm a pilot.

SALESPERSON: That makes sense. I like to be in control too. (Aside) So you're a pilot. What kind? (At first this might seem like a choices question but look what happens).

CUSTOMER: I'm a glider pilot. I fly every weekend.

SALESPERSON: That's neat. I have always wanted to learn more about flying in a glider.

> "You might notice who is doing all the talking ... the customer."

At this point the salesperson has learned a great deal about his customer, in terms of what he needs and what he is like personally. The two have even struck up some areas of common interest and now the salesperson is in position to move the process forward to the next development step. You might notice who is doing all the talking. It's the customer. And who is in control: it's the salesperson. And to top it off, it all took place in less than five minutes.

Some Notes On Note Taking

For some reason some salespeople find taking notes in front of a customer difficult. There's no logical reason for that feeling. Taking notes reinforces your customer's feelings of trust because it shows that you value his or her words and that you are mindful of the need for attention to details. The notes also help you remember the proper sequence of steps in the sales process and help you move through them properly and in good order.

Don't jump around from section to section on the form. Follow the order from top to bottom and follow the sequence of the questions. If a particular is not specifically asked, make sure to make a note of what the customer says in the appropriate space on the form.

Also, it's a good idea to ask for permission to take your notes. Explain your very logical reasons and be friendly. This helps put your customer at ease with the process and also gives reassurance that he or she still has some control or power in the situation.

Objective And General Situation

The way you handle acquiring this information (and, of course what you do with it) is critical. I do not use that word lightly.

Question: *What is the objective of this call or visit?*

Your customer will usually arrive with an idea of his or her need. This may be very specific: "I need a Ford Ranger with four-wheel-drive, high clearance, skid plates, a front-end winch and I want the extended cab." Or very general. "I need something for the kid to take to college."

Whatever level, the idea is almost always focused entirely on the solution to a perceived problem. For example: "I want some information on pricing" or "I would like to know what all you folks have to offer."

*Your goal here is simple yet maybe counter intuitive to most. Your job here is to simply build trust and make a **positive** first impression. How? Listen. Period. Just listen. Take off the shark hat and just listen.*

CUSTOMER: I'd like some information on pricing, please.

YOU: So you would like information on our prices. Is that right?

CUSTOMER: Yes, that's right.

YOU: I would be happy to help you with that. Do you mind if I ask you a question?

If the customer is just looking for information, it might go like this:

CUSTOMER: Well, I would just like to know what you folks offer.

YOU: So you would like to know what we offer. Is that right?

CUSTOMER: Yes, that's right.

YOU: I would be happy to tell you what we offer. Do you mind if I ask you a question? What is your situation?

Maybe this sounds too simple but let me explain. By using this simple tactic, look what you have accomplished:

1) You have listened to the customer
2) You have agreed to give them what they want
3) You have taken control of the process
4) You have asked them to start saying more about their situation

Pretty neat, huh?

The second part of the question is the time constraint under which you must work. Handled properly, this isn't much of a challenge. **First, you only address time if it is brought up by the customer.** If he or she is dropping by during the lunch hour, you probably have less than an hour to work with. Don't worry about digging out this information too much. Generally, the nervous customer is all too willing to let you know: "Well, I just have a few minutes. Then I have to get back to the 'salt mines,' you know."

Acknowledge the time constraint and make reassurances that you can accomplish what needs to be done within that timeframe. If more time is needed, then just set up an appointment at a time more conducive to his or her schedule and for you to close the sale. Using the VALUE MATCH approach, it will go like this:

YOU: So you are short on time? Is that right? What do you mean you are short on time?

HER: I have about 40 minutes.

YOU: So if I can help you in 40 minutes, will that work?

HER: That will work fine.

Question: *What is the general situation?*

Resist the urge to ask detailed questions this early in your presentation. You'll only intimidate your customer. In-depth questioning will come later. This is the time to gather general information that focuses on the main issues. Be sure to keep things general at this point. Keeping things general this early also has the benefit of keeping your customers at ease. They don't feel "assaulted" with personal questions, but at the same time you are getting them in a comfortable frame of mind in answering your inquiries.

Question: *How do you feel in general about the situation?*

At this point, you begin shifting their impression of you from that of a salesperson to that of a friend. This question allows you to empathize with your customer. You begin to connect on the basis of *feelings and issues* rather than *solutions to problems*.

From Business to Rapport

These questions help identify what the customer knows about your firm, products and/or services. This is particularly important because it begins moving the conversation from *business* to *rapport*. It also helps you to build credibility in your company or firm. As well, these questions help discover whether the person you're speaking with is the final decision maker, one of two or more decision makers, or just someone gathering information for the real decision maker who is behind the scenes. Obviously, this bit of information affects every aspect of your presentation from this point onward. You don't want to waste the effort closing someone who cannot be closed because he or she or they lack the power to say "yes".

Question: *What do you know about us?*

It is important to discover whether the information the customer may have is positive and might be helpful in moving the sales process forward. Having to overcome a negative image is a lot more difficult than building on a positive image. But it is also a lot easier to overcome such a negative image if you know what you are dealing with.

Question: *What attributes are you looking for in the company you will work with?*

This is a clarifying question for the previous question. The question should encourage the customer to elaborate on the information mentioned in the previous answer. The aim is to gain more clarity on how the customer knows about the company and what might be influencing him or her to be doing business with you.

Question: *Why is that important to you?*

This question also allows you to empathize with your prospect and continue the transition from solutions to feelings and issues. At the same time, you need to be aware of who will be making the ultimate decision in the sales process. You may also ask:
- **Who is involved in the decision process?**
- **Who will have the responsibility to sort through the details?**
- **How is that process working for you?**

You may notice in each case the questions move the customer from talking about things from a factual perspective to an emotional view.

Sharing Personal Values

These questions are designed to help you learn something personal about the customer. These questions can range from work to hobbies to family. You can pick and choose what is most appropriate for this situation or person.

While it might seem that you're just shooting the breeze with the customer, this is actually one of the most important steps in the sales process. In fact, all of this information is extremely valuable. These types of open-ended questions are designed to help you begin to learn and understand something about the personal life and personal values of the customer.

Basically, you're trying to find out what makes this person "tick." Once those values are uncovered, you can relate to those values that match yours. This is the essence of rapport building and of the VALUE MATCH process.

You can relate and share important information that truly connects with your customer and helps builds rapport and the bonds of trust. You want the customer thinking: "Hey, in a lot of ways, this salesperson is a lot like me. I think I could get to like you."

Have these questions in your mind and ready to be asked. But remember that these questions are only samples and need to be fitted into the particular situation. Often they don't even need to be specifically asked. You will notice that the customer will often provide the answers before you have the chance to ask the question.

Remember, the customer wants to talk, to be heard and to be understood. Once they discover you really are interested in their situation, they'll be more than willing to continue the conversation. You will notice that nowhere have I suggested that you the salesperson start answering questions and volunteering information. With a little practice you can make this process work for you.

Playing Detective, Seriously

Often the customer will comment on or mention certain things early in the conversation that can be used as markers. This is a set of *clues* from which you can formulate and ask additional questions. Initially, these clues will be on "easy" subjects such as hobbies, interests, or the basics of work. You always look for the clues and ask for more with clarifying questions. Prioritize the answers and ask more value-added questions. Again, *question everything*.

- **What do you like to do in your spare time?**
- **What do you enjoy most about your job?**
- **What sort of hobbies do you enjoy?**
- **What is your family situation?**

You see, questions provide clues, which provide reasons for more questions, which give you even more clues. The values your customer expresses then allow you to match those with your own. They allow you to build a relationship with the customer based on those shared values and enable you to build the foundation of friendship and trust.

By using VALUE MATCH principles and a little strategy, you can conquer the challenge of customer dominance and place yourself in control.

Additional Considerations For Building Rapport

A VALUE MATCH salesperson must be focused and in control. You have to remain intent upon the focus of your customer. As long as you are listening to the customer, you are on the right track. But at the same time you have to be aware of, considering and planning for a wide array of concerns and options. You need to trust in the process. My favorite saying is: "Listening (and you could say selling) is not a thinking man's sport." Listening, staying on the customer's agenda, selling only requires that you respect the customer, provide a forum for them to share their thoughts, attitudes, feelings, and then help them. Now we have set the stage for our sales process. We are ready to move to the next step: Uncovering needs and offering a solution.

These are some of the major considerations you will need to keep in "top of the mind" awareness:

- Basically your customer will want to discuss two things: the features and price of your product or service. Again, your customer will be focused on what he or she believes is the solution to the problem.
- The salesperson must reassure the customer that the customer's words are being heard and understood. Such basic phrases as "I understand" or "I see" work well, as does restating what has just been said.
- A salesperson must take the responsibility of moving the conversation from business (there's that fixation on the *solution* again) towards building rapport (*feelings and issues*)
- You must help your customer allow you inside the circle of trust.
- Once inside that circle, it's very easy for your customer to leap right back out again. This can happen at any time during the presentation, even when you think things are going along marvelously. The salesperson has to help the customer share and stay focused on the topics that are inside the circle.
- Take notes. It is impossible for any salesperson to remember everything he or she needs to take from the conversation. Besides, as noted earlier, note taking reassures the customer of your professionalism.
- Realize that in the sales process one step *follows* another. You can't skip a single step. And you can't hurry through one either. Every step is built upon a foundation of the one before it. Make sure all your steps are solid or you're sure to fall and fail.
- Building rapport is more than a step in and of itself. When you build rapport by discussing topics on a personal level with a customer, you are also establishing *compatibility* and *trust*.
- Start building rapport from the first instant of the first contact, whether that's a handshake, eye contact across the showroom floor, a phone call or an e-mail response to an inquiry. You've got about ten seconds. Make them count.
- One of your biggest challenges is the customer's fixation on his or her *perceived solution* to the problem rather than the emotional issues behind that need.

- **To really serve that customer, you must encourage him or her to open up and share what is needed to build rapport. You will need skill, patience and confidence to make this happen.**

Some salespersons have a misconception about rapport building and question why we need to go through this process. They ask questions such as:

- **Doesn't this all take too much time? Time we could be using to sell?**

   Answer: If we do not build rapport, the process will come to a halt and seem very time consuming indeed. Research shows that in cases where rapport building is skipped, the overall process can take two to three times as long.

- **Isn't this stuff (work, hobbies, etc.) none of my business?**

   Answer: This is usually a personal misperception. Most customers are more than willing to talk about their personal lives and don't see it as an intrusion. For those that do at first, it just means that the rapport-building process might take a little longer.

- **I don't like taking notes while someone is talking to me. Do I really need to take notes?**

   Answer: YES YOU DO! Note-taking reinforces the listening model. You cannot effectively listen if you are not taking notes because you cannot possibly remember everything someone says. If you think the customer is uncomfortable talking while you are writing, ask permission to take notes before starting.

Other salespersons want to build rapport but they don't know how. They then make the mistake of not bothering to build rapport. This is further complicated by the fact your customer may try to create barriers to rapport-building because he or she feels it's the best way to keep a "safe" distance.

At the same time, if you do skip rapport building and simply deal with what the customer says he or she wants, that customer may feel uncomfortable at the fact you're getting down to business too quickly and not paying enough attention to how he or she feels. On the other hand, be careful about building rapport for too long. That might give your customer the impression you're wasting his or her time. The table below gives four steps for making the transition from rapport-building to business.

Four Steps for Transitioning From Business to Rapport		
	In This Step You Will:	**Example**
1	Acknowledge and empathize with the customer's situation	*"I understand that what you need right now is some information about our firm so that you can make some informed decisions as to what you need."*
2	Outline the process	*"I know your time is valuable. If I can take a minute to ask a couple of questions, I can make sure to give you the information you require."*
3	Establish a time-frame for the meeting	*"The questions will just take a minute and then I can give you the right information."*
4	Get agreement from the customer to participate in the process	*"There are several things I'd like to know. Will that work for you? And, if you don't mind, I'm going to take some notes."*

Curiosity Fulfilled The Cat

As author Desmond Morris noted in the quote above, we humans are a curious species. In all senses of that word! Better yet, we are a *questioning* species. From when we first learn to talk, we are constantly asking: "Why? How? Where? How come?" We always want to know more and that is our best and most basic survival tactic.

That's true for sales, too. VALUE MATCH professionals use their questioning skills to build rapport, trust and credibility with their potential customers. We do this so that we can turn those good folks into people with whom we can do business—on a long term basis. We do this by matching their unique values with our own unique values and those of our product or service.

Using the VALUE MATCH model you will be able to establish rapport and build toward trust from the very first instant of the very first contact. You will be able to maintain that rapport and trust through the process to a mutually successful close and into a long-term relationship with a satisfied customer. It doesn't get any better than that!

In the next chapter, we will look at the next step in the VALUE MATCH sales process: the establishing of the customer's true needs. We will look at the 10 "Must Knows" about a customer that allow a salesperson to determine what those true needs are rather than what a customer might first say they are. Again, we will also look at invaluable VALUE MATCH tools that, if properly implemented and followed, will make the process easier and simpler—the VALUE MATCH Balanced Scorecard forms three to five.

VALUE CHECK

- The keys to making a positive first impression are: use the customer's name frequently, the importance of touch, the process, your environment, hygiene and dress, and etiquette for over-the-phone contacts.
- How to be and stay in control.
- Beyond product and service, customers want four things from a salesperson: (1) to be noticed, (2) to be appreciated, (3) to work with a trusted friend, and (4) to make judgments based on first impressions.
- Using the VALUE MATCH Balanced Scorecard to build rapport and credibility
- How to overcome zingers and THE BRET CLOSE.
- One of your greatest challenges is the customer's unawareness of the need for discussing personal information.
- A customer will want to discuss facts. A salesperson must encourage the customer to discuss feelings and issues.
- Take notes. No one can remember every important fact, word or key phrase said during a presentation.
- Use the VALUE MATCH Personal/Relationship Inquiry form to help with your note taking.
- Building rapport isn't a time-consuming waste. When you don't build rapport, your presentation will inevitably come to a screaming, screeching halt. When you invest the time to build rapport, you set the stage for a successful conclusion for you and your customer.

*He who wants to persuade
should put his trust
not in the right argument,
but in the right word.
The power of sound has always
been greater than the power of sense.*

—Joseph Conrad

CHAPTER NINE:

DEVELOPING NEEDS

*A prudent question
is one-half of wisdom.*

—Francis Bacon

*We all enter the world
with fairly simple needs:
to be protected, to be nurtured,
to be loved unconditionally, and to belong.*

—Louise Hart

The Next Step: Discovering the Customer's Needs

Values Unlocked In This Chapter

In the previous chapter, we took a significant leap, going from theory to applying the Value Match principles in real life selling situations. We have learned to meet the customer where he or she is, his or her need to gather information, and how we can reassure them that we will be able to help them, through the process of building a <u>relationship of trust</u>. In this chapter, we will look at the next practical step in the VALUE MATCH sales process: the discovering of the customer's true needs. I call this the "To Tell You The Truth" process and we talked about this a little earlier, the process that leads to the "That's amazing!" remark from the customer. We will look at the 10 "Must Knows" about a customer that allow a salesperson to determine what those true needs are rather than what a customer might first say they are. Again, we will also look at two invaluable VALUE MATCH tools that, if properly implemented and followed, will make the process easier and simpler—the VALUE MATCH Needs Inquiry Form and the relevant Balanced Scorecard forms.

Among the values unlocked in this chapter are:
- Ten "Must Knows"
- **The VALUE MATCH Needs Inquiry Form Overview**
- **The Needs Form Step-By-Step**
- **The Balanced ScoreCard Forms**

Note: In Chapter Eight, the focus needed to be on building rapport and trust. We did this by redirecting the customers using the VALUE MATCH tactics: "I'd be happy to help you with that... Do you mind if I ask you a question …" This was followed by the asking of "good" VALUE MATCH questions (that are open-ended and carefully scripted, with my favorite one to get things off to the right start being: " What is your situation?"). These "good" VALUE MATCH questions guide the customer to answering questions, and sharing information, and allow you to **LISTEN**. In baseball terms, we're on base. In VALUE MATCH terms, we're in the Relationship Bubble or Inner Circle.

Now in this chapter, we have the opportunity to start selling. Now selling is not telling. Selling is once more asking questions. But now we have other carefully scripted questions to move to second and third base. Here, the goal is to have the customer say: "TO TELL THE TRUTH". This means the discovering of real needs which in turn allows us to do a powerful presentation. That, in turn, allows our customer to say: "THAT'S AMAZING! What are the chances that you have exactly what I am looking for," after you have done the perfect presentation.

Okay, you've established rapport and a relationship of trust. Immediately after you've done that, move on quickly to the next step: Discovering the customer's needs. This part of the sales process is very powerful. I sometimes warn trainees to do a gut check on their definition of a salesperson. Used for good, this Value Matching skill is great, but if you are not comfortable with the integrity of being a salesperson, it is not so great. As I have mentioned before, it can be used for good or evil.

You might be thinking: "It's about time. I was wondering when I could start selling." Well, hold on. Let's just do a quick check. I said <u>sell</u> not <u>tell</u>. The next step in the VALUE MATCH Sales process includes leveraging the rapport and trust you have managed to build to begin to discover what the true needs of the customer are.

You see, up until now, the customer has not yet volunteered the "true" situation or the "real" issues. Sure, they may have told you in general what they want. But if 20 years of sales experience has taught me anything it usually translates into: "I'm just looking around," "I need to gather more information," "I wanted to find out what it costs," "We'll be ready to move on this in a couple of months." You get the picture. If you have been selling for long, you have heard it all.

Every customer has <u>real</u> needs that you must address. When you identify needs early on, you will find it easy to create a "good fit" between the potential customer and what you are selling. If you ignore those needs and are determined to simply move ahead with your own sales agenda without feedback, you may find the potential customer sliding out the door or slamming the phone down.

In this chapter and in the Values Discovery stage of the VALUE MATCH sales process, you are ready to take your relationship to a whole new level. And if successful, the customer will actually <u>tell you what to sell them</u> and <u>how to present it</u> in a way that will be <u>perfect for them</u>. In this chapter, we will outline the process step-by-step and show you how you can put yourself in position to make a powerful presentation of your product or service that will match exactly what the customer wants. .

> "Every customer has real needs that you must address"

Will's Ten "Must Knows"

Although each customer is unique and must be treated as such, all customers (nay, all humans) share some basic needs. You can start to identify these basic needs by discovering ten items I call the "must knows." These are key facts about your customer that you may want to uncover if you want to keep the sales process going with you remaining in control. These are:

- *Referral source* This answers the question: "How did you hear about us?" It's an important topic because it tells you how well or how poorly your referral sources are performing. If the answer is "from your advertising," then you know that your marketing program is working, or at least some part of it is. If you're advertising like crazy and aren't hearing that answer, then you know to rethink some of that marketing. And if you hear someone's name mentioned as a referral source, you need to contact that person and provide him or her with a hearty "thank you."

- *The home or office situation* You need to know what kind of support for dealing with the current situation is back home or back at the office. There are always unseen and unfelt influencers in a situation. Who are they? How much influence do they exercise? Can you become the most trusted of all those influencers? How?

- *Decision maker* Knowing who can and cannot say "yes" to a presentation is essential information for all the obvious reasons. Is your prospect the ultimate decision maker or are others involved? Who? How many? Will they be coming by for a presentation? Can you arrange a presentation for the actual decision maker? If you can't see the decision maker, how can you best work around that situation?

- *Knowledge* Determine how much your customer knows about your product or service. The simplest and most effective way is to just ask: "What do you folks know about the Ajax line of cars and trucks?" Assessing the client's level of knowledge lets you tailor your presentation to their specific level of need. Again, you never talk down to a customer, but your presentation to a young, first-time auto buyer will vary considerably from your presentation to the automobile mechanic who owns his or her own repair shop down the street.

At the same time, it is extremely important that you learn your customer's knowledge level. A person's ego will often keep him or her from expressing an honest evaluation of their knowledge and experience. All that does, however, is build a barrier between the person in need and the most qualified person to provide a solution to that need. Always explore, gently and carefully, to determine how much he or she actually knows about your product or service—and similar products and services.

- *Competition* A customer will shop around. It's no secret, so go ahead and ask: "Where else have you folks looked? What else have you looked at?" That's valuable information. If they've shopped around, that's good. They've got it out of their system and that puts you in a very good position. If not, you will need to work on building a sense of urgency so they'll be encouraged to buy now. Either way, the information is important to help determine the direction of the remainder of your presentation.
- *Urgency* There's always some level of urgency, so just ask: "What has recently occurred to motivate you to inquire today?" Again, the answers will point you in a specific direction. For example, the answer: "Oh, Bob's just got 'new car fever' again" will be handled entirely differently from: "Oh, Bob's car was smashed to bits by a meteor this morning." Each customer has a definite need, but a different level of urgency that you must first discover and then address.
- *Decision Impact* The "family" might actually be the traditional nuclear family, an extended family or people back at the place of work. You must determine who is involved in the purchase and precisely how much this person or these persons are involved. Will the family (or committee, etc.) simply "rubber stamp" the recommendation of your customer? Or will there be an intensive round of discussion, investigation and decision making? How will the decision impact the others involved? How should you structure your presentation—and at whom should you aim that presentation?
- *Product* What are the issues or challenges the customer is trying to address with this purchase or service? Why it is important

to try to address it? How will your product or service help them? What will be the most important benefit of your product or service to the customer? What if any are the weaknesses of your product or service? What are needs the customer may have that your product does not or will not meet? What are the most important needs of the customer? Why are these needs the most important?

- *Support Services* How are the product or services needs of your customer being met at the moment? Are they being met at all? How satisfactorily? What are the problems, challenges or concerns? Knowing where the customer is at present will help you point out where he or she should or could be.
- *Lifestyle* General questions about lifestyle, such as hobbies and interests, provide a basis for connecting with your customer. You discover common ground and use it to continue discovering needs. Lifestyle questions also allow you to "plug in" your product to that lifestyle in very realistic, easy-to-visualize ways. Knowing the lifestyle of your customer helps make your presentation "real" in the context of that lifestyle. The customer doesn't have to rely on abstract arguments or lists of benefits and features. He or she can simply imagine the product or service as it applies to their lifestyle.

Again, sales is a step-by-step process and you must take those steps one at a time and in proper order. Getting the ten "must knows" down before you proceed builds a firm foundation for the next step.

It also allows you to quickly match your customer's values. Matching your customer's values means that you determine if he or she will be a good fit for what you have to offer. If you match those values early, your sales efficiency will increase dramatically. You will be able to focus your limited and valuable time on qualified leads, the salesperson's dream customers.

Face it. No salesperson wants to spend hours working with a lead only to find that the potential customer's values do not match those of the firm. The sooner you find out whether a customer is qualified, the sooner you can determine how much time to invest in the lead.

This brings us to the next tools in the VALUE MATCH toolkit: the next set of VALUE MATCH Balanced Scorecards.

Balanced Scorecard VALUE MATCH Process—To Build Value, Discover Urgency, and Uncover Customer Hot Buttons

I want to introduce you to the next set of powerful sales tools, the VALUE MATCH Balanced Scorecards for <u>building value</u>, <u>discovering urgency</u>, and <u>uncovering customer hot buttons</u>. Used properly, these forms will improve your ability and effectiveness in leading customers through the process of identifying, clarifying and prioritizing needs.

These are the third, fourth and fifth forms respectively of the Balanced Scorecard VALUE MATCH Process. These forms offer you the opportunity to keep score as a way to determine how well you are doing in the creation of value for your customer and discovering situation urgency. Successfully completing these important skills and tactics with a customer can lead to <u>creating and matching value</u>, <u>uncovering urgency</u>, and <u>finding customer hot buttons</u> during the VALUE MATCH Process. Circle the score for each task if accomplished, and total the score at the bottom of each form.

Remember:
- Get the answer to the "Get Honest Question."
- Take the opportunity to tell about the overall offerings of the firm
- Identify the Emotional Solution
- Be prepared for Zingers.

Balanced ScoreCard™: Discovering Urgency	
	Be ready to take notes. Have both the VALUE MATCH Needs Inquiry Form and the Balanced Scorecard Urgency Form with you.
	Question: How long have you been in your current situation?
	Question: What has recently occurred to motivate you to shop or buy now?
	Response Skill: So, what I hear you saying is <Repeat what customer said>. What do you mean by that (use key words or phrases)? Repeat answer.
	Response Skill: So, <Repeat answer and ask>. What optimal solution are you looking for?
	Response Skill: "VALUE MATCH" (Relate what they have just shared to one or more of the special services/amenities you offer)
	Special service #1
	Special service #2
	Special service #3
	Special service #4
Overcoming Zingers	
	Identify and repeat the zinger.
	Ask what is meant by the zinger.
	Why do you ask about <here mention the particular zinger>?
	Answer the zinger, remembering that the answer must lead back to the process.
	Tie Down
	Total

Remember:
- Find out what is most important and why it is important to the customer.
- Take the opportunity to describe the product/amenities/features values that are important.
- Tie Down interest.
- Be prepared for Zingers.

Balanced ScoreCard™: Customer Hot Buttons

	Be ready to take notes. Have the VALUE MATCH Needs Inquiry Form and the Balanced Scorecard Discovering Customer Hot Buttons form with you.
	Question: "What amenities or additional features will be most important to you ?"
	Move towards or point to the amenities or additional features they have expressed interest in.
	Response Skill: So, What I hear you saying is <Repeat what customer said> How do you feel about that?
	Question: Why is that important to you? **(Listen)**
	Response Skill: "VALUE MATCH" (Relate what they have just shared to one or more of the amenities)
	Amenity or additional feature #1 (discuss and elaborate)
	Amenity or additional feature #2 (discuss and elaborate)
	Amenity or additional feature #3 (discuss and elaborate)
	Amenity or additional feature #4 (discuss and elaborate)
	Tie Down
Overcoming Zingers	
	Identify and repeat the zinger.
	Ask what is meant by the zinger.
	Why do you ask about <here mention the particular zinger>?
	Answer the zinger
	Total

Remember:
- **Listen to the "what" and the "why"**
- **Take the opportunity to tell the story in a way that matches what is important to the customer**
- **Be prepared for Zingers.**

<td colspan="2" align="center">## Balanced ScoreCard™: Building Value</td>
	Be ready to take notes. Have both the VALUE MATCH Needs Inquiry Form and the Balanced Scorecard Building Value form with you.
	Question: What will be important to you about the products/services offered? What do you like most about those products/services?
	Response Skill: "So, what I hear you saying is <Repeat what customer said>. What do you mean by that (use key words or phrases). Repeat answer.
	Question: Why is that important to you? **(Listen to the Answer)**
	Response Skill: "VALUE MATCH" (Relate what they have just shared to one or more of special features offered)
	Feature #1 (discuss and elaborate)
	Feature #2 (discuss and elaborate)
	Feature #3 (discuss and elaborate)
	Feature #4 (discuss and elaborate)
<td colspan="2">## Overcoming Zingers</td>
	Identify and repeat the zinger.
	Ask what is meant by the zinger.
	Why do you ask about <here mention the particular zinger>?
	Answer the zinger, remembering that the answer must lead back to the process.
	Tie Down
	Total

Each section of the VALUE MATCH process form is designed to help you move the conversation from to to get to the
TO TELL YOU THE TRUTH
platform and from there to a further position of knowledge. You begin moving your customer off his or her focus on the solution, and on to the more important issue of feelings, where the real selling takes place. Below is a summing up of the process.

VALUE MATCH PROCESS SUMMARY

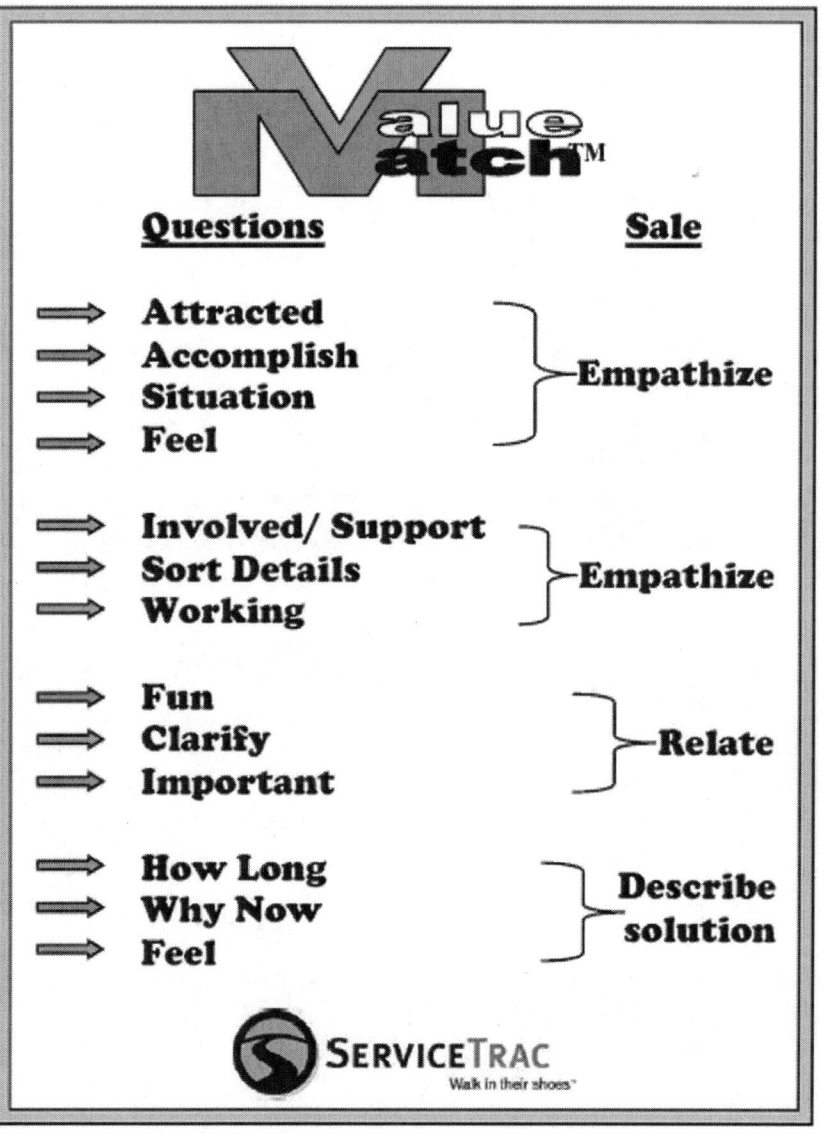

At the end of each section, salespeople should be prepared with three skills:
- The **Tie down** – confirm with the prospect (customer) that they can get what they have described they would be **interested in.**
- Be careful not to start telling until all questions have been exhausted
- Be ready for Zingers.

As noted above, the idea here is to move the conversation forward from facts to emotion, keeping in mind that customers make purchases based on emotion and then justify them with facts and figures. With that in mind, let's take a more in-depth look at each section of the Needs Inquiry Form.

Here Is A Little More Explanation

Urgency of The Situation: TO TELL YOU THE TRUTH

Question: What has recently occurred to motivate you to inquire today?

The first section of the form deals with Your goal here is to determine specifically what has caused the urgency of the current situation. For example, a customer could easily say: "Oh, Bob's having a case of his annual 'new car fever.' We're just shopping." That could very well be. But it's just as possible that their old car is actually on its last legs and they are in desperate need of reliable transportation to get to work, run household errands and get the kids to school on time.

What do they need? One of the first things to ask is: "How long has the current situation been going on?" We need to use our new VALUE MATCH sales skills and customers generally will volunteer if there are any pressing issues and critical timelines.

The car may have been on its "last legs" for some time and the family is well-prepared for making a major purchase. They could have shopped around via the newspaper and the Internet, have conducted in-depth product research, and may have a good idea of their product needs.

On the other hand, the car could have fallen apart first thing that morning and they're in full panic mode. Once you have this information, you'll know what kind of pressure is driving their decision-making process. You'll also have a good idea of the critical timing issues involved and what your next steps should be.

Question: How do you feel about the situation?

This helps develop the purpose of the visit and refine your client's sense of urgency. Only when you have identified the feelings of your customer can you discover his or her values so that you can begin the process of matching them with your own and with those of your product. Feelings, not facts, are key to your success. This is a very important point, a very **BIG** point to keep in mind.

Question: What solution are you looking for?

Usually a customer will tell you exactly what is needed with very little prompting, sometimes without any prompting at all. "Oh, the car just 'blew up' this morning and we're in a real bind." This is an excellent moment to make a trial close. **"So, if you could get into a new car this morning that would be exactly what you need right now. Is that correct?"** Depending upon the customer's level of urgency, you could close the sale right then and there. And wouldn't that be great!

What is key here is that, if we have rapport and trust, we can put the skills to use full throttle: ask questions about the customer's needs and peel the onion, so to speak. You are helping the customer describe the solution in terms of his or her feelings. So you can present the solution in terms of their feelings. Here's an example:

SALESPERSON: Why Now?

CUSTOMER: We think we're ready.

SALESPERSON: When you say ready, what do you mean?

CUSTOMER: Well, to tell you the truth… our car isn't running well and we don't want to put more money into it.

SALESPERSON: How do you feel about that?

CUSTOMER: We want to stabilize our expenses and know what it costs each month.

SALESPERSON: I am so glad you shared that. So, what solution are you looking for?

CUSTOMER: A payment we can afford.

SALESPERSON: So, if we can get the car you want and get the payment that you feel you can afford, will that work?

CUSTOMER: That's amazing, that is exactly what we want.

The Role Of "Family"

"Family" could be mom, dad and the kids or it could just as easily be the gang at work, a special committee set up just to make this purchase, or just the boss. The second set of questions, numbers three through five, encourage your customer to discuss the role of family members or office personnel in the buying decision.

Question: How are you involved? How is it affecting your life?

These two questions address the family or office implications of the decision and the impact of such a decision on all involved. Here, you are trying to discover how much your customer is involved in the product to be purchased. For example, if the customer arrived with "marching orders" to buy a new car, is he (or she) a purchasing agent who will never use the vehicle or one of the people who will actually be driving it?

This information will help target your presentation, especially in the areas of support services that might be required. A purchasing agent might not be very concerned about lumbar support in the driver's seat. But that might be very important to the individual who will spend hours behind the wheel on the open road.

Question: What changes would you like to see?

This questions lets you begin to see into the mindset of your customer. Their answer isn't necessarily the stated reason for the visit, "just shopping," but should be closer to the truth. "Our vehicle became a 'non-car' this morning. Help!"

Determining Product/Service Needs

These questions are designed to ferret out the real product or service needs of your customer. Specifically, these questions target the customer's values. There's no reason to "tap dance" around this subject. Just ask the question.

Question: What are your (your product) needs? How are these needs currently being met? What needs are most critical?

Chances are, you'll be surprised. The customer will actually answer: "I need a car so I can get to work tomorrow." Of course, as a VALUE MATCH salesperson we know that the solution of "get to work" translates to the emotional issue of "feed my family" or "see that young Biff gets that scholarship" or "pay for little Polly's braces so she will smile again, meet Prince Charming and live happily ever after."

If the family (office) needs were well met by the previous product, before that meteor hit, then you can get a pretty good idea of how the customer feels about your product or service in general. If they mention problems, you get an idea of the obstacles you have to overcome to make your presentation.

If "the old car" was great, but the folks are in due to that unfortunate meteor incident, you can develop a clear definition of just what "great" means. If they start in on: "Yeah, but you know, a CD stereo system would have been nice," then that might steer you toward a more upscale model.

If the customer is not providing much information, then it is up to you to prompt him or her with suggestions such as: "How satisfied were you with your previous vehicle? How would you like to move up a bit?" The ideal thing is to talk about material and topics the customer has already mentioned or hinted at. That is the secret to staying on their agenda.

Determining Support Service Needs

These questions prompt you to identify support service needs and how satisfied the customer is with those services at present as well as what he or she might be looking for in the future.

Question: What types of support services are being provided at this time? How are they currently being provided? What services are most important?

These questions allow you to determine the current level of service being provided, if at all, and how well those services meet the needs of your customer. Handled properly, you will also gain a pretty good idea of what the customer is really looking for and the priority they assign to different values related to that service. For example:

YOU: How well are those needs being met?

CUSTOMER: Oh, they're fine.

YOU: So, what I'm hearing is that your current provider is doing a fine job. When you say "fine" what do you mean?

CUSTOMER: Well, to be honest, what we really need is _____ _____ _____.

Whatever fills that blank gives you a solid clue as to a certain level of dissatisfaction, not matter how small, that you can pursue. Once those unmet needs are identified and prioritized, you can begin matching values to them.

Discussing Lifestyle Needs

The final questions encourage your customer to discuss lifestyle needs with respect to the products and/or services at hand. These are the activities, hobbies and interests that make life more interesting, the "spice of life," in other words.

Question: How does the decision fit into your lifestyle? What is happening now? What features or amenities would have the most impact on you personally?

Most likely your customer has more than one interest. You might even get a list of five or so, or even more. In some situations you can explore and prioritize the issues or items mentioned by simply restating what is said and asking: "Out of the items you mentioned, which is the most important to you?" In so doing you can discover what is the most important to your customer? When you discover a customer's lifestyle and are able to match that lifestyle or values with your product or service, you are very near to closing the sale.

At the end of each question, I like to ask why what they have shared is important to them and why they care about it. This helps the customer to show their feelings. More importantly, it helps the salesperson present the solution in the "ambient light" of the customer's feelings, thus making the solution all the more palatable. In simpler terms, it helps the customer relate to what you are sharing because it is painted in terms of their own feelings.

In the next chapter, we will look at the next step in the VALUE MATCH sales process: the importance of presenting. This is where we take all this information and discoveries and put them to good use. We will look at how you can tell a "Different and Better Story." We will also look at the final VALUE MATCH Balanced Scorecard form, Getting Into A "Closing Posture."

VALUE CHECK

- The 10 "Must Knows" that let a salesperson determine a customer's true needs
- The use of the VALUE MATCH Needs Inquiry Form in helping to establish a customer's needs
- The importance of taking it one step at a time and following the proper flow
- The importance of matching values ASAP
- Moving the conversation forward from facts to emotions
- The VALUE MATCH Needs form explained step-by-step, question by question and section by section
- The Balanced Scorecard forms as complements to the VALUE MATCH Needs form

Communication is a continual balancing act, juggling the conflicting needs for intimacy and independence. To survive in the world, we have to act in concert with others, but to survive as ourselves, rather than simply as cogs in a wheel, we have to act alone.

—Deborah Tannen

CHAPTER TEN:

THE PRESENTATION

*Nobody's born with
great presentation skills.
But everyone has the potential.*

—**Robert Keiper**

*There is one story and one story only
that will prove worth your telling.*

—**Robert Graves**

How To Make Yourself Presentable Or The Ol' Game Of Pitch And Catch

Values Unlocked In This Chapter

Whether trying to succeed in sales, managing personnel, or just getting along with people, presentation is the key. What is important here is that the power in a presentation is to **present** the solution in the ambient light of the customers' feelings and to describe it in their words exactly. A win here is when the customer says: "That's Amazing! What are the chances you have exactly what I wanted?"

In this chapter you'll learn about:
- Telling your own different and better story
- Linking company values with customer values
- Focusing your presentation on customer values
- Tailoring presentation to match customer's hot buttons
- Effectively presenting yourself and your organization in a sales situation
- Using the VALUE MATCH Balanced Scorecard "Closing Posture" form to better prepare yourself for the actual close.

Tell A Different And Better Story

Once you have successfully identified the true values and needs, you are in a better position to pinpoint the specific features and benefits of your product that match the unique needs and values of the customer. One step naturally follows another.

Presenting a different and better story doesn't mean you have to be different and better in every category. You do this by:
- **Pinpointing customer values**
- **Highlighting product strengths**
- **Powerfully matching the values of your customer with the strengths of your product or service.**

One of the characteristics of our consumer society in recent years has been a dramatic shift from easily distinguishable products to "cookie cutter" products and services. The real differences are in many cases practically non-existent. I have heard automobile dealers, for example, bemoaning the fact that the production of so many look-a-like products has had a negative impact on the power of brand loyalty.

I remember walking into a parking lot near my home and being struck by the sight of ten or twelve recent model, four-door sedans. Several U.S. manufacturers were represented, as were a number of European and Pacific Rim models. Except for small details, such as wheel covers or headlight alignment, they could have been punched out by the same cookie cutter. What is the poor consumer supposed to think when it's time to make a purchase from all these "different" brands?

Again, that's where the VALUE MATCH salesperson shines.

The way you tell a different and better story is to match the unique features of your product to the unique needs of your customer. You do that by providing the answers to three concerns the customers have:

#1 Relationship: "Do I feel really comfortable with this salesperson?"

#2 Product: "Does the product and sales person meet my specific needs?"

#3 Service: "Can and will they help me after I've signed the check?"

You face a considerable challenge. The nature of your business or the type of product or service you provide offers no protection from it. More than ever before it is our duty as salespeople to inform our customers about how and why our story is different and better than the story being told by the competition.

> **The only way to honestly and effectively tell a different and better story is by understanding the values of the customer.**

Our personal integrity is a key element in making all this work – for us, our company and customer.

State it. Show it. Prove it. And state it again (there's that buyer's remorse showing up). Where are you different and better? What is your proof of this? Why does it matter to your customer?

The story really is different because we've made an investment in discovering and then matching our customers' unique values. Our story is better because it relates specifically to the problem and the value filters of that individual customer. Done correctly, this is a story no one else will ever hear. It's a story no other person <u>can</u> ever hear because you have made the investment to make certain every unique customer is served with a unique solution to his or her problem.

Know Your Mission, Your Vision And Your Values

Your product or service represents a lot of different values. Some of them precisely match the needs, wants, and, most important, the values of your customer. Before you know why your story is different and better, you have to develop a clear understanding of your organization's mission, vision and values. That only makes sense.

A VALUE MATCH salesperson must be able to answer these three questions—and not in a vague way either but fully and honestly:

Exactly, how are you different and better?

What proof or evidence do you have that you are different and better?

Why does it matter to the customer?

That's a pretty good series of questions. And you'd better be prepared to answer them. Even if your customer doesn't verbalize these questions, he or she will certainly be thinking them. Providing answers at the appropriate times will enhance your credibility and increase your chances of gaining the customer's trust, thereby making it easier to enter his or her inner circle.

In addition, you must keep up on the latest changes in your company. In today's high tech world of Internet research your customers can do research unlike that of any previous generation. They **WILL** research your products and be very knowledgeable before they ever meet you. Any discrepancies between what you tell them and what they already know will give off unpleasant warning signals.

In most cases, customers are going to drop some serious cash and they won't be doing this lightly. To keep an advantage over your competition you will need to be continuously updated and educated on changes in your company and the industry at large. It's much like continuing education.

Another essential aspect of staying ahead is fully understanding your competitors and your competitors' products or services. That's the only way you can prepare to discover why and how your product is different and better. And never forget that "different and better" isn't a generic phrase. Its meaning changes with every prospect because everyone is different and arrives with different wants and needs. When you use VALUE MATCH techniques, you will match your unique product values to those of your customer, thus proving that your product really is different and better.

For Example: Good Mission and Vision Statements

Here are excerpts from a few examples of good, well-considered corporate mission and vision statements. Pay particular attention to the fact that they are concise, easy to understand and mercifully free of the meaningless boilerplate statements you find in so many similar corporate documents. Notice also that they form a continuum, a never-ending circle composed of customers, employees and investors, each serving and being served by the other.

XEROX

"Xerox, the Document Company, will be the leader in the global document market, providing Document Services that enhance business productivity ..."

"Xerox Values"

- We succeed through satisfied customers
- We aspire to deliver quality and excellence in all that we do
- We require premium return on assets.
- We use technology to deliver market leadership.
- We value our employees.
- We behave responsibly as a corporate citizen.

"Strategic Direction"

"Xerox, the Document Company, will be the leader in the global document market, providing Document Services that enhance business productivity..."

It is impossible for anyone in the company (or outside the company) to misunderstand the Xerox mission, vision and values. They're expressed briefly and eloquently and in an understandable English.

Here's an even more concise statement from Northwestern Mutual Life Insurance:

> ### "The Northwestern Mutual Way"
> "The ambition of The Northwestern has been less to be large than to be safe; its aim is to rank first in benefits to policy owners rather than first in size. Valuing quality above quantity, it has preferred to secure its business under certain salutary restrictions and limitations rather than to write a much larger business at the possible sacrifice of those valuable points which have made the Northwestern pre-eminently the policy owner's company."

Incidentally, "The Northwestern Mutual Way" was written in 1888. Here's one final example from Intel:

> ## Intel
>
> <u>Our Mission</u>
>
> "Do a great job for our customers, employees, and stockholders by being the preeminent building block supplier to the computing industry."
>
> <u>Our Values</u>
>
> "... Partnerships with our customers and suppliers are essential to our mutual success ..."
>
> "... We are results oriented ..."
>
> "The complexity of our work and tough business environment demands a high degree of self-discipline and cooperation ..."
>
> "A productive and challenging work environment is key to our success ..."
>
> "... Our business requires continuous improvement of our performance to our Mission and Values ..."
>
> "... To succeed we must maintain our innovative environment."
>
> <u>Our Objectives</u>
>
> "1. Strengthen our number one position in the microprocessor market segment"
>
> "2. Make the PC THE ubiquitous interactive device ..."
>
> "3. Do the right things right ..."

Now those are missions, visions and values you can go out and really sell!

Carving Your Niche

Every organization has to carve its own special niche in the marketplace and every salesperson within that organization must understand and be able to articulate what that market niche is. It could be a large, broad-based niche serving a wide audience, such as a full-service automobile dealership. Or it could be something much narrower in focus, such as a dealership specializing in a limited number of high-end, pricey import cars. Everyone and every organization has a niche. The sooner you find and fill yours, the better for you, your organization and your customer.

This includes knowing such things as:
- **Organization's mission**—where is the organization going?
- **Organization's vision**—how is the organization going to get there?
- **Organization's values**—for what does the organization stand?
- **Customer's values**—what do your customers want?
- **Who are your customers?**
- **Who is your competition?**

Make A WOW! Presentation

As a VALUE MATCH sales professional, you have the skills to connect the "must knows" mentioned in the previous chapter with the values of your customer, focusing specifically on each customer's hot buttons. Regardless of how exciting a given feature, benefit, service factor or amenity may be, if it doesn't push a customer hot button it is of little value except as support information.

Regardless of the extraordinary good gas mileage on the car you're selling, if the customer is most interested in safety then safety is what you must promote. Regardless of how secure the investment, if your customer's hot button is financial growth then growth is the feature you must concentrate on. If your customer is most concerned about insurance liability, all the presenting in the world on price will not help you close the sale.

Always determine your customer's hot buttons and structure your presentation accordingly. If you're unsure of how to determine a customer's hot bottoms, go back to the specific section in Chapter Nine and re-examine the VALUE MATCH Needs Inquiry Form and the Balanced Scorecard Forms, especially the Uncover Customer Hot Bottoms form. Once you've done that, you're ready to make a WOW! presentation.

The Four Components Of A WOW! Presentation

The WOW! presentation takes place in four distinct stages, or steps. These four components are:

- ***The Warm Up*** Do everything in your power to create a relaxed and comfortable environment that is conducive to effective selling. This includes a warm and sincere greeting, a private or at least a quiet setting, arrangements that you will not be interrupted, mood music, refreshments and so on. If you can think of something specific that will warm up your prospect or customer, then do it. The objective is to provide the optimum setting during your sales situation.

- ***WIIFM*** This acronym stands for "What's In It For Me?" Your customer's needs and values should be your preeminent concern. Drop your own pre-conceived agenda and keep your presentation focused on the agenda and values of your customer. The last thing a customer wants at this point is to listen to your concerns and agenda if they don't coincide with his or hers.

- ***Give 'Em A Show!*** Be enthusiastic. Be convincing. Make it exciting. Go the extra mile, be prepared and leave nothing to chance. Remember, brochures, videos and computer programs are good support. But they don't sell. They sell. Only a salesperson can sell and the ones who sell the best are VALUE MATCH salespersons.

One of your best "show biz" techniques is storytelling. Not only are relevant stories an excellent way to illustrate a point, they also provide a context for understanding. "Oh, now I see what you mean," is often the customer's first comment after being told a story. And that's the whole point – that they see what you mean.

- *Involve Your Customer* Selling is a two-way communication. You can't sell successfully by lecturing, by talking at someone. You have to talk the person. Pause to ask questions and check with your customer to make sure everything is proceeding on track. Watch for those yellow caution lights. Don't barrel through it when you encounter one. Instead, stop and slowly backtrack until the issue has been satisfied. Clearing up issues as they occur means you don't have a pile-up at the end.

Power Up Your Presentation With Enthusiasm

A VALUE MATCH sales professional is always prepared to demonstrate or elaborate on his or her product or service. But the professional also does it with genuine, heartfelt excitement, with an attitude that exudes confidence and get-up-and-go. Your presentation is the power of your sale, so it is important that you do everything possible to add power to your presentation. Enthusiasm is your key.

Studies prove that optimistic, the-glass-is-half-full people achieve more than pessimistic, the-glass-is-half-empty people. For example, a study of Metropolitan Life Insurance salespeople in the mid-eighties showed that:

- **Optimists consistently outsold pessimists from the beginning.**
- **Optimists continued to outsell pessimists over the long-term.**
- **Optimists earned greater longevity at work than pessimists.**
- **Optimists were less likely to quit than pessimists.**

Why are these results so consistent? The answer is twofold. First, optimists really don't think in terms of "failure." They also know that challenges are there to be overcome. More than that, they know, really know down deep in their hearts that they will overcome them. Success is the inevitable outcome.

Second, enthusiastic people know that persistence is key to success and unwavering optimism is essential to maintaining a successful, goal-centered career. No matter what happens, they just keep trying… and trying… and trying… until all that trying turns into succeeding.

At the same time, you need to be honest and sincere! "The medium is the message," as Marshall McLuhan so famously said. People believe 10% of what they hear, 20% of what they see, And never try to fake sincerity. You won't be able to get away with it for long, if at all. This is especially true around children and seniors who can smell a phony a mile away.

Remember:
- **Only the motivated can motivate.**
- **Get excited because your excitement matters.**
- **Sweat the details.**

A VALUE MATCH sales professional is always prepared to share with the customer the details and information knowledge they have about the product or service they represent but they also recognize that selling is not telling. I will let you in on a little secret I have successfully used for many years that helps me keep control of the presentation and keep the presentation focused on the customer: Whenever you feel the urge to talk just ask a question. Preferably an open ended question, one that would elicit some great feedback from the customer and would give you clues and information that you will be able to listen to the VALUE MATCH way and in so doing, gather what you need to focus your own presentation on just the right information.

This is a wonderful rule and if you can master it, the rule works miracles. Even for those of you that do presentations or speeches for large groups. Try asking the audience who they are and what they want to learn from the time they are about to invest with you. You will be amazed at what they suggest and if you are listening, know your material and have confidence, it will be amazing, your presentation will be exactly on point and all will walk away satisfied and impressed. I have been using this skill for some time now and it really works. Try it and you will be happy you did.

Tool #5: The VALUE MATCH Balanced Scorecard "Closing Posture" Form

One of the best ways to ascertain whether you're ready for the "closing arguments" of your presentation is to go through the "Get Into A Closing Posture" form with a customer. This form serves as a summing up of all that has gone on before, a step-by-step reminder of what information you've gathered and the importance of that information.

Again, successfully completing these key skills and tactics with a customer can <u>get you into a closing posture</u> during the VALUE MATCH Process. Circle the score for each task accomplished, and total the score at the bottom. Be honest and try to achieve the maximum score whenever possible because the closer you get to the maximum the better chance you have of closing the sale.

Remember:
- **Put yourself in a closing posture**
- **Present the hot buttons and tie down each one**
- **Ask for a specific next action step**
- **Watch for yellow lights**
- **Be prepared to overcome objections: Repeat > Reassure > Resume**

Balanced ScoreCard™: Closing Posture

	Have your notes ready. Make sure you have the VALUE MATCH Balanced Scorecard "Closing Posture" form ready on your clipboard. Sharpen those pencils!
	Use your notes to summarize the customer's situation.
	Summarize the customer's urgency.
	Summarize the customer's hot buttons for product, service, amenities, etc.
	Throughout summary, confirm what you have identified as hot really holds an interest for the customer.
	Question: What is going to be the most important issue or feature in your decision to purchase the product (service)?
	Response Skill: "That's amazing! Based on what you have shared, I have exactly what you are looking for. Would you like to see some of the products (services) I have in mind?"
	Question: "If indeed I can show you the product (service) that matches everything you and I have discovered that you are looking for, would you be in the position to buy today?"
	Tie Down
Overcoming Objections	
	Hear the objection. Assure the customer by repeating the objection.
	Ask what they mean by <their objection>
	Why do you ask about <here mention the particular objection>?
	Answer the objection, remembering that the answer must lead back to the process.
	Total

In the next chapter, we will look at an next extremely crucial step in the VALUE MATCH sales process: the actual closing. This is that dreaded moment (well, dreaded by some salespeople, in any case) where you discover whether or not you've succeeded in your sales pitch. We will look at the importance of the step-by-step process leading to the close, as well as some particular types of closes and which one you think is the best for you.

VALUE CHECK

- Presenting a different and better story doesn't mean you have to be different and better in every category, just in areas important to your customer.
- You tell a different and better story by: (1) pinpointing customer values, (2) highlighting product strengths, and (3) powerfully matching the values of your customer with the strengths of your product or service.
- Your customer wants answers to three basic concerns: (1) Relationship – "Do I feel really comfortable with this salesperson?" (2) Product – "Does it meet my specific needs?" (3) Service – "Can and will they help me after I've signed the check?"
- A VALUE MATCH salesperson provides the answers to these three questions: (1) How are you different and better? (2) What is your proof? (3) Why does it matter if you are different and better?
- Every person and every organization must find and fill a niche in the marketplace.
- The four components of a WOW! Presentation are: (1) the warm up, (2) What's in it for me, (3) Give 'em a show, and (4) involve your customer.
- People believe 10% of what they hear, 20% of what they see, and 70% of who you are.
- Using the Balanced Scorecard "Closing Posture" Form can help you sum up the customer situation and prepare you for the all-important close.

The first law of story-telling....
Every man is bound to leave a story
better than he found it.

—Mary Augusta Ward

CHAPTER ELEVEN:

CLOSING ARGUMENTS

> *What has always boggled my mind is why such a negative word such as "close" has been used to commemorate the "opening" of a new account.*
>
> **—John W. Thrasher**

> *Selling is the art of asking the right questions to achieve the string of minor yeses that will lead to the final yes. The final sale is nothing more than the sum total of all your minor yeses, isn't that right?*
>
> **—Tom Lanza**

How To Close (Open) A Sale, Naturally

Values Unlocked In This Chapter

In this chapter, we look at the next natural step in the VALUE MATCH sales process: the oft-dreaded but inevitable end of the sales process, the closing. In this chapter, you will learn about:

- Why you shouldn't dread the closing
- Goal-focusing techniques
- Passing the self-administered test
- Never a discouraging word
- Trial closes and their kin
- Types of closes
- The art of listening

The Closing Ceremonies

If there's one word more than any other that seems to really strike terror in the hearts of many salespeople—and in particular, beginning salespeople, it would have to be "closing." I've actually heard salespeople say: "But, I just can't ask someone for money!" Or even more commonly: "But what if she says 'no'? I couldn't stand the thought of being rejected!"

Well, that's too bad because there's absolutely no reason at all to fear or put off the close of a sale. (I was going to say "avoid" but you can't really avoid it, can you? With or without you, the sale is going to come to a close).

When you go through all the presentation steps in proper order, when you execute each as it should be carried out, when you've done everything successfully, the closing should be so natural as to appear effortless. Often it effortless. That much-dreaded closing just becomes the natural end of a successful and pleasant sales experience. Handled properly, both customer and salesperson come out winners, truly a "win-win" situation.

In fact, in a recent retail customer survey, consumers who hadn't purchased an item after they'd gone shopping were asked why they didn't buy the product or service they had been examining. The most common answer was: "We weren't asked."

Not that they couldn't make up their minds. Not that they didn't find the right the product or service. Not that they didn't like the salesperson or the surroundings. But because they hadn't been "asked" to buy the product. The truth is that, unless you speak up, the customer may not buy. Makes sense, right? They don't know you're ready to sell the product to them.

> "When you've done everything successfully, the closing should be so natural as to appear effortless"

Focus On Two Goals

Although the close might be effortless, you still need to work hard to get to that point. During the latter part of your presentation, as things are winding down toward the successful culmination of your efforts, clear your mind of all distractions. Focus as intensely as possible on two key goals:

- **Goal #1: Help your customer take the next action step.**
- **Goal #2: Uncover your customer's fears so that you can continue to keep the process moving forward.**

Passing Your Own Closing Test

Before you can make your **heartfelt recommendation to the person** you **now consider a friend**, before you can successfully close a sale, before **you can recommend** that the customer-friend **take the next best action step**, you need to pass the following test. This is one only you can administer, so there's no cheating possible. (Unless you count lying to yourself, which is only cheating yourself. Like cheating at golf.)

Prior to closing, you must be able to answer the following questions in a truthful manner:
- **Do I believe in what I am doing?**
- **Have I built trust and a rapport with my customer?**
- **How deeply do I feel that my recommendation is the specific solution my customer needs?**
- **Have I suggested the next, best and most appropriate action step in the process?**

This isn't a "pass/fail" test where failure gets you a dunce cap and a trip to the corner. But it is, as they say at NASA, a "go/no-go" test. Going ahead when you're not ready is a surefire, tried-and-true formula for disaster.

In fact, if for whatever reason you don't feel comfortable moving on to the next step with your customer, that's a pretty sure sign that you're picking up on one of those "yellow lights" I mentioned previously. Among those yellow lights or warning signals are:

- **Folded arms**
- **Rolling eyes**
- **Little/no conversation**
- **Looking at watch**
- **Stiff posture**
- **Lots of objections**
- **Walking away**
- **No facial expression**
- **Interruption of conversation at inappropriate times**
- **Asking many questions**

That very wise, incredibly perceptive subconscious mind of yours is probably sending a signal that you haven't answered all the questions correctly. Or that the customer hasn't understood all of the ramifications of what you've been saying. Or that you've simply confused him or her by moving too quickly. The thing to do is slow down at a yellow light. Assess the situation and start rebuilding or reinforcing so you can help your customer take that next logical step. You might even have to back up a light or two to make sure you're on the same page as to customer (pardon the mixed metaphor).

Through The Customer's Eyes

If you're still intimidated by the thought of asking for the close, here's something important to consider. Try looking at it through the customer's eyes and ask yourself: What is happening in your customer's mind when you do not make a heartfelt recommendation? What does that customer think or imagine when you don't even make an effort to close?

Several thoughts come to mind right off the bat—and none of them are very pleasant:

"This salesperson doesn't care."
"This salesperson isn't confident."
"This salesperson is keeping something from me."
"This product or service isn't any good."

How can you get someone to accept a heartfelt recommendation when he or she believes your heart just isn't in it? Believe me, that customer will start looking for someone who does care. As we have pointed out throughout the course of this book, people buy on heartfelt recommendations from someone they like and trust.

Making a purchase is just not possible when customers believe you don't care about them. Or don't care about making the sale. Regardless of your real motives or fears, whether you're being paranoid for fear of a "no" or not sincere, over-prolonging, attempting to avoid or even refusing to close the deal sends a clear and unpleasant message:

"I just don't care enough about you or your situation to continue this any further."

What kind of negative messages are you sending when you show such a lack of confidence?

Again, it doesn't matter if you appear nervous because you're intimidated by closing, the fear of failure, or a harsh lecture from your supervisor. The customer will perceive your nervousness as a lack of confidence in your product or service. The customer's attitude becomes: "Well, if their own salespeople don't believe in this product, I surely ain't buying it!"

These problems are easily avoided.

Closing A Deal, Opening A Friendship

It is essential to remember one key fact: Closing isn't the final step in the sales process—at least not if you've done things right. So you close one deal and immediately have the possibility of opening another. Each customer represents a relationship that should be valued and preserved.

After all, you don't want to sell him, her or them this one widget only. You don't want it to be a one-shot deal. You want to sell them their next one and the one after that—and maybe bigger and better ones, too. Moreover, you want to sell the other members of their family, their friends, neighbors and acquaintances, too. You want to create as long-lasting a relationship as possible with as many customers as possible—all from one close, if possible!

Here are a few other important points to keep in mind when it comes to the art of closing:

- **The Numbers Game:** Sure, sales is a numbers game. But, just like in any sport, nobody wins every game all the time. If you're doing your level best to serve the needs of your customer, and if you're learning from your mistakes, never let a "no" discourage you. Press on. Even the top performing salespeople **earn** "no" a lot more often than "yes." I emphasize the word "earn" in that sentence because you work hard for them—be it "no" or "yes.". You really do earn them. Rejection—of the product or service and not you personally—is just a natural part of the process. And remember this very important point: Every time you hear a "no," you are one step closer to earning the inevitable "yes."
- **The faster you fail, the faster you succeed** Never be afraid of failure. It too is a natural part of the process and must not be feared. Too many in this profession are so afraid of failing that they actually create the very condition for the failure they're working so hard to avoid. The fear becomes a self-fulfilling prophecy. Instead, learn to replace your fear by jumping right in there with enthusiasm—especially after a failure. Fail as fast as you can. That's how you learn, grow, and eventually succeed.
- **Ask for commitment:** Until you ask for a commitment from your customer, you have not given that customer a reason or an

opportunity to fully express his or her concerns. Objections, often serious ones, can remain hidden for any number of reasons. You can't address what you don't know and sometimes the only way to know more is to ask for the close. Look at it this way. Closing is an excellent way to gather valuable information from your customer. In that sense, it's an excellent research tool. And why should you be afraid of learning more about your customer's real needs?

- **Ask and then... silence!:** This is a key point. I've heard too many stories and have seen too many salespeople actually talking the customer out of buying. The salesperson gets nervous, starts yapping away and pretty soon the customer has lost interest. Or thinks the salesperson is trying to hide something with rapid-fire talk. Think about it. How can a customer respond when you're talking a mile a minute? He or she can't get a word in edgewise. And that word may very well be "yes."
- **Be helpful and encouraging:** Help your customers over the hurdle of making the right decision. Don't push, but be there with a helpful, encouraging hand. Reinforce the wisdom of the purchase and how it is the unique solution to their unique problem. You don't want an argument over objections, you just want to help your customers express their concerns so that you may answer them.
- **Yellow light warning:** Keep an eye out for those yellow lights. They can turn up at any time. Be sensitive to the needs of a customer who puts on the brakes. There's always a reason. Three types of actions are certain clues to a yellow light:

1. Sudden changes in body language: Things like folded arms, loss of eye contact, a tapping foot, or cracking knuckles show the customer is no longer relaxed and may be looking for a way out of the close.
2. Questions that address facts rather than values: You have worked hard to match your values and those of the customer and that is where the sale has been coming from. If the customer begins to question only facts and figures, you're losing that value match. Take a step back and get to that common ground. From there you'll be able to move once again toward the close.

3. A general uneasiness in your customer's overall demeanor. You may notice the customer looking at his or her watch, hemming and hawing or stumbling with his or her words. This is once again a time to backup, rematch your values and head toward the close.

If you're open and aware, you'll recognize the signs.

- **Always ask three times:** In closing, always ask at least three times. Studies have shown that the customer needs to have the opportunity to express his or her questions and concerns and most often the customer has several questions he or she has not expressed. The closing questions give the customer the chance to not only express the concerns or questions but also give you the opportunity to help the customer clear those concerns and questions up and respond to them. By asking for a decision several times you are actually doing the customer a great service and helping him or her through the buying process. That said, it is important that you allow plenty of time for this process to occur. So you must start asking for a decision early in the presentation and plan time for you to help the customer overcome his or her objections one at a time while still leaving time at the end to take care of the paper work and get a check. Always plan enough time in your presentation to ask three times.
- **Timing:** In closing, always be aware of timing. Try to make sure that you will have enough time at the appropriate moment for closing. Do all you can to make certain your customer isn't distracted. You don't want to build up to a good close only to hear: "I have to get back to the office... I have to go pick up my carpool... Oh, shucks! I've got to go!" or some other reason for leaving. You can take care of such problems simply by asking your customer's time frame up front and then scheduling your presentation accordingly.•

- **Check = Commitment:** Remember, regardless of what anyone says, Over the years, I have developed a simple but effective motto: When someone gives you a check they stop shopping and they start planning. I learned this simple lesson early in my life when I sold carpet while going through school. I would show a nice couple the carpet they needed and answer all of their questions and eventually, I would ask them if they would like to buy the carpet. To which they would say: " Sure, that sounds great. Let us go home and think about it and then we will come back tomorrow and give you the deposit." As you might already know, that did not happen very often. Why? Because the well intentioned folks would see Joe's Carpet Barn on the way home and think to themselves: "Maybe we should just go in there and see what Joe has to offer." They were still shopping. I soon learned that I needed to help these couples by not only asking them to buy the carpet but also to require that they give me a small deposit to get the process started. This usually helped them really pin down their decision and if there were any misgivings or questions you can be sure they were asked. But, once the check was given and the folks were on there way, guess what? They did not see Joe's sign but did stop at Sam's furniture warehouse to start the process of buying the new furniture that went with the new carpet. Always remember, when folks give you a check they stop shopping and start planning. Always ask for a check.

> "When someone gives you a check they stop shopping and start planning"

Remember:

> "A close is when a salesperson makes a heartfelt recommendation to a friend to take the next best action step."

> "If you have built a relationship with the customer from your first contact and you "pass the test," you shouldn't be afraid to close."

The Trial Close

A VALUE MATCH salesperson isn't closing all the time. But he or she **is** looking for closing opportunities all the time.

The Trial Close is a good example of this constant probing. It can be used throughout the process to gauge your customer's level of interest and excitement—and to determine his or her value priorities. For example: "Would you like that in red or in blue… So a delivery on January 14 would be the best date for you… Should we plan on delivery by rail or truck …"

What you're looking for are positive answers to help determine whether to actually close or continue the process. Trial closes not only get agreement on features your customer may (or may not) like, they also gather information. You can use the trial close method as many times as needed during your presentation, if necessary.

You can use a process close to help lower the pressure during your presentation. For instance, "The next step in the process is …"

A VALUE MATCH salesperson always assumes the sale, that the answer is "yes." Optimism and enthusiasm, in other words. This type of selling becomes easy with a simple change in your words and phraseology. For example, you don't say: "If you buy…" Instead, you say: "When you buy…."

The idea is to have your word pictures throughout the presentation paint lovely, exciting images of your customer already using your product or service. In short order, your customer is making those same assumptions right along with you. And he or she starts to feel that they need the product or service.

Never forget that You want them. They're the best way to tell what your customer is really thinking and, more importantly, what he or she is feeling. You can't handle an objection until and unless it comes up. That's part of your job, to ferret out all those objections so you can effectively handle them and then go about the business of closing. Every objection moves you one step closer to a successful conclusion. You have to help your customer get it off his or her chest.

Types of Closes: Get To Know Them Well

There are many different ways to close a deal, depending on the particular situation or conditions. If you have been following the VALUE MATCH process step by step, you will know instinctively which one to use. Below are several types of closings that are used fairly commonly. Some of these are fairly new. Others have been around since the times of the first used-wheel salesperson.

Many of these techniques were introduced in the 1920s by E.K. Strong, considered by some as the father of modern selling and an advocate of matching closing to both the customer and the situation. Of course, these are templates. How well they actually work in a particular situation depends entirely on you.

The If-Then Close

One excellent technique is called the "If-Then" close. For example, let's assume Mr. Smith has raised an objection by saying: "The cost of this house just seems a bit high to me." The VALUE MATCH salesperson responds with: "Mr. Smith, is your only concern that the price seems a bit high? Is that right? When you say, a 'bit high' what does that mean, Mr. Smith? And Mr. Smith's answer: "Well, I want to make sure that the overall price fits into my budget." Then you respond in turn with the if-then close: "So **if** we could overcome your concern about your budget, **then** you would be willing to move forward?"

The Ben Franklin Close

The "Ben Franklin" close works well in many tough situations and it has the added benefit of the active participation of your customer in the process. Basically, you take pen to paper (or keyboard to computer screen these days) and list all the pros and cons involved in making the decision.

Naturally, as a top salesperson selling a top product or service, you will be able to list a lot more positive reasons than negative ones. Once your customer sees how overbalanced the pros are compared to the cons, you can move on to: "I think we can safely say that your best move is the one we're discussing. Let's go ahead and take the next step in the process, shall we?"

The "Hypothetical Question" Close

The "Hypothetical Question" close typically asks: "If you found the ideal Whatchamacallit today, would you be willing to make a down payment today?" Of course, if the customer is at all serious about the purchase he or she will agree. That's the reason they're investing their time with you in the first place. As a VALUE MATCH sales professional, you'll be able to discover their unique values, match them to your product and prove that, yes, you have found the ideal Whatchamacallit today.

Take Away Close

This is one of my personal favorites. Sometimes it is useful to inspire the customer to explore his or her feelings of what life might be like without the product or service you have suggested. Sometimes, a little jolt of reality will help the customer stop rationalizing and start being more realistic about what his or her real needs are and get the customer thinking of how your product or service will help meet that need. This close goes something like this.

Salesperson: Come to think of it Mrs. Smith, I am not sure we have that sweater in your size. You might need to think of another color. You know… Maybe I can check at another store and see if they have one? Would you like me to check?

Mrs. Smith: Yes, do that.

While you are checking Mrs. Smith suddenly realizes that she likes the sweater more than she was letting on. When you come back, Mrs. Smith is showing her enthusiasm and will be a little more receptive to your request: "Should we ring this up?"

The Either Or Close

This closing technique works very well if you have helped the customer narrow his or her choice to a couple of strong contenders. Then as soon as you can ask the customer, you say: "So, it looks like you really feel that both A and B would fit your requirements. Is that right? Which one should we go forward with?" This is close to the assumptive close and helps you to check if you are in the ballpark. It also suggests to the customer that now is the time to start narrowing the field and move to the next step.

The Urgency Close

The Urgency close is one of the most misunderstood and misused closing techniques in the book. The reason? Most salespeople have not been taught to use it properly. The thing to remember with the Urgency close is to always make sure you use their urgency not yours. That means that the fact that your prices are going up tomorrow, that you are selling fast and your inventory is drying up quickly, that your schedule won't permit you to meet again for some time, while very compelling are not " their reasons". It is true that your urgency issues can be used but only after their urgency has been discovered, illuminated and confirmed. If you do not focus on their reasons for needing the product or service first before you highlight your reasons, you may very well get answers like this: "Well, if it is meant to be then it will still be there tomorrow. Oh well, it may not be the right time."

Here is an example of the right way to use the Urgency close.

Salesperson: Well Mr. Doolittle, do I understand you correctly? Do you need to find a new snow blower by this weekend because yours does not work and you are concerned about the storm coming this weekend?

Customer: Yes, that is right. I do need to make a decision this week so I have something to work with this weekend.

Salesperson: Well, it sounds to me like you feel the J5 Snow Eater is the one you like and I should let you know now that I only have one left in stock. Should we start the paper work so we can get it ready for you to have this weekend?

Always remember: Use their urgency not yours. It will work much better. Also remember: You need to have their urgency to use it. At the end of the sales process is not the time to try to get those reasons. Check what I shared in earlier chapters when we talked about asking the Get Honest question. The time to ask the customer to be honest with you and share the "Why Now" answer is the best time to gather this information and now is the time to use it most effectively.

The Process Close

The Process close is one of my favorites and I think most sales people like to have this one handy too. It is easy and I think the appeal of this close is that it takes the pressure of asking the customer off of the shoulders of the sales person and suggests that the sales person is basically facilitating the sales process and helping the customer to understand the sales process. The Process close simply asks the sales person to suggest to the customer that if they are interested in the product or service and " Think" that they may want to move forward that there is a process that needs to be followed and that the sales person wants to make sure that the customer does not get surprised and is well informed.

It goes something like this.

Sales Person: Well Mr. Stay Well, it appears that you are interested in our Spring Well mattress and box spring, am I on target? If you think that you may want to purchase the mattress I should let you know what the process is. (This works well if you are selling items that people do not buy every day like cars, houses, beds and furniture). The first step in the process is that you pick out what you like, then check to see if we have some in stock (opportunity for the take away close) and then you can put down a deposit and I can set up the delivery. The delivery times are set up first come first serve (urgency close). So if you think there is a chance that you will want to have this by this weekend, then we should start the process now. How does that sound to you?

I like the next step close because the process not the salesperson is putting the pressure on the customer to make a decision.

The Next Step close

I call this one the next logical step close. It is very close to the process close but with this twist: When using the Next Step close you make sure that it is the next logical step for the customer, not you. Sometimes getting the check is really not the next thing the customer needs to do to get to the point where he or she is ready to make a commitment. This close also works well as a trial close. It goes something like this:

Sales Person: Well Mrs. Stay Fit, I can see that you like the model K mountain bike, is that right? And you want to purchase one for you and your husband, right? And you want to make sure that your husband will be comfortable with your choice? It sounds like the next step here is to let your husband have a chance to get excited about the bike like you have. Can I make a suggestion? Why don't we bring a couple of bikes to your home and let you two ride them around for a while and see how you both like your decision? (puppy dog close). To set that up the next step is to set up the delivery, when should I do that for you? (next step close).

As you can see, many of these closes can be used in conjunction with one another to really power up your closing efforts.

The Columbo Close

OK, you have probably realized by now that I love closing. It is fun and I love the challenge. This is my all time favorite close. Now remember that the reason you ask for a close is not to get a yes but to get all the no's so you can get to the yes. Sometimes it is not easy for you to get into a situation where the customer feels comfortable to tell you why they are not yet ready to make a decision. Sometimes customers have not taken the time to really figure out for themselves exactly what is holding them back from making a decision. Sometimes the store or the shop is not the right place for them to express their feelings. They may have their guard up when they are on your turf.

For all these reasons and probably a whole bunch more, the Columbo close is a real neat tool. Basically the Columbo close works just like old Columbo did in his hit series that millions watched in the 70s. Columbo was a curious investigator who delighted in disarming the people he was investigating by casually asking questions and portraying himself as a very friendly and somewhat slow cop. He would ask questions about everything under the sun and most of the time the questions seemed to be unrelated to the case which very often irritated the person being investigated.

Then at some point, Columbo would say goodbye and head for the door. The person being investigated would seem to relax as he or she felt the trial by irrelevant questioning was over. It was at that moment that Columbo would use his trademark tactic of stopping at the open door and say: "I have just one more question." Then he would ask a very direct question related to the crime and some condemning piece of information or evidence and ask for an explanation.

As you might expect, the person being investigated was usually very surprised and unprepared and, to everyone's amazement, would give away something that he or she had not wanted to give up. In some cases it would be a stuttering or a look of embarrassment or sometimes a real juicy fact that had heretofore been kept hidden.

Let me give you an example how this might work in the selling process. A year or so ago I had a customer who had asked me to give him a proposal to provide Sales Training for his company. I quickly responded to his request and then was surprised that he did not act on it and send it back signed with a deposit. In fact he did not even give me a real reason for not acting. He simply said he did not have time to get to it and would let me know when he was ready.

This is where old Columbo comes in. One evening I was in the office and decided to call my friend. He was a hard worker and I knew he would be in the office late. I was right and I reached him after a couple of rings. I told him I was just touching base and then proceeded to ask him about everything under the sun except our pending agreement. I asked about his job and his family and how things were. We talked for 10 to 15 minutes and had a nice chat. I said I was going to sign off and say goodbye and he did the same.

Just before I hung up the phone, I said: "Bill (not his real name), I have a question. Why are you holding off on signing the training agreement? He then replied: "You know, I feel the price is too high and I do not have that much in my budget." I replied: "You know, I am confused. When we talked and you shared what your numbers were, we discussed the budget on a per person basis and you thought it sounded right." Bill then said: "Let me look at that again. I have your agreement right here." Lo and behold, he looked at it again and decided right on the spot that he could live with the number and gave his approval to go ahead.

Now I realize that this may sound a little tricky but remember my first rule: Always have integrity in every aspect of selling. That rule still applies here. I think this technique, used correctly, can really help the customer by giving him or her an opportunity to think about and verbalize the reason or reasons he or she has been holding back or postponing a decision. So you could say that this technique, like all of these closing techniques, is just a tool we have at our disposal to help the sales process and the customer get to where he or she wants to go and get the service, product or help that he or she needed.

Every professional salesperson should know several different closes

These are just a few examples of closes and there are many more. I am always surprised when I conduct sales training to find that many salespeople have not taken the time to learn and master these important tools. Now, I am not suggesting that these closing techniques will replace VALUE MATCH selling but I do believe that closing is an important part of the process and the more comfortable a salesperson is with closing and asking for the close the more successful he or she will be.

I can think of at least two reasons. First, studies show that most customers need to be asked to make a decision at least 4 to 5 times before they buy. They can either be asked by you or by your competitors. You can make the choice. Second, if you have determined that you would like it to be by you, then you will need to be prepared to ask in a few different ways, don't you think?

It might be a little silly if you used the same approach more than once. I made the commitment early in my own sales career to learn and master at least ten closing techniques. I did this by learning them one at a time. I would memorize the words and then commit to using the specific close for the next several weeks. It was painful at first, but as I continued to practice each close in real life situations, I began to get more comfortable and then soon changed a word or two to make it fit my style and personality. Today, I can rattle off more than 20 different closes and I am comfortable using them when the time arises. Remember, learn as many closes as you can and get to the point where you are comfortable using them on demand. It will be a real asset.

> "Every professional salesperson should know several different closes"

Don't Forget To Listen

Even though you feel you are winding down the process to a successful close, it is important that you continue to In fact, it is probably more important than ever and you need to be on high alert if you don't want to lose the sale so close to the end. We've all had the terrible experience while fishing of almost having the trophy fish in the boat and then losing it because of inattention.

For example, often the customer's stated objection isn't the real objection. Keep your customer talking. Keep (politely) probing for hidden objections. Question your customer. Clarify what has been said. Restate what has been said to make sure you're on the same page. Make certain you understand the real objection and the values associated with that objection. That's what the VALUE MATCH forms are all about. Then you can move on to handling the objection and getting it out of the way of your close.

Also remember, if the objection is something you can touch, something physical, it's outside the circle of trust. That means you're working outside too and you have to work your way back in. Inside the circle is where all the real action takes place. That's the territory of the VALUE MATCH sales professional.

Also remember, being a master at closing will not replace being able to pass the closing test. If you:

1. Do not believe that the product or service is the best solution for the customer.
2. Have not made a firm recommendation
3. Have not really connected to the customer and have not established real trust
4. Have not suggested the next appropriate step for Them not You,

Then all the closing techniques in the world won't make a difference.

"If you can touch it you are in trouble"

In my experience, when a sale is not going as well as I think it should, I ask myself these important questions—and give honest answers. More often than not, I can't pass this test and I need to go back to the basics to get things back on track.

In the next chapter, we will look at objections and how to handle them. We will learn that most objections are good things, and how the majority of objections are actually not expressed and, when they are expressed, they are lies of various kinds, designed to try to hide the customer's real issues and protect him or her from having to make a decision.

VALUE CHECK

- If all the steps of the sales process are followed properly and in order, the closing should be so easy as to seem effortless.
- During the latter part of your presentation, focus on two goals: (1) Help your customer take the next action step, and (2) Uncover your customer's fears so that you can continue to keep the process moving forward.
- If you can't answer the following questions correctly, you can't close: (1) Do I believe in what I am doing? (2) Have I built trust with my customer? (3) How deeply do I feel that my recommendation is the specific solution my customer needs? (4) Have I suggested the next, best and appropriate action step?
- When you don't make the effort to close, your customer is left with two thoughts: (1) You don't care about solving their problem and/or (2) you aren't confident about your product or service.
- The faster you fail, the faster you succeed.
- Closing isn't the end, it is the beginning of a relationship.
- After you ask for the close, wait for the answer. Don't talk your customer out of a sale you've already made.
- Make sure you arrange to have enough time to close the sale.
- Objections are good.
- Listen, really listen, to your customer all the way through the sales process. Always be alert for "yellow lights" and hidden objections.

Inherently, each one of us has the substance within to achieve whatever our goals and dreams define. What is missing from each of us is the training, education, knowledge and insight to utilize what we already have.

— Mark Twain

CHAPTER TWELVE:

HANDLING OBJECTIONS

*Objections are a common element in any culture.
Courtroom lawyers raise objections to the statements
of competing lawyers. Theater audiences object
when films break during a showing.
And prospects object to what salespeople tell them.*

—Robin Peterson

*Handling objections is the art of gentle persuasion.
You must appeal to the person's gentler side,
his emotions and feeling. Tug at his heartstrings
since once the heart agrees, the head has to give way.*

—Ajay Arora

It's Zinger Time!

Values Unlocked In This Chapter

In this chapter, we take a close look at objections and how to handle them. We learn that most objections are good things, and how the majority of objections are actually lies that cover up the real fears the customer has to move forward. Among the values unlocked in this chapter are:

- **That most objections are lies or cover ups of customer fears**
- **Minor and major objections**
- **How objections are a good thing**
- **The Triangulate Method of handling objections**
- **When to start handling objections**
- **The Feel, Felt, Found Method**
- **The third party testimonial**
- **Five objection-handling tips**
- **Handling five common objections**

Allied with closing as a fearful experience in the minds of many salespeople is the task of handling objections. In every sales training I have ever done I am alerted right up front that one of the most important issues the sales people have trouble with is overcoming objections. If you feel this way, I want you to reorient your thinking about this important subject.

In this chapter, you'll learn how to understand which objections are really a problem, which ones can actually help you make the sale, and which ones are a helpful warning sign that you need to regroup and patch up a mistake you may have made along the way.

Objections can be a positive part of the sales process and in fact can be a helpful road sign in the sales process to let you know how and if you should proceed. You just need to learn how to recognize and work with the different types. In this chapter I will show you how to recognize the nuances of objections and how to learn and practice specific, proven methods for overcoming them and closing the sale.

I am going to let you in on a little secret: I am going to tell you how to overcome any objection. In fact, I am going to show you how you can use the VALUE MATCH skills you have been learning and hopefully practicing to set it up so the customer tells you how to overcome their own objection.

You see, the customer always knows exactly what the question is and what the answer to that question is. The skilled salesperson's role is to help them go through the process of verbalizing the real objection and their answer to it. You will know when this works because you will say something like: *"That is a great idea! You mean, if I can do that then you would be willing to move forward?"*

Does this sound fun? Well, trust me, it is. What do you say we get started?

What Are Objections? LIES

Let's start with a definition.

The first and most important thing that you always want to remember about objections is that the initially expressed objections are always a LIE. As in: not the truth! Now I know this may surprise and even offend some of you, so let me explain. These lies or untruths fall into at several categories and are used for different reasons.

The first category and probably the one with the smallest number in it is the real lie. It is the objection offered with no real truth to it and designed by the customer merely as a negotiating tool to see if you will take the bait. It is usually tendered as a negotiating method in the hopes that you will get nervous and change the deal in favor of the customer. This might consist of telling the salesperson that he's found a Whatchamacallit at a better price when he knows full well he's done no such thing.

The second type of objection is more common and is used by a customer simply because he or she has not really thought through what the real reason for feeling uncomfortable. So the customer says the first thing that comes to mind which usually is on the surface: "Oh, I've decided we really don't need one after all. Not at that price."

The third and most common lie is used when the customer does not want to share the real objection because he or she feels it exposes a vulnerability. Customers know that salespeople are trained to overcome objections and will overcome theirs if they tell you the truth. So they lie and toss out a false objection to cover the real one. This commonly occurs when a customer is concerned about being able to afford something but doesn't want the salesperson to know about those kinds of problems and thus starts to make objections related to a perceived product or service fault.

The biggest challenge salespeople face in overcoming objections is that they make the mistake of taking what is said and immediately trying to overcome it. Naturally, this is not going to work because you cannot overcome something that does not exist. Something that is a lie.

Let me share an example: Mary has listened to Bob the salesman tell her about the newest vacuum cleaner model in a demonstration in her home. Bob is excited because Mary has been very quiet which he interprets as giving him buying signals. So he goes in for the close and says: "Well, Mary, I can leave this with you if you can give me a check for the special sales price of $250. What do you think?" Mary: "I need to think about it."

> "The biggest challenge salespeople face in overcoming objections is the mistake of taking what is said and immediately trying to overcome it"

Bob has been trained to overcome this objection and launches into his technique of telling Mary that many people he has shown this to have felt this way and they eventually come around and then been sorry they did not do it sooner. Especially as the special price might go higher.

Mary seems unimpressed. The challenge is that Mary does not really need to think about it. Mary knows exactly how she feels. She wants to go to the appliances store and check out what their prices are and what features they have to offer and compare. She does not want to tell Bob because she wants to do this and does not want him to interfere.

Bob, on the other hand, could easily get Mary to tell him the truth with a very simple technique. You guessed it. Use his VALUE MATCH Listening Skills and say: "Mary, I heard you say you need to think about it, is that right? What do you mean by think about it?" If Mary has some trust in Bob, she will probably tell Bob the truth and then Bob can use his skill to help her work through the need to do some more shopping.

It sounds simple doesn't it? It is and, in this chapter, we will give you several more ideas how to recognize and overcome objections. But just remember …. Objections are always LIES. If you keep that in mind, you will be fine. If you are not convinced yet just walk through the exercise below and see how it comes out. Then try it out on some others you know, and I believe you will understand this principle.

1. Think of a decision you were asked to make recently that you said "no" to.
2. Think of what you gave as the reason for saying "no".
3. Now think of the real reason: What were your true feelings at the time?
4. Ask yourself why you did not give the person the real reason.

There are some rules of the road we need to visit before we go too far or get too deep here. We have just covered the fact that most if not all objections are at the very least cover-ups of the real issues. Taking that into consideration we need to be sure to get to the bottom of any objection, to get to the real objection, before we attempt to work on or overcome it. We will work on this more towards the end of this chapter.

Another way of looking at this: The first objection to surface is a **minor objection**. In reality, it's just a way for a customer to stall your presentation. That's not necessarily a problem. Sometimes a customer just needs a few extra minutes to consider some point of your presentation. These minor objections can often be handled quite easily provided you allow your customer the breathing space he or she needs.

An excellent way to handle an objection of this type is to postpone the answer and to reassure the customer: "I'll address that very point a bit later in my presentation. Is that okay with you?" You'll discover that, as you continue through your presentation, the objection often disappears.

The second type of objection is called a **major objection or a condition**. This is an obstacle that you cannot overcome. Or can only overcome with great difficulty. For example, if your customer just doesn't have or can't get enough money to buy your product or service, you can't close the sale at that point. If you're about to sell a house, but your customer is suddenly called up by the military for a year's service overseas, you've probably run into a major obstacle.

Remember: That doesn't mean you can ignore it. Ignoring an objection, no matter how minor or trivial you might feel it is, is a surefire way of losing a sale. Just remember a minor objection is one you can answer. So… just handle it.

Let's end this section with a brief summing up of some key points:
- **When a customer objects, he or she has a question or may have concerns**
- **An objection is something that, if not handle properly, can stall the sales process**
- **A customer's objections and concerns are a normal part of the buying process**
- **Objections and concerns are part of the psychology of decision making**
- **Objections are usually questions or requests for more information.**
- **How the salesperson handles this stage of the sales process often dramatically affects the success or failure of the sale**
- **Salespersons frequently here objections when presenting solutions to the customer.**
- **Objections can, however, occur at any time during the sales process. So, be prepared to handle objections effectively at any time**

- **Salespeople need to remember that the customer is much more likely to believe himself or herself so you should attempt to help them answer the objections themselves**
- **Objections are a good thing! Don't be surprised or taken aback by an objection. Be happy. Customers don't volunteer objections unless you have attempted to close and they are seriously thinking of buying.**

Objections Are Good!

"Objections are an essential part of every presentation you make"

You want them. You can't do your job, helping your customer, without them. Objections are an essential part of every presentation you make. Even though they can sometimes prove to be a challenge, the VALUE MATCH salesperson actually embraces objections because they are such a powerful force in helping close the sale. It's like clearing the air after a storm.

When one of your customers raises an objection, he or she has a question or some concern about your product, service or perhaps your presentation. It should be treated with that level of respect, but with only the normal level of fear or concern. If you panic, act flustered or show frustration, you can actually create the thing you fear most – a lost sale.

If not handled properly, a minor objection can stall the sales process, sometimes indefinitely. How you handle objections will affect every aspect of your presentation from the moment the objection is brought up. Whether disaster happens or you effectively address the concern is really up to you and how you react to the request for information. More than anything else, the difference between a stalled or lost sale and a successful continuation of your presentation is your

Never forget that objections are an expected part of the sales process. They're just a part of the psychology of decision-making. You can't avoid them and, in fact, you shouldn't even try. While they may occur at any time during your presentation and you should be prepared to answer them at any time. You will hear them most often, however, while you are presenting solutions: "Well, yes, Mr. Salesperson, but we don't want to spend that much money… We don't have enough time… We're just not ready today …" and on.

Play Lead The Follower

Whenever possible, lead your customer so that he or she will provide the answer to his or her own objection. You can learn to do this with a little practice. The advantage is that, when the customer supplies the answer to the objection, No matter how sincere you may be, no matter how persuasive, no matter how much trust you've built, customers believe themselves more than they believe salespeople. Don't be offended by that. It's just common human psychology. Don't work against it. Work with it.

Don't be surprised or let them throw you. Expect and be prepared to address them. Think of objections as gifts, gifts of valuable information that you can use to help your customer obtain the product or service he or she needs.

Handling Objections With The Triangulate Method

Of course, there are all types of ways for handling and overcoming objections. Every sales and marketing textbook includes a list and a Google of the Internet will bring up literally thousands of web sites devoted to the subject. And I'm sure these are all valid ways of doing it.

But one method for handling and overcoming objections called the "Triangulate Method" has proved particularly adaptable to VALUE MATCH principles. In this situation you create a triangle of yourself, your customer and the objection. Once the key or true objection is identified, you "join the customer's team" to help him or her resolve the issue. Below is a graphic of the "Triangulate Method."

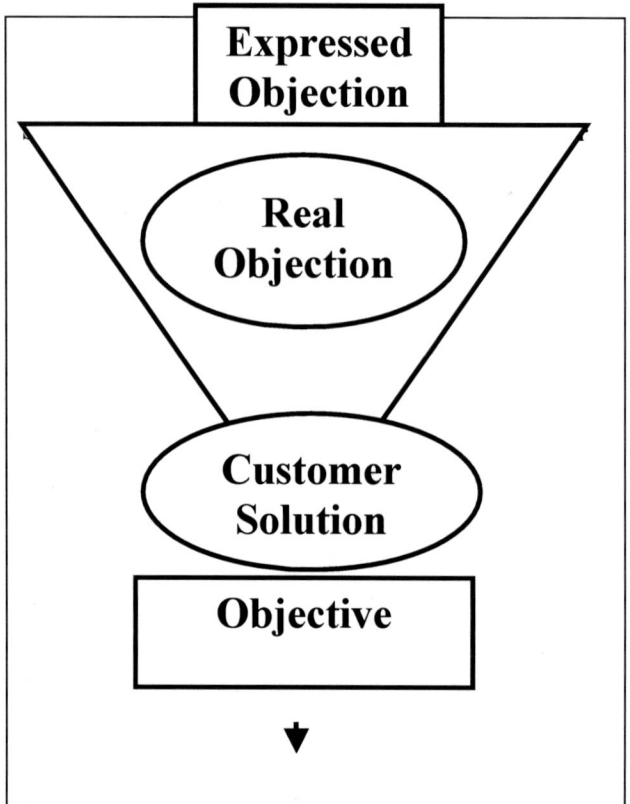

The Triangulate Method for Resolving Objections.

One of the reasons we like to employ the Triangulate Method is because customers are often very vague about the words they use. They usually know what they mean or what they want to say, but we might be left uncertain. Salespeople need to use their questioning skills to clarify the customer's central objection.

Here's part of a presentation to show you how it works. In this case, a customer is seeking an assisted living facility for his mother, a very important and delicate decision to be making. Definitely not widget country! Let's see how our VALUE MATCH salesperson uses the Triangulate Method to handle the objections.

CUSTOMER: I can't imagine how anyone could be happy in such a small apartment.

SALESPERSON: If I hear you correctly, you're asking about how anyone could be happy in such a small apartment? Is that right?

CUSTOMER: Yes.

SALESPERSON: What do you mean by that?

CUSTOMER: I just don't see how we could get all of mom's furniture in that small apartment.

SALESPERSON: So, you don't know how you could get all of your mom's furniture in the apartment. Is that right?

CUSTOMER: Yes, that's exactly right.

> "What's the simplest and most direct way to get an answer? Ask a question!

[Realize that there could be and probably are multiple concerns, which could affect the closing of your sale. These must be (1) discovered, (2) prioritized, and (3) addressed. Which of all the objections are the most important? Which is the single most important objection? Again, all you really have to do is ask intelligent questions and then listen to what your customer tells you.]

SALESPERSON: You've expressed a number of concerns today. Two seem to be most important to you: price and apartment size. Do I have that right?

CUSTOMER: Yes, I'd say those are the "big two."

SALESPERSON: Of the two, which would you say is most important?

CUSTOMER: Both. I'm concerned about each.

SALESPERSON: If there were one concern more important to you than the other, which would that be?

CUSTOMER: Well, if push comes to shove, I'd have to say the size is my biggest concern. As I mentioned, I am not sure if my mom can get all of her furniture in the apartment.

[Professional salespeople are communicators. We know, understand and are skilled at using words. Most customers aren't trained communicators. They may be experts in their fields, but words usually aren't their tools of the trade. They aren't always as precise or as informative as we'd like them to be. They may be sure of their meaning, but the way they may have expressed that meaning could easily leave you in the dark. Again, this is where your questioning skills come in to play. Clarify what you have just heard to make sure you have pinpointed the central objection. In our example, the salesperson has identified the size of the apartment as the chief objection. Notice how our salesperson keeps questioning.]

SALESPERSON: How do you feel she will manage the transition from a big house to the apartment we just visited?

CUSTOMER: I think it'll be tough. She has so many lovely things she'd like to bring with her.

SALESPERSON: So you think the transition will be difficult because she has so many lovely things. I certainly understand. So many of our residents have lovely things in their rooms. Your concern really is about having room for some of her things. Is that right?

CUSTOMER: Yes.

[]SALESPERSON: I realize that it is important for you and your mom that she have enough room to have some of her nice things. What ideas do you have about what we can we do to make you feel more comfortable with this situation?

Customer: Well, if you could help us figure out how much we can actually get into the apartment and help us find out what to do with the things we cannot bring, that would be very helpful.

Sales person: That is a great idea. I think we can help with that and, if we do that, are you prepared to move forward?

Customer: If you can provide that help, then we are ready to move forward.

If handled properly, the Triangulate Method can be extremely effective, especially when combined with VALUE MATCH strategies and tactics. But you have to practice. You have to be patient and completely focused on your customer. You have to really listen to everything your customer tells you with the same level of intensity that you use during the Building Rapport and Developing Needs phase.

Remember that not every single objection can be overcome. The success rate can never be 100%. There will always be the objection or obstacle that no salesperson could possible expect (military service, for example, or your customer's sudden bankruptcy). But, by using the Triangulate Method, you will handle any objection that can be overcome.

Here are several other objection-handling methods that a trained VALUE MATCH salesperson can use:

The Feel-Felt-Found Method

Salesperson Say that you understand how he or she feels that way if you were placed in that position.

Why? It is virtually impossible and very presumptuous to claim to know how someone else feels. Even if you and the customer have experienced similar situations, your reaction and theirs may be entirely different. By stating that you could understand how they feel you are not only showing compassion, but you are showing that you truly do respect the personal experiences and their reaction to such experiences.

Cavalry-To-The-Rescue Method

Sometimes a customer just keeps bringing up objections. No matter how many you answer successfully, no matter how well you answer them, and even if you've backtracked to make sure you haven't skipped an important step, they just keep coming. At moments like these, it's time to bring in the cavalry – in the shape of an independent third-party testimonial.

This is one of the most powerful and effective techniques available for overcoming objections. But it requires planning, coordination and a respect for the time of the third party. This third party can be your sales manager or one of your most satisfied customers. You want an outside expert, someone not involved directly in your sales process, to support your statements.

Bring in or call up the "cavalry" and let this person speak directly with your customer. Encourage him or her to ask the tough questions and not to hold back. You have one shot using this technique, so don't waste it by allowing your customer to be timid. Once the outside expert has answered the objection, you then ask for the order.

When To Begin Handling Objections

The key is to know your product, your customer and your competition. That way, you'll be prepared when the inevitable objection comes up. Thus prepared, you'll be able to anticipate many of the objections that customers will bring up throughout the process—and even some most customers wouldn't think of raising!

Of course, every salesperson can't overcome every objection every time. Some objections just can't be overcome: "Well, Miss Salesperson, I should have mentioned this earlier, but we really can't afford anything right now. We're just shopping around so we can buy when our money situation improves."

If further research shows that statement to be true, stop the sales process and move on to a real customer, someone you really can help. Obviously, you will disengage with appropriate respect and courtesy. Not only is that the decent thing to do, but your failed prospect of today may acquire enough money at some point to actually become a customer of the future. Also, even someone who can't afford to make a purchase can be a source of referrals.

Five Tips On Handling Objections

Here are some handy tips that can help you handle and overcome objections—and seal the deal:

- **Tip #1:** Make sure your customer has stated his or her real objection and not a minor objection. Use the VALUE MATCH Communication Model to help ferret out this information.
- **Tip #2:** After you've made efforts to address the objection, ask for the close again. Be patient. You may have to do this as many as three or four times before you and your customer are comfortable moving toward the next step.
- **Tip #3:** If you're encountering too many objections, that's a sure sign that you probably have skipped a step somewhere in the process. Above-average resistance means it's time to backtrack,

find out where the problem is, and address it before you attempt to move on again.
- **Tip #4:** If the primary objection is a feature, that is, if it is physical and something you can touch, then you have not discovered your customer's real values. Again, backtrack and determine your customer's real values.
- **Tip #5:** Before attempting to address any objection, make sure you know the objection. For any number of good and not-so-good reasons, many customers keep these hidden. Or at least they keep them hidden until they can spring them on you at an unexpected moment. Keep the VALUE MATCH Model in mind: listen, question, restate, and clarify.

How To Answer Five Common Objections

Here are some ideas for handling the five most common objections. You hear these across the board, in all industries and in all situations. Keep in mind there's no such thing as a "pat" answer for a given objection. Learn these answers and then adapt them to your individual business, your individual style and, most importantly, to your individual customer.

Objection #1: No immediate need

> "Well, I'll have to talk this over with my husband (wife, significant other, co-workers, boss, family, etc.). This is such a big decision, you know."

To answer this objection, review all your qualifying information, especially the urgency of need. Did you assess the need accurately? Is there something you missed? Do you need to backtrack and cover some important details? After your mental review, act accordingly and press on.

Objection #2: Customer questions quality of your product or service

> "Look, I'll be straight with you. I've checked around, and word on the street has it your company is rated rather poorly."

That's pretty straight-forward, and you should welcome that kind of openness. It's much easier to address than some of the wishy-washy and unfocused questions put out by your more timid customers. With the latter you sometimes have to struggle to get a completely honest answer. Like pulling teeth. The main thing to remember is that, if quality is a problem, you have to discover it. Get it out in the open.

Remember also that people buy based on emotion and justify later with the facts. What you are really dealing with here is perceived value and quality. Perceived value is important to the equation and perceived quality is a major component of value.

Here's how you build a strategy for handling this objection. First, honestly assess the quality of your product. Know fully your strengths and what may be perceived as weaknesses so you can discuss each in a positive way. Learn how to turn those perceptions into reality. Two, really know your competition. Evaluate how you stack up against them point-by-point, feature-by-feature, and benefit-by-benefit. You should be able to do this with your eyes shut. The less you know, the easier it is for you to be blindsided; the more you know, the more you can be prepared for any objection. Third, clearly understand what feelings the customer has about the quality and what the real objection is before you attempt to overcome it.

Objection #3: Your customer has found another option

> **"We're really impressed with what you've got here. But we believe XYZ Company is better for our specific needs."**

Customers usually have lots of options, especially these days when the Internet has opened up a true worldwide marketplace. Smart customers shop around—both in person and by phone or Internet searches. That's only wise. And, face it, you do it too with your own purchases. Sometimes, during their searches, they'll come across a product or service that they believe makes a better choice than your own.

The first step is to list all the options your customer has. Or get him or her to list them. Once that's done, explain in appropriate detail why your product is the best or why it at least merits serious consideration. Step two is to know your competition inside and out. Once you know their strengths and weaknesses you can compensate with your own. Again, this requires a lot of knowledge and a salesperson who isn't afraid to do his or her homework.

Objection #4: Customers say they lack the funds.

> "Don't think for a second we don't like your offering. We love it, really! But I'm afraid we'll have to go for something a bit more in our price range."

Sometimes this is a legitimate concern, but generally this objection hides a deeper and more serious concern. They make a somewhat embarrassing statement about not having enough money to hide an objection that is even more difficult to discuss. When you hear this objection, you're probably hearing someone looking for an easy way out of the sales presentation. (But first make sure you determine whether or not money is a real issue.)

You have to get your customer to bring up and discuss this hidden objection. Otherwise, there's no way you can address it. First, review the financial qualifying information, then think back on your customer's responses during your presentation. (This is where the VALUE MATCH and Balanced Scorecard forms come in handy). Did you miss a clue that price is a serious issue? Were there any hints at a deeper, hidden concern? What questions can you use to discover this vital information?

Objection #5: The timing isn't right

> "We're not ready to make a buying decision right now."

When you hear something like this, it could be a clue that you've pushed to your close too quickly. Your customer isn't ready yet to become a purchaser. Maybe you've caught them a bit off guard and they're feeling defensive. Perhaps they suddenly think you're just going for a sale rather than trying to solve their problem. Maybe you've just rushed ahead and left them behind. They might just be lost somewhere back in the process.

Always assess the situation throughout your presentation. When is the best time for the next step? When is the appropriate moment to close? Am I being too pushy? Are they ready for the close right now?

Assess yourself as well as your performance. Am I trying too hard to be Salesperson of the Month? Am I helping a customer, or shooting for a bonus? Have other customers felt I'm being pushy? What's my true motive in this specific situation?

As you can see, there's a simple method to handling any of the most common types of objections customers can throw at you. Once you've learned how to do this effectively, the number of deals you close successfully will increase exponentially.

In the next chapter, we'll wrap everything up, put it all in perspective, and send you out to do your stuff as a fully qualified VALUE MATCH salesperson. That means someone who can sell himself or herself—be it in a business or personal relationship.

Balance ScoreCard™
ValueMatch™ Process

"Make Money"
Goal: **Finalize the Close**

Successfully completing these important skills and tactics with a prospect can <u>help the salesperson finalize the close</u>" during the ValueMatch™ Process. Circle the score for each task accomplished, and total the score at the bottom.

1	Summarize the customer's situation. Empathize and gain agreement.
1	Summarize the customer's urgency. Reconfirm urgency and tie to action step.
1	Summarize the hot buttons for location, amenities, neighborhood, and home.
1	Throughout summary, confirm what you have identified as "hot" really holds an interest to the customer. At closing, confirm you did indeed find what they wanted in a specific home!
	Note: Closing Strategy: Be prepared to ask the prospect to move forward and take the next step in the process at least three times.
	Optional Closing Questions
1	Optional Question 1: If indeed I have shown you a house that meets the criteria we have discussed, can you think of any reason not to take the next step in the process?
1	Optional Question 2: Is there anything you can think of that we have left out that would keep you from moving forward?
1	Optional Question 3: Are there any questions you have or information I need to clarify in order for you to move forward?
	Note: Stalling Strategy: If you have asked for the close at least three times and listened through each objection, and the prospect still feels they need to take more time, be prepared to come to an agreement on the next step (i.e. Offer to provide information that would be helpful, and set an appointment to meet as soon as appropriate.).
2	Tie Down. "Why don't we start the process to move into your new home?" "The next step of the process is..." "Your earnest money check and a signature is all we will need to get the process started."
	Can you pass the closing test?
	Heart felt
	Recommendation
	To a friend
	To take the next best action step
	Total (max score = 9)

©2006

VALUE CHECK

- Objections are good things.
- There are only two kinds of objections: minor and major. Minor objections are often stalling techniques and can be easily addressed. Major objections are obstacles that cannot be overcome.
- An objection is a request for information.
- Lead your customer so that he or she provides the answer to the objection.
- The Triangulate Method creates a triangle of the salesperson, the customer and the customer's objection. Once the objection is isolated, the sales-person joins the customer's "team" to help come up with a solution.
- Never tell a customer you know how he or she feels. Say you could understand that feeling.
- When objections keep piling up, you may need to call in a third-party testimonial.
- Handling objections begins immediately, during the building rapport phase of the sales process.
- Five tips for handling objections are: (1) Make sure your customer has stated his or her real objection and not a minor objection. (2) After you've made efforts to address the objection, ask for the close again. (3) Above-average resistance means it's time to backtrack, find out where the problem is, and address it before you attempt to move on again. (4) If the primary objection is a feature, then you have not discovered your customer's real values. Backtrack and determine your customer's real values. (5) Before attempting to address any objection, make sure you know the *real* objection.
- To answer the "no immediate need" objection, review all your qualifying information, especially the urgency of need
- To answer an objection about the quality of your product or service, assess the quality of your product and know your competition.

- To answer the "found another option" objection, list all the options your customer has and explain why yours is the best or why it merits serious consideration. Then know your competition inside and out so you can compensate for strengths and weaknesses.
- To address a customer who says he or she doesn't have the funds to make the purchase, review the financial qualifying information, then think back on your customer's responses during your presentation to see if you missed an important clue.

If you don't sell, it's not the product that's wrong, it's you.

—**Estée Lauder**

The VALUE MATCH Sales Model

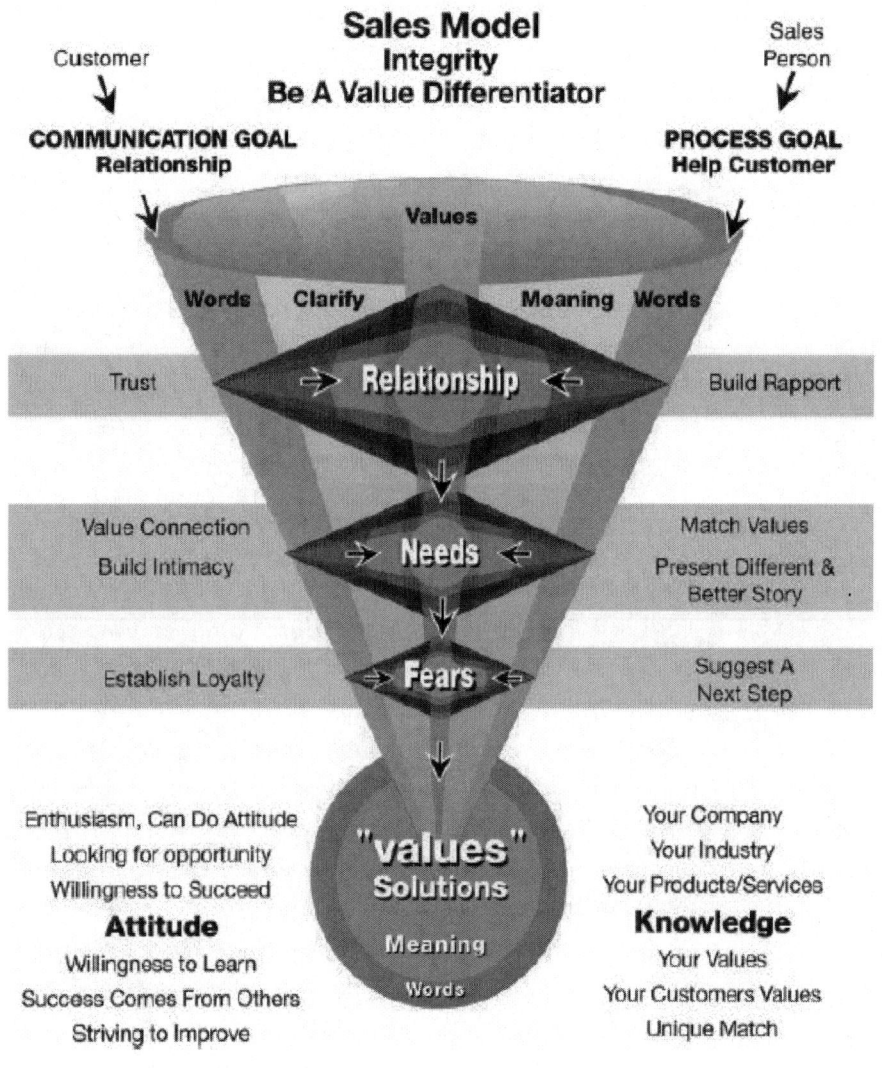

AFTERWORD

There you have it: I have guided you through the VALUE MATCH process step-by-step. Together, we have taken the journey leading to a deeper understanding of what it means to communicate with another person on a level beyond the surface one, beyond the level where "Everybody Lies!" Together, we have tried to keep in mind the question that set the entire journey off: What is it that keeps individuals from reaching their full potential?

As you have seen, the steps are simple, easy to learn and just as easy to apply. I promised at the very start that this would be a simple process but also a revolutionary one and I think I kept that promise: simple and revolutionary. But at the end of the process (which, by the way, is really only the beginning of the journey), we have seen how the taking of each individual step leads to new and expanded vistas, to new ways of looking at the world around you. We have seen how each step builds on the preceding one and fits into the one following it. And we have seen how the cumulative effect of following each step leads to a revolutionary discovery: the ability to tap into the limitless potential we all have inside of us.

In this book, we have looked in detail at how to use the VALUE MATCH process in the noble profession of selling, the time-honored art of acting as the inter-mediary between the selling and buying of products and services, be they your own or someone else's. We have learned that, in the selling

> "What is it that keeps individuals from reaching their full potential?"

process, the salesperson has to overcome a fundamental truth about the vast majority of human communication: the fact that, as the title says, "Everybody Lies." Everybody speaks in code. Once the salesperson comes to understand that, then he or she is able to come up with the code breaking "equipment" to interpret what the person is really saying and to give that person what he or she <u>REALLY</u> wants, what he or she is <u>REALLY</u> looking for.

The beautiful, wonderful thing about the VALUE MATCH process, however, is that it is not only valuable for use in the selling process. It's not just a one-trick pony that salespeople keep in their library of sales techniques (although every salesperson should definitely keep it close by for reference purposes). It can be used in each and every facet of a person's life. It can be adapted for everything from how to carry on successful job interviews and negotiations, to dating and personal counseling, from efficient interoffice communication to the world of political discourse (especially the world of political discourse!).

Most importantly, the VALUE MATCH process can be used for any type of relationship, be it personal or professional. In the future, it is my sincere hope and desire to be able to lead you through a number of individual relationships using a variation of the VALUE MATCH process introduced here. It is my hope and desire to be able to provide you with the specific, tailor-made code breaking equipment for any communications situation, thus enabling you to lead a life that fulfills its full potential, that makes you proud.

God willing, and if you'll let me.
According to the ancient Chinese proverb:
"A journey of a thousand miles
must begin with a single step."

—John F. Kennedy

VALUEMATCH ™ INQUIRY WORKSHEET

Name _____ Phone # (____) _____
Date of Contact _____ CS Name ___ _____
What would you like to accomplish on our call today? _____

	Clues (Words)	Definition	Values
Build Rapport	What do you want to accomplish on our call today?		How do you feel about the situation? Empathize/Relate **3**
	Who else in involved in this situation with you?	Who has the responsibility of sorting through the details?	How is that working for you? Empathize/Relate **2**
Build Trust	What do you do for fun? Is there anything else?	Which one is most important to you?	What about _____ is important to you? Empathize/Relate **1**
Discover Urgency	Recap/Summarize **1 2 3** How long have you been involved in your current situation?	What has recently occurred to motivate you to contact us now? What do you mean by that? ****DIG IN**** *Get them to tell the truth*	How do you feel about this? Can you describe the ideal solution?
	Based on what you have shared with me, Mr./Mrs. _____, there is at least 1 community which is a perfect match for you. May I make a suggestion? *Wait for answer* **YES-** We need to get you down here to see it for yourself. What do you think?		**Yes-** *Flip page over* **No-** *Do not turn page over unless customer has expressed agreement to visit.*

© ServiceTRAC, LLC. February 2006

Value Match System

Preferred Guest Getaway- A way for customers to see and experience the community for themselves.
Includes: Discounted hotel room, personalized tour and limited access to community features.

	Clues (Words)	**Situation**	**Solutions**
P/S/L	Summarize customer's ideal solution Ask questions to fill in any gaps (price, style, location)	(Name of community) will fit very nicely. State why using interests, situation and ideal solution.	Why is that going to be important? Tie down (find the best day/date for them to come down)
Closing Posture	Identify day/date of their arrival. If unable, get day/date of return call to schedule a visit.		

Notes:

Next Action Steps:

Objections Expressed:

Name _____
Address _____
　　　　　Number and Street　　　　　　　　　City　　　　　　　　State　　　　Zip Code
Home Phone (____)_____　Cell Phone (____)_____　Work Phone (____)_____
Type of Contact ☐ In-Call ☐ Call-Out　　☐ Email _____

© ServiceTRAC, LLC. February 2006

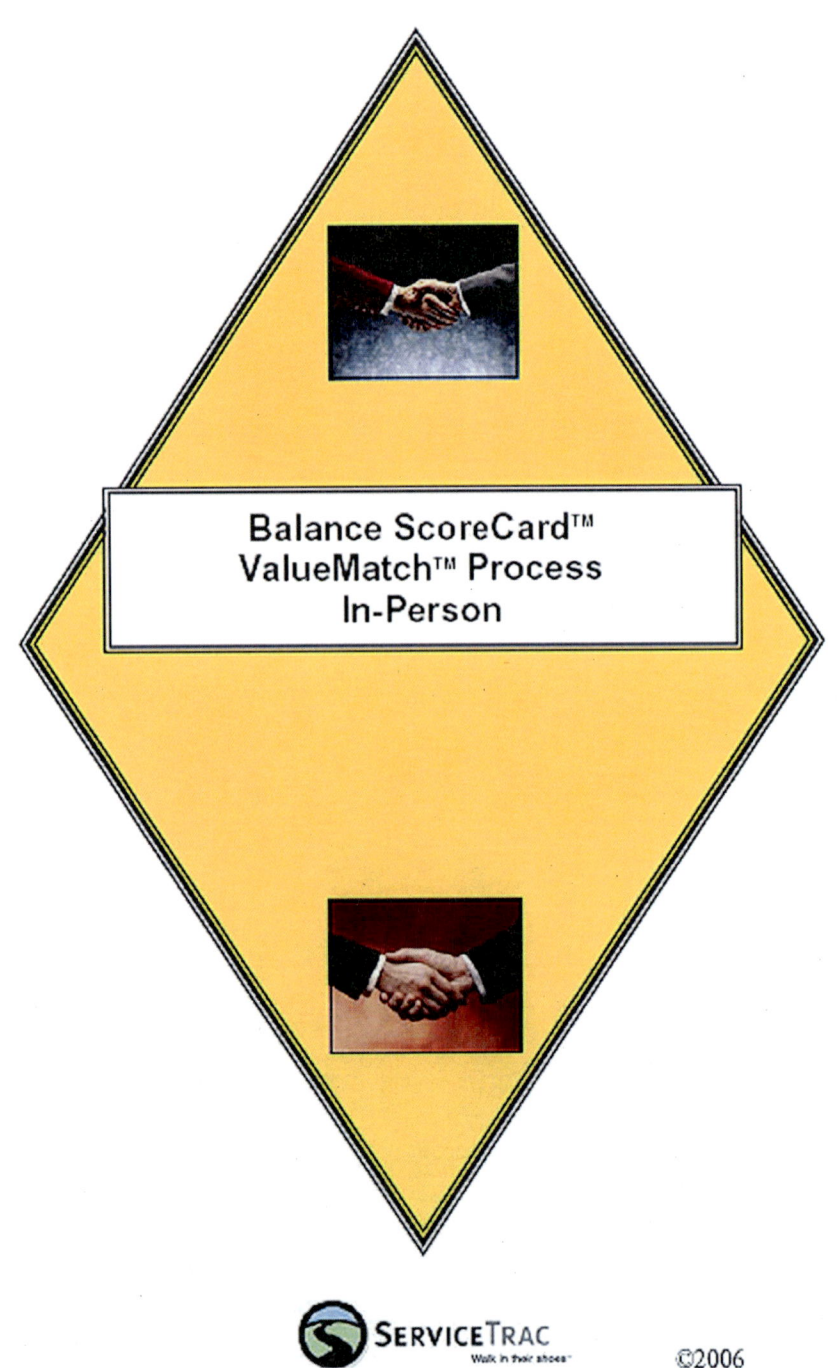

Value Match System

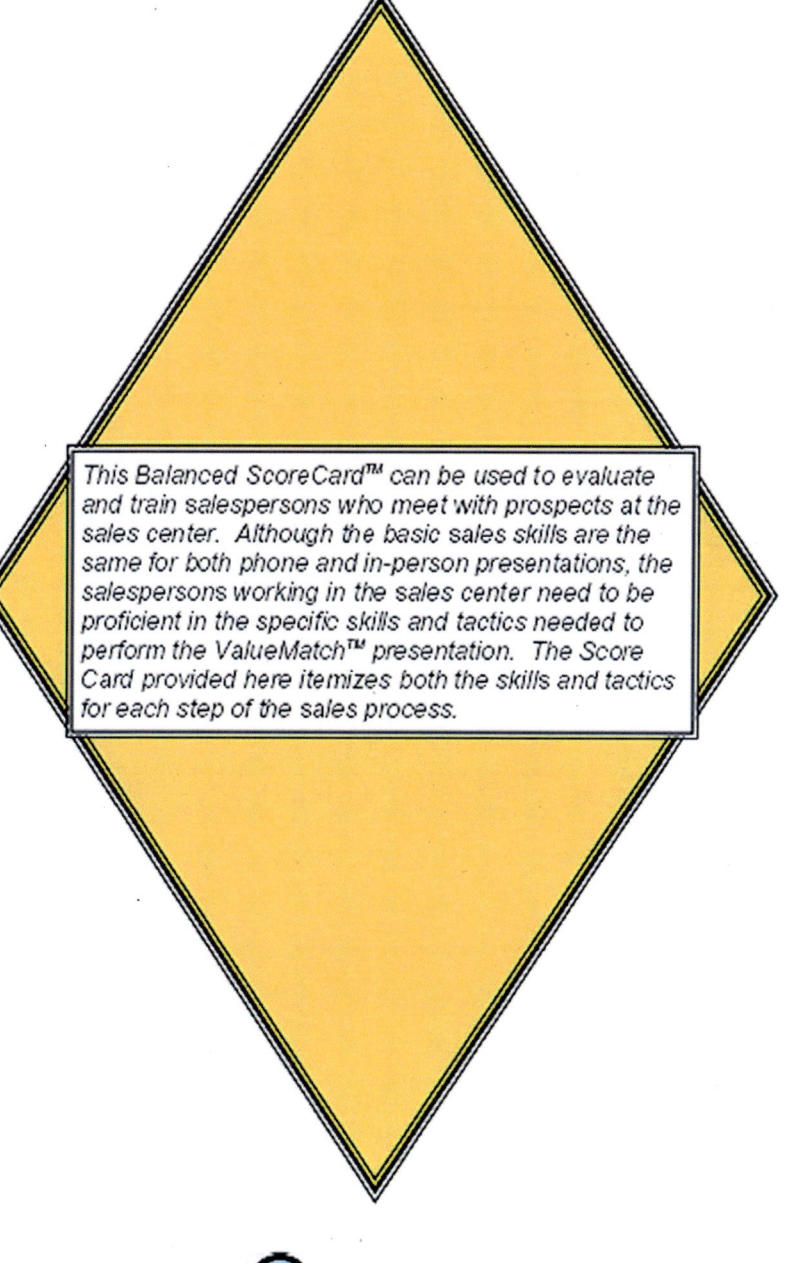

This Balanced ScoreCard™ can be used to evaluate and train salespersons who meet with prospects at the sales center. Although the basic sales skills are the same for both phone and in-person presentations, the salespersons working in the sales center need to be proficient in the specific skills and tactics needed to perform the ValueMatch™ presentation. The Score Card provided here itemizes both the skills and tactics for each step of the sales process.

©2006

Balance ScoreCard™ ValueMatch™ Process

The Greeting
Goal: **To Build Rapport**

Successfully completing these important skills and tactics with a prospect can lead to building <u>stronger rapport and trust</u> during the ValueMatch™ Process. Circle the score for each task if accomplished, and total the score at the bottom.

1	Take notes.
1	Meet at the door (no wait) and shake hands.
1	Make introductions (positive, upbeat, smiling) and carry clipboard and guest card with you.
1	Question: What attracted you to the community?
1	Question: What would you like to accomplish today?
3	Response Skill: "So, <Repeat what is said>. I would be happy to help you with that. Do you mind if I ask a question first?"
1	Option 1: Question: What is your situation? (Listen to the Answer)
3	Response Skill: "So, <Repeat what is said>. How do you feel about the situation?"
1	Listen to the answer and empathize.
2	Tie Down. Move towards the [company] Story Board.
	Overcoming Zingers (Bonus)
1	Identify and repeat the zinger.
1	Ask what is meant by the zinger.
1	Why do you ask <about the zinger>?
1	Answer the zinger remembering that the answer leads back to the process.
	Total (max score=19)

©2006

Balance ScoreCard™
ValueMatch™ Process

The Builder Story
Goal: **To Build Credibility**

Successfully completing these important skills and tactics with a prospect can lead to <u>building credibility</u> during the ValueMatch™ Process. Circle the score for each task accomplished, and total the score at the bottom.

1	Take Notes!	
1	Move towards the [company] Story Board	
1	Question: What do you know about [company]?" "What will be important to you about a builder you select or work with?"	
3	Response Skill: "So, What I hear you saying is <Repeat what is said>. What do you mean by that (use key words or phrases). Repeat answer.	
1	Question: Why is that important to you? (Listen to the Answer)	
3	Response Skill: "ValueMatch" (Relate to what they have just shared to one or more points of the [company] Story.)	
1	Feature #1 (6-8 families move to a [company] community everyday.)	
1	Feature #2 ([company] was voted "America's Best Builder 2004.")	
1	Feature #3 ([company] is the area's largest homebuilder.)	
1	Feature #4 ([company] has been in business for more than 60 years.)	
	Overcoming Zingers (Bonus)	
1	Identify and repeat the zinger.	
1	Ask what is meant by the zinger.	
1	Why do you ask <about the zinger>?	
1	Answer the zinger remembering that the answer leads back to the process.	
2	Tie Down.	
	Total (max score = 20)	

©2006

Balance ScoreCard™ ValueMatch™ Process

The Locator Map
Goal: **To Build Value**

Successfully completing these important skills and tactics with a prospect can lead to <u>building value</u> during the ValueMatch™ Process. Circle the score for each task accomplished, and total the score at the bottom.

1	Take Notes!
1	Move towards the Locator Map.
1	Question: "What will be important to you about the area you move to? What has attracted you to this area?"
3	Response Skill: "So, What I hear you saying is <Repeat what is said>. What do you mean by that (use key words or phrases). Repeat answer.
1	Question: Why is that important to you? (Listen to the Answer)
3	Response Skill: "ValueMatch" (Relate to what they have just shared to one or more of the Area's special features)
1	Area feature #1
1	Area feature #2
1	Area feature #3
1	Area feature #4
2	Tie Down.
	Overcoming Zingers (Bonus)
1	Identify and repeat the zinger.
1	Ask what is meant by the zinger.
1	Why do you ask <about the zinger>?
1	Answer the zinger remembering that the answer leads back to the process.
	Total (max score = 20)

©2006

Balance ScoreCard™
ValueMatch™ Process

The Locator Map (cont.)
Goal: **To Discover Urgency**

Successfully completing these important skills and tactics with a prospect can lead to discovering urgency during the ValueMatch™ Process. Circle the score for each task accomplished, and total the score at the bottom.

1	Take Notes!
1	Question: "How long have you been in your current situation? Or looking for a new home?"
2	Question: What has recently occurred to motivate you to shop or buy now?
3	Response Skill: "So, What I hear you saying is <Repeat what is said>. What do you mean by that (use key words or phrases). Repeat answer. Repeat process.
1	Question: "Why is that important to you" <or> "How do you feel about that?"
1	Response Skill: "So, <Repeat answer and ask>. What is the optimal solution are you looking for?"
3	Response Skill: "ValueMatch" (Relate to what they have just shared to one or more of the special features of your community)
1	Community feature (or optimal solution) #1
1	Community feature (or optimal solution) #2
1	Community feature (or optimal solution) #3
1	Community feature (or optimal solution) #4
2	Tie Down.
	Overcoming Zingers (Bonus)
1	Identify and repeat the zinger.
1	Ask what is meant by the zinger.
1	Why do you ask <about the zinger>?
1	Answer the zinger remembering that the answer leads back to the process.
	Total (max score = 22)

©2006

Balance ScoreCard™
ValueMatch™ Process

The Amenities Board
Goal: Discover Customer Hot Buttons

Successfully completing these important skills and tactics with a prospect can lead to <u>discovering your prospects' hot buttons</u> during the ValueMatch™ Process. Circle the score for each task if completed successfully, and total the score at the bottom.

1	Take Notes!
1	Move towards the Amenities Board.
1	Question: "When you think of amenities, which ones are most important to you?" "What are some of the things you like to do in your spare time?"
3	Response Skill: "So, What I hear you saying is <Repeat what is said> "What do you mean by that?" "Which one is most important to you?"
1	Question: Why is that important to you? (Listen to the Answer)
1	Response Skill: "ValueMatch" (Relate to what they have just shared to one or more of the Amenities)
1	Amenity #1
1	Amenity #2
1	Amenity #3
1	Amenity #4
2	Tie Down. So if you had <repeat the most important amenity> available to you, would that be important
	Overcoming Zingers
1	Identify and repeat the zinger.
1	Ask what is meant by the zinger.
1	Why do you ask <about the zinger>?
1	Answer the zinger remembering that the answer leads back to the process.
	Total (max score = 18)

©2006

Balance ScoreCard™
ValueMatch™ Process
TOPO Overview
Goal: **Discover Most Important Neighborhood Features**

Successfully completing these important skills and tactics with a prospect can lead to <u>discovering what neighborhood features are most important</u> during the ValueMatch™ Process. Circle the score for each task accomplished, and total the score at the bottom.

1	Take Notes!
1	Move towards the Site Board.
1	Question: "What about the neighborhood will be most important to you?" "What type of neighborhood is important to you?"
3	Response Skill: "So, What I hear you saying is <Repeat what is said>. What do you mean by that?
1	Question: Why is that important to you? (Listen to the Answer)
3	Response Skill: "ValueMatch" (Relate to what they have just shared to one or more of the Neighborhood special features)
1	Neighborhood Special Feature #1
1	Neighborhood Special Feature #2
1	Neighborhood Special Feature #3
1	Neighborhood Special Feature #4
2	Tie Down. So, it sounds like we have the type of neighborhood you are looking for. Is that right?
	Overcoming Zingers
1	Identify and repeat the zinger.
1	Ask what is meant by the zinger.
1	Why do you ask <about the zinger>?
1	Answer the zinger remembering that the answer leads back to the process.
	Total (max score = 20)

Page 7

©2006

Balance ScoreCard™
ValueMatch™ Process

The Product
Goal: **Discover Most Important Home Features**

Successfully completing these important skills and tactics with a prospect can lead to <u>discovering what home features are most important</u> during the ValueMatch™ Process. Circle the score for each task accomplished, and total the score at the bottom.

1	Take Notes!
1	Move towards the Home Board.
1	Question: "So, you told me your interest is in a _____ style of home. Is that right? What type of home most interests you?" "What are some of the specific features of the home you are interested in?"
3	Response Skill: "So, What I hear you saying is <Repeat what is said>. What do you mean by that?
1	Question: Why is that important to you? (Listen to the Answer)
3	Response Skill: "ValueMatch" (Relate to what they have just shared to one or more of the Home's special features)
1	Home Special Feature #1
1	Home Special Feature #2
1	Home Special Feature #3
1	Home Special Feature #4
2	Tie Down. So, it sounds like our Model _____ would fit your need.
	Overcoming Zingers (Bonus)
1	Identify and repeat the zinger.
1	Ask what is meant by the zinger.
1	Why do you ask <about the zinger>?
1	Answer the zinger remembering that the answer leads back to the process.
	Total (max score = 20)

©2006

Balance ScoreCard™
ValueMatch™ Process

"Have Fun"
Goal: **Gaining Agreement**

Successfully completing these important skills and tactics with a prospect can <u>help the salesperson progress towards the "closing posture"</u> during the ValueMatch™ Process. Circle the score for each task accomplished, and total the score at the bottom.

1	Summarize the customer's situation.
1	Summarize the customer's urgency.
1	Summarize the hot buttons for location, amenities, site, and home.
1	Throughout summary, confirm what you have identified as "hot" really holds an interest to the customer.
1	Question: "What is going to be the most important issue or feature in your decision to purchase a new home?"
3	Response Skill: "That's amazing! Based on what you have shared, I have exactly what you are looking for. Would you like to see some of the homes I have in mind?"
1	Question: "If indeed I can show you the home that matches everything you and I have discovered that you are looking for, would that be something you could get excited about?"
2	Tie Down.
	Overcoming Objections
1	Hear the objection. Assure the customer by repeating the objection.
1	Ask what they mean by <their objection>
1	Why do you ask <about the objection>?
1	Resume the process, remembering that the answer needs to lead back to the process.
	Total (max score = 15)

©2006

Balance ScoreCard™ ValueMatch™ Process

"Make Money"
Goal: **Finalize the Close**

Successfully completing these important skills and tactics with a prospect can <u>help the salesperson finalize the close</u> during the ValueMatch™ Process. Circle the score for each task accomplished, and total the score at the bottom.

1	Summarize the customer's situation. Empathize and gain agreement.
1	Summarize the customer's urgency. Reconfirm urgency and tie to action step.
1	Summarize the hot buttons for location, amenities, neighborhood, and home.
1	Throughout summary, confirm what you have identified as "hot" really holds an interest to the customer. At closing, confirm you did indeed find what they wanted in a specific home!
	Note: Closing Strategy: Be prepared to ask the prospect to move forward and take the next step in the process at least three times.
	Optional Closing Questions
1	Optional Question 1: If indeed I have shown you a house that meets the criteria we have discussed, can you think of any reason not to take the next step in the process?
1	Optional Question 2: Is there anything you can think of that we have left out that would keep you from moving forward?
1	Optional Question 3: Are there any questions you have or information I need to clarify in order for you to move forward?
	Note: Stalling Strategy: If you have asked for the close at least three times and listened through each objection, and the prospect still feels they need to take more time, be prepared to come to an agreement on the next step (i.e. Offer to provide information that would be helpful, and set an appointment to meet as soon as appropriate.).
2	Tie Down. "Why don't we start the process to move into your new home?" "The next step of the process is…" "Your earnest money check and a signature is all we will need to get the process started."
	Can you pass the closing test?
	Heart felt
	Recommendation
	To a friend
	To take the next best action step
	Total (max score = 9)

©2006

ValueMatch™
The Greeting

Goal: Make a positive first impression.

✻ What attracted you to the community?

✻ What would you like to accomplish today?

✻ What is your situation?

✻ How do you feel about that?

✼✼ *Empathize* ✼✼

©2006– ServiceTrac, LLC.

ValueMatch™
The Builder Story
Goal: To build credibility.

* What is important to you about a builder?
* What do you mean by that?
* Why is that important to you?

Personalized Presentation

Tie down.

©2006 ServiceTrac, LLC.

ValueMatch™

The Location
Goal: To build value.

* What will be important to you about the area to which you move?

* What attracted you to the area?

* What do you mean by that?

* Why is that important to you?

Personalized Presentation

Tie down.

©2006– ServiceTrac, LLC.

ValueMatch™

The Real Situation

Goal: To discover urgency.

* How long have you been in your current situation or looking for a new home?

* What has recently occurred to motivate you to shop or buy now?

* What do you mean by that?

* Why is that important to you?

* Describe the optimal solution.

Personalized Presentation

Tie down.

©2006 ServiceTrac, LLC.

ValueMatch™

The Community Lifestyle

Goal: To discover amenity hot buttons.

* Which amenities are most important to you?

* What do you like to do in your spare time?

* What do you mean by that?

* Why is that important to you?

Personalized Presentation

Tie down.

©2006– ServiceTrac, LLC.

ValueMatch™

The Neighborhood

Goal: To discover most important neighborhood features.

* What about the neighborhood will be most important to you?

* What type of neighborhood is important to you?

* What do you mean by that?

* Why is that important to you?

Personalized Presentation

Tie down.

©2006– ServiceTrac, LLC.

ValueMatch™

The Model

Goal: To discover most important home features.

* What type of home are you interested in?

* What feature about the home will be important to you?

* What do you mean by that?

* Why is that important to you?

Personalized Presentation

Tie down.

©2006– ServiceTrac, LLC.

ValueMatch™

Make Money

Goal: Finalize the close.

* Empathize and gain agreement on situation.

* Summarize the hot buttons for locations, amenities, neighborhood and home.

* Reconfirm urgency and tie to action step.

Optional Closing Questions

* If indeed I have shown you a house that meets the criteria we have discussed, can you think of any reason not to take the next step in the process?

* Is there anything you can think of that we have left out which would keep you from moving forward?

* Are there any questions you have or information I need to clarify in order for you to move forward?

Heartfelt, Recommendation, To A Friend,
Take The Next Best Action Step

©2006– ServiceTrac, LLC.

ValueMatch™

The Builder Story

Goal: Identify Decision Process.

* Who else is involved in this decision with you?

* Who has the responsibility to make the final decision.

* How is that working?

Personalized Presentation

Tie down.

©2006– ServiceTrac, LLC.

ISBN 1412089964-4